T0311461

"Elizabeth Mamukwa's book is a multi-layered revelation: it practically demonstrates how to build and empower local knowledge communities; it is a solid pointer towards the much needed evolution of universities to become innovation platforms and catalysts for the production of relevant knowledge in the public and communal space; it is also an inspiring key to the renewal of societies, in particular of their capacity to innovate; and, finally, it has the power to enable a veritable renaissance of authentic knowledge creation in Zimbabwe, if not for Africa as a whole. For anyone working in the field of social innovation and societal renewal, I strongly recommend reading this important book."

– Professor Alexander Schieffer, Co-Founder, Trans4m Center for Integral Development, Switzerland; Co-Founder, Home for Humanity, France; Co-Series Editor of the Routledge Transformation and Innovation Series

"This book could not have been published at a better time for Africa, and Zimbabwe in particular. The whole education system is being reengineered to focus more on innovation and industrialisation, having realised that education that was being generated was not creating the knowledge that was necessary for innovation and transformation of our societies. In *Integral Knowledge Creation and Innovation*, Dr Mamukwa gives an exposé of this seemingly complex concept yet something that was lost from our indigenous knowledge systems embedded in the Ubuntu philosophy. The emphasis on knowledge creation not for its sake but for innovation is quite apt to prepare the African reader for the pending fourth industrial revolution. The book emphasises the need for collaboration in this knowledge creation. Collaboration is now the way to go regardless of the sector or industry one is in, and the concept of multi-disciplinary approaches to problem-solving promoted here is the way to go in this era. I like the concept of Communiversity introduced in this book that places knowledge creation and innovation in the right context of communities to ensure relevance, ownership and sustainability of research outputs. This concept, if supported, could prove complementary if not more effective than the innovation hubs being established at most conventional universities."

– Moses Chundu, Lecturer, Economics Department, University of Zimbabwe and Executive Director, Africa Leadership & Management Academy

"A timely and exceedingly valuable publication intended for scholars and social scientists engaged in research, innovation and knowledge creation. The book comprehensively captures the narratives on knowledge creation through the Mode 1 and Mode 2 University. The mode 1 being the more traditional format of university education while the Mode 2 is relatively contemporary, putting emphasis on trans-disciplinary approaches that transcends local and national boundaries. This resource draws exciting contrasts in Knowledge Creation from all corners of the globe. This text is indeed a must-read for you as it extends the frontiers of knowledge in research and innovation."

– Professor David D. Chakuchichi, Dean of Student Affairs, Zimbabwe Open University

"Dr Elizabeth Mamukwa in this book shares readily knowledge she acquired through her doctoral and post-doctoral research journeys. The former culminated in her Calabash of Knowledge Creation/*Denhe re Ruzivo* innovation and the latter being a revelation of concepts such as technopreneurship at the Harare Institute of Technology and numerous work-based innovations from the mode 2 Da Vinci Institute of Technology. The book, which is structured along the 4 Cs concept, the acronym for **C**all, **C**ontext,

Co-Creation and Contribution, raises consciousness and know-how on the subject of Knowledge Creation and Development in order to empower individuals, communities and many organisations. Dr Mamukwa skilfully weaves knowledge with philosophy and religion and challenges individuals and organisations to collaborate, albeit from different perspectives, in taking knowledge creation and the encouragement and promotion of innovation to a higher level of impacting communities."

"In the process she consolidates indigenous and exogenous knowledge rhythms taking into consideration learnings from the four corners of the earth, North, South, East and West, with a view to coming up with better knowledge systems. The book will thus be very relevant to the entire business community, the knowledge industry and to academia."

– *Passmore Matupire (PhD)*

Integral Knowledge Creation and Innovation

This work focuses on the creation of new knowledge, and how this has happened throughout all ages, as far back as the time of ancient philosophy to today. A product of integral research, it covers the process of creating new knowledge, leveraging existing knowledge, sometimes resulting in cutthroat innovations. It also includes knowledge systems such as conventional university systems to Mode 2 university concepts, culminating on integral research to innovation.

This book will help the reader to realise that the subject of knowledge creation is no longer business as usual. Many innovations have been created for human benefit in general, but such innovations may have benefited only parts of society. The challenge in the world is that, while new innovations may be brilliant, there are sections of society who continue to slip into poverty. Modern innovators must also consider such communities and come up with appropriate interventions. This book will open the eyes of innovators to new possibilities. In addition, the subject of knowledge should not be an elitist affair. One may stand to gain a lot by seeing the knowledge in other people, whatever their station in life. This realisation can enable serious innovators to widen their scope in terms of the sources of existing knowledge which can be improved and reassessed as new knowledge. Such existing knowledge can be identified by engaging the very communities that may be affected by a problem or challenge. Such communities will have had time to interrogate their situations and think of possible solutions to such, although they might not have the economic capacity to implement such solutions. This is always a useful starting point if one is seeking a solution to a community problem.

This book will be useful to students interested in the subject of knowledge and innovation, from undergraduate to PhD level. It will also benefit captains of industry, executives and managers who are interested in improving their knowledge improvement cycles in their companies.

Elizabeth Mamukwa is Research Director at the Pundutso Research Institute. She was the chief editor for *Integral Green Zimbabwe* (2014). She began her career as a schoolteacher and then moved to Industry and Commerce in the Human Resources discipline. She has worked in five corporates in the Agriculture, Engineering, Manufacturing and Telecommunications sectors, rising to the position of Human Resources Director. She also does some consulting work.

Transformation and Innovation

Series editors: Ronnie Lessem, Alexander Schieffer

This series on enterprise transformation and social innovation comprises a range of books informing practitioners, consultants, organisation developers, development agents and academics how businesses and other organisations, as well as the discipline of economics itself, can and will have to be transformed. The series prepares the ground for viable twenty-first-century enterprises and a sustainable macroeconomic system. A new kind of R&D, involving social, as well as technological innovation, needs to be supported by integrated and participative action research in the social sciences. Focusing on new, emerging kinds of public, social and sustainable entrepreneurship originating from all corners of the world and from different cultures, books in this series will help those operating at the interface between enterprise and society to mediate between the two and will help schools teaching management and economics to re-engage with their founding principles.

Evolving Work
Employing Self and Community
Ronnie Lessem and Tony Bradley

Integral Finance – Akhuwat
A Case Study of the Solidarity Economy
Muhammad Amjad Saqib and Aneeqa Malik

Emergency Preparedness through Community Cohesion
An Integral Approach to Resilience
Jean Parker

Integral Knowledge Creation and Innovation
Empowering Knowledge Communities
Elizabeth Mamukwa

For more information about this series, please visit
www.routledge.com/business/series/TANDI

Integral Knowledge Creation and Innovation

Empowering Knowledge Communities

Elizabeth Mamukwa

Routledge
Taylor & Francis Group

LONDON AND NEW YORK

First published 2021
by Routledge
2 Park Square, Milton Park, Abingdon, Oxon OX14 4RN

and by Routledge
52 Vanderbilt Avenue, New York, NY 10017

Routledge is an imprint of the Taylor & Francis Group, an informa business

British Library Cataloguing-in-Publication Data
A catalogue record for this book is available from the British Library

Library of Congress Cataloging-in-Publication Data
A catalog record has been requested for this book

ISBN: 978-1-138-31651-5 (hbk)
ISBN: 978-0-367-53295-6 (pbk)
ISBN: 978-0-429-45562-9 (ebk)

Typeset in Bembo
by Newgen Publishing UK

Contents

Figures

Foreword

New ways of harnessing knowledge through innovation – the tip of the iceberg

In this book, the author brings to the fore the nature of knowledge and how this has evolved, even from the time of ancient philosophers. Perhaps more than the concept of knowledge itself, Mamukwa focuses on how new knowledge can be consciously created. In this regard, she dwells on the work done by the Harare Institute of Technology as well as the Da Vinci Institute. She also shares the research that she carried out which culminated in the development of the Calabash of Knowledge Creation.

What is fascinating is the way Mamukwa takes the past, present and future of knowledge creation by capturing early physical inventions that we now take for granted such as the aeroplane and the combine harvester, right through to more recent intellectual ones such as the leadership pipeline, Nonaka and Takeuchi's model, David Kolb's Learning Styles and the Four Worlds Model.

The story does not end there, as Mamukwa raises the issue of a Research Academy and Communiversity (the future), which will be the culmination of all the work that has happened. She describes the Research Academy as the place where new knowledge will be created, not only by the researchers, but in conjunction with the communities affected by a problem or challenge and would hence be interested in the solution. This is an interesting dimension and one that makes a lot of sense. According to Mamukwa, the creation of a Research Academy must be followed by a Communiversity where communities can be taught about the new forms of knowledge created at the Research Academy. This is an opportunity to "commercialise" the new knowledge so that it benefits as many people as possible. This is an exciting approach to knowledge creation, where, instead of worrying about patent rights, focus is placed on making sure more people are exposed to an innovation and are allowed to benefit from it.

This book makes a very interesting read.

Engineer Quinton Kanhukamwe
Vice Chancellor – The Harare Institute of Technology

Prologue

Introduction: The Mode 2 University

Among other things, this book lends prominence to the concept of a "Mode 2" University (Gibbons et al., 1994). I and many others benefited from the Mode 2 system as individuals undertaking our PhD's in Technology, Innovation, People and Systems (TIPS) through the Da Vinci Institute program, as we shall see, originally articulated in *Integral Green Zimbabwe* (Mamukwa, Lessem & Schieffer, 2014). It has become increasingly clear to me that a Mode 2 approach is well placed for knowledge creation and innovation. The very essence of Mode 2 speaks to this.

According to Nowotny (Nowotny et al., 2001), Mode 2 involves a multi-disciplinary approach to research, which Da Vinci students from a multiplicity of disciplines, are doing. In Zimbabwe, the PhD grouping run by Da Vinci/Trans4M has students from all walks of life carrying out research along the same lines. Students come from backgrounds such as Human Resources, Telecommunications, Non-Governmental Organizations (NGOs), Manufacturing and Consultancy, to name only a few. This makes research truly multi-disciplinary.

Nowotny further postulates that Mode 2 is trans-disciplinary in nature, mobilising both theoretical perspectives and practical methodologies to solve societal problems. *Transdisciplinary Research* is defined, for example, by the Harvard Transdisciplinary Research in Energetics and Cancer Center (www.hsph.harvard.edu/trec/about-us/definitions/) as "research efforts conducted by investigators from different disciplines working jointly to create new conceptual, theoretical, methodological, and translational innovations that integrate and move beyond discipline-specific approaches to address a common problem". Nowotny also emphasises that the Mode 2 approach is primarily generated in the context of application. Now, we have a number of Zimbabwean PhD Students who have used the Mode 2 approach to carry out research. This has worked at an individual level. "Success" stories include the invention of Integral Ubuntu Leadership by Passmore Matupire (Matupire, 2017), Industrial Ecology Model by Joshua Chinyuku, Kushanya Mumamisha (Community Based Tourism) by Kennedy Mandevhani and the Calabash of

Knowledge Creation by Elizabeth Mamukwa (Mamukwa, Lessem & Schieffer, 2014). Individually the success stories have been indeed a reality. The challenge has been harnessing these brains and efforts and innovations to work in a collective sense. While the innovations were brilliant, the scale of implementation makes such innovations problematic. Unless a more meaningful model of sharing such knowledge is identified and implemented, it will reach only a handful of people.

I can just imagine the powerhouse that could be created by conjoining the activities and actions of such individuals into a single system. The results could be quite an explosion of not only the innovations but also the transformation to human existence. The tragedy is that, such working together has so far mostly happened in the figment of our imagination. While this book is about how different institutions and corporates have taken different and varied approaches to knowledge creation and innovation, and while there is evidence of such approaches, there has been little evidence, hitherto, of such individuals and organisations working meaningfully together to take knowledge creation and innovation to a higher level. It is rather like the power situation in Zimbabwe in 2019, when electricity was only available for seven hours per day at night. Most households individually invested in power solutions, be it generator, gas or renewable (solar) power. It boggles the mind what could have happened had all these resources been harnessed together to come up with a wholesome, symbiotic solution. The power utility could easily have lost its position as a monopoly in the industry. So too could be the power of conscious collaboration in knowledge creation and innovation.

Evolution of Mode 2 to Communiversity

To foster such working together in order to achieve more for the communities we exist in, we are now consciously evolving the Mode 2 further into what has been termed a Communiversity (Lessem, Adodo & Bradley, 2019). This will involve a collective emphasis on a Nhakanomics (Lessem, Mawere & Taranhike 2019) Research Academy catalysed by Pundutso locally and Trans4m Communiversity Associates (TCA) globally, as the so called Pilgrimium, with Learning Communities and Socioeconomic Laboratories that also participate in, and benefit from this Communiversity. This will enable the results from the Research Academy (when constituted) to be actualised through the communities and laboratories, at a much higher scale. This way communities stand to benefit from tried and tested solutions to community challenges, through a Communiversity. Such a Communiversity's focus will therefore not merely be on awarding degrees and certificates (though there is no reason why this too cannot happen), but more on the overall Process for Holistic Development (PHD), or indeed regeneration in and of a particular society. The Communiversity will instill structure and systems in the sharing of the research-and-innovation outcomes. Success will be measured by the effectiveness of solutions birthed from the Integral Research (Lessem & Schieffer, 2010) and practically implemented in communities and society. Such an establishment, as indicated, will have laboratories to work in to produce the desired knowledge. These laboratories can be academic, such as Da Vinci Institute and Harare Institute of Technology (HIT); commercial such as Providence Human Capital (PHC), Schweppes and others; and community based, such as the Taranhike Homestead in Buhera, Mamina small scale farmers project, and Chivhu, to mention a few. The model will be that institutionalized research is carried out and tested in these laboratories, and the outcomes implemented by imparting such to communities through the Communiversity, altogether mediated by a local-global Pilgrimium, in a particular society, in our case that of Zimbabwe. Such could equally take place, say, in Nigeria (Adodo A, 2017), our lead Communiversity case in Africa, or indeed in South Africa.

Conclusion: Individual to inter-institutional

It is very exciting, to see that the subject of knowledge creation and innovation is very much alive today. Symbiotic or not, the institutions that have taken this on board, such as Da Vinci Institute in South Africa and Harare Institute of Technology in Zimbabwe, or Pax Herbals in Nigeria, are not only contributing extremely meaningfully to the Body of Knowledge, but are also bringing practical solutions to businesses and communities (it is my view that HIT will positively impact Zimbabwe by continuing to bring solutions that result in import substitution). As Integral Research continues, now on a collectively based, inter-institutional level, so too will the innovations coming out of such, resulting in an avalanche of benefits to communities. This is where the Communiversity will find its niche.

References

Adodo, A. (2017). *Integral Community Enterprise in Africa*. New York: Routledge.

Ash, R. (1974). *The Wright Brothers*. London: Wayland.

Brands, H. W. (2010). The First American: The Life and Times of Benjamin Franklin. New York: Random House Digital.

Gibbons, M., Limoges, C., Nowotny, H., Schwartzman, S., Scott, P. & Trow, M. (1994) *The New Production of Knowledge: The Dynamics of Science and Research in Contemporary Societies*. London: Sage.

Lessem, R., Adodo, A. & Bradley, T. (2019). *The Idea of the Communiversity: Releasing the Natural, Cultural, Technological and Economic GENE-ius of Societies*. Manchester: Beacon Books and Media Ltd.

Lessem, R., Mawere, M. & Taranhike, D. S. (2019). *Nhakanomics: Harvesting Knowledge and Value for Re-generation through Social Innovation*. Harare: Talent Research Publishing.

Lessem, R. & Schieffer, A. (2010). *Integral Research and Innovation: Transforming Enterprise and Society*. Farnham, England: Gower.

Mamukwa, E., Lessem, R. & Schieffer, A. (2014). *Integral Green Zimbabwe: An African Phoenix Rising.* Farnham, Surrey: Gower.

Matupire, P. M. (2017). *Integral Ubuntu Leadership* New York: Routledge.

Nowotny, H., Scott, P. & Gibbons, M. (2001). *Rethinking Science: Knowledge and the Public in an Age of Uncertainty.* Cambridge: Polity Press. Available at www.hsph.harvard.edu/trec/about-us/definitions/ (accessed on 30 July 2019).

1 Introducing knowledge creation

The subject of knowledge creation and development has gained momentum in recent years. The issue of harnessing knowledge became the bane of my life as Human Resources Director in a manufacturing enterprise in a hyper-inflationary economy. The challenges of skills retention became enormous. The choice of topic for doctoral research became obvious, given the passion to improve knowledge systems at workplaces, resulting in a model for knowledge transfer and creation. This model's applicability is not only limited to workplaces, but to families, communities and other arms of society.

Working with three groups of co-researchers (Cooperative Inquiry Groups) within and outside my company we developed the Calabash of Knowledge Creation *(Denhe re Ruzivo)*. This model was tested and utilised in three corporate, public listed manufacturing companies in Zimbabwe.

One of these Cooperative Inquiry groups developed into the Pundutso Centre for Integral Development, which has begun to engage with the Zimbabwean Society following the CARE rhythm of Community Activation, Catalysation, Research-to-Innovation and Education (Knowledge Embodiment).

This book serves three purposes:

- First, it is an opportunity to share my research journey and the knowledge that I acquired when I read for my PhD degree.
- Second, I seek to share the work done by two unique universities, namely the Harare Institute of Technology in Zimbabwe and the DaVinci Institute in South Africa. In the process I will dwell on the Mode 2 University.
- Finally, I will use this platform to share two innovations, namely the Calabash of Knowledge Creation/Denhe re Ruzivo, which was the innovation that came out of the research that I carried out, and the Pundutso Centre for Integral Development, which was an unintended and yet very pertinent outcome of the same research process. I will go further and share some of the innovations that Pundutso seeks to share.

Furthermore, I will articulate the concepts that will be contained in the book and outline their relevance thereof. Such concepts will encompass the 4Cs, the CARE concept (Community Activation, Awakening Consciousness

[Catalysation], Research-to-Innovation and Embodiment of Knowledge [Education]), the GENE (Grounding, Emergence, Navigation and Effecting), and OFET (Origination, Foundation, Emancipation and Transformation) concepts and Integral Worlds Model and how all this will link with the research trajectory which resulted in the outcomes that will be shared in the book. In fact, the book is structured according to the 4 Cs concept of Call, Context, Co-Creation and Contribution. A summary of the Calabash of Knowledge Creation will also be given, focusing on how this was created and why it is important.

The interest in the Mode 2 University and what it embodies will also be accorded prominence in this book. Of particular attention will be the work done by the Da Vinci Institute and how this has gone a long way in developing people, organisations and countries.

This book then, is on the most part inspired by research carried out for a PhD Thesis on Knowledge Creation and Development. It will cover, among other things, the factors that are critical for sharing existing knowledge, as well as developing new knowledge concerning existing situations and factors in workplaces, institutions and communities. The book is premised on the fact that knowledge is not static, but is forever evolving; therefore, the creation of knowledge will happen anyway with or without our interference, but a well thought out and structured knowledge creation and development strategy can result in more useful, productive and relevant new knowledge. It is further influenced by the realisation that the best way to improve knowledge is to do so as a community, and not individually. Working as a team of people impacted by a common problem through the trajectory of action research has proven to be one sure way of coming up with knowledge that is relevant and practical (Mamukwa, Lessem and Schieffer, 2014; Matupire, 2017; Lessem and Schieffer, 2010).

The question that begs to be asked is, why knowledge creation? Literature on the most part concerns itself with competitive advantage in the corporate world and other such arguments for knowledge creation. However, knowledge creation goes far beyond making glass, tinning fruit, manufacturing equipment and other such activities. In my view, it is the essence of human livelihood and survival. It is true that knowledge creation has become critical in manufacturing and other industrial entities, because a greater part of the world has become industrialised and many people now depend on the activities of such for jobs and consumable products. However, life goes beyond commerce and industry. Knowledge Creation is equally relevant in the village and rural communities, as well as in peri-urban situations.

Knowledge is therefore relevant in any set up that involves the existence of people. Its necessity encompasses a range of reasons, including finding better and faster ways of doing things, coming up with new ways of making people more comfortable as well as coming up with innovations that promote a complete life for individuals and communities, regardless of where they are situated. Examples of more recent innovations are the mobile phone which has made communication easier for all people, rich and poor, urban and rural, old and young; the internet which has brought information closer to people and made transactions simpler and more convenient through mobile and internet banking, to give just two examples.

To dig further in history, many years ago in America the first aeroplane was invented by the Wright brothers (Ash, 1974), and this has revolutionized travel. There are other inventions that have made life easier and more convenient for us, such as the catheter which was invented by Benjamin Franklin (Brands, 2000), the concept of mass production which was invented by Eli Whitney (Lakwete, 2004), and other "simpler" conveniences whose inventers may not have become famous, such as the salt shaker, the teapot, sticky-notes and staplers used in the office.

People develop new knowledge for a number of reasons. Sometimes those who develop and produce knew knowledge do so when there are burning issues in an individual's mind, or in a community, when they are frustrated by something that takes long or is difficult to do, when they have a vision that others may not share, and when there are life and death health issues. If there is a message that I hope this book will send, it is that innovations and the creation of new knowledge does not need to be a calling. The approach to knowledge creation taken by this book is that communities have the power to take charge of their situations and collectively review their existing knowledge and create new knowledge, to the benefit of not only one specific community but to be shared with other communities. Such communities then, enjoy the satisfaction of leaving a footprint, a legacy.

This book will give prominence to Integral Research (Lessem and Schieffer, 2010) as a practical way of identifying a shared problem and coming up with a solution as a team, group or community. This creates a participatory approach to the said research and gives the process a wealth of contributions from colleagues who identify with the problem. As such research seeks to develop solutions to identified existing problems, the chances of using the developed solutions are higher than in conventional research (which of course has its own merits). In the latter, sadly the bulk of the results of research by Master's and Doctoral students in such universities tend to gather dust on a bookshelf somewhere. In action research, the chances are that by the time the research is completed there is an entire community operationalising the results of the research.

There are a number of questions that will be answered in this book regarding the subject of Knowledge Creation and Development. The first question is WHY? Why should we bother ourselves at all with the subject of Knowledge Creation? The next is WHO? Who should be interested in involving themselves in Knowledge Creation and Development? "WHO" in this context is not necessarily limited to people. Through a process of personification, "WHO" includes corporate organisations, institutions, schools, farms, factories, and any such entities where people are gathered for productive purposes. Then there is the "WHAT". This can be looked at from a number of angles. "WHAT" is the starting point for Knowledge Creation? "WHAT' is the raw material. "WHAT" is the measure of success when Knowledge creation is happening as it should.

"WHAT" highlights the benefits and rewards that Knowledge Creation and Development yields to those who make the effort. Finally, there is the "WHEN". When should Knowledge Creation and Development be carried out?

This book is also inspired by the work done by Nonaka and Takeuchi in their work with the SECI Model (Socialise, Externalise, Combine, Internalise) (Nonaka and Takeuchi, 1995), as well as by Nowotny, Scott and Gibbons (2001, 2003) in their work on Mode 2 Universities.

In this book then, focus will be placed on creating and developing knowledge in communities, including the world of work, whatever it is perceived to be.

The aim of this book is to raise consciousness and know-how on the subject of Knowledge Creation and Development to empower individuals, communities and organisations. Such consciousness will assist by empowering knowledge workers, researchers and organisations to utilise the resources within their structures in the quest to share knowledge, improve such knowledge and create higher level and more appropriate knowledge in communities and the world of work. Such empowerment will ensure that, while knowledge is shared and is made communal, the creation of new knowledge is equally shared. This way, a culture of active participation in influencing the knowledge that is important to us is developed and strengthened. Knowledge sharing, creation and development should then cease to be elitist, but becomes an area of interest for all concerned in any relevant establishment. This way, the process of knowledge development and creation is enriched by the involvement of all people across the structures, and not just senior level leaders or management.

The book will also bring prominence to the Mode 2 University as a means of promoting the creation of new knowledge through an educational process, and a comparison will be made with the Mode 1 University (the conventional university). To this end, particular attention will be accorded to the Da Vinci Institute as an example of a functional Mode 2 University, and its epistemological differences with the Mode 1 University analysed. Their programs will be put to scrutiny, and their success stories highlighted.

I would want to clarify that, much as I, like many African academics, may feel that the African people were disenfranchised by colonisation, and that they were "forced" to abandon their own knowledge systems in favour of those brought by the colonial masters, that is not the spirit of this book. Instead, emphasis may be placed here and there on the consolidation of indigenous and exogenous knowledge rhythms. History has happened and we are here now, exposed to both indigenous and exogenous knowledge. I sincerely believe that the opportunity that is staring us in the face is how we can get the best deal out of this situation by maximising on the best of both worlds. In other words, we should not accept everything that is indigenous as good and everything exogenous as bad (or vice versa), but seek to take what is good and where possible combine it and hopefully come up with even better knowledge systems.

The book is a four-part exposition with thirteen chapters. The parts are aligned to the 4 Cs (Call, Context, Co-creation and Contribution).

References

Ash, R. (1974). *The Wright Brothers*. London: Wayland.

Brands, H. W. (2010). The First American: The Life and Times of Benjamin Franklin.

Gibbons, M., Limoges, C., Nowotny, H., Schwartzman, S., Scott, P. & M. Trow (1994). *The New Production of Knowledge: The Dynamics of Science and Research in Contemporary Societies*. London: Sage.

Lakwete, A. (2004). *Inventing the Cotton Gin: Machine and Myth in Antebellum America*. Baltimore, MD: Johns Hopkins University Press.

Lessem, R. & Schieffer, A. (2010). *Integral Research and Innovation: Transforming Enterprise and Society*. Farnham, England: Gower.

Mamukwa, E., Lessem, R. & Schieffer, A. (2014). *Integral Green Zimbabwe: An African Phoenix Rising*. Farnham, England: Gower.

Matupire, P. M. (2017). *Integral Ubuntu Leadership*. Farnham, Oxon: Routledge.

Nonaka, I. (1990). *Management of Knowledge Creation*. Tokyo: Nihon Keizai Shinbun-sha.

Nowotny, H., Scott, P. & Gibbons, M. (2001). *Rethinking Science: Knowledge and the Public in an Age of Uncertainty*. Cambridge: Polity Press.

Nowotny, H., Scott, P. & Gibbons, M. (2003). Mode 2 Revisited: The New Production of Knowledge. *Minerva*, 41, 179–194.

Part I

The call

Why knowledge creation

2 Why knowledge creation and innovation

Introduction

This chapter seeks to bring to the fore the different sources of knowledge creation and development. There are different needs in human communities that lead to the creation of new knowledge and the development and improvement of existing knowledge.

However, before we get our teeth into this matter it is necessary to have clarity on what knowledge creation, knowledge development and innovation is.

Knowledge creation is the ongoing combination and transfer of different kinds of knowledge, old and new. This happens as users of knowledge interpret the knowledge while using it and continue seeking new and better ways of doing things. In this arena ideas are created to improve customer experience and make life easier for the users of such knowledge. The process involves practicing and learning and changing aspects of the knowledge to improve the impact of such knowledge on the users. New concepts are constantly formed during the process of knowledge creation (Nonaka, 1990).

Knowledge development can be the constant improvement of knowledge and knowledge systems to meet certain needs. This is what has led to the continuous improvement of computers for example, as a result of developing knowledge to make things better and more efficient.

Innovation, on the other hand, can be a totally new invention, a system, a prototype or totally new way of doing things. Innovation is associated with ground-breaking inventions with significant impact on people and society.

What catalyses knowledge creation and innovation?

Knowledge creation is a result of need, and therefore becomes necessary when there is an unmet need, or when a particular need cannot be met with existing knowledge.

Among individuals, families, businesses, communities and even countries, wherever people exist, there are a number of issues or needs that provide the catalysis or urging for existing knowledge to be improved and developed further, as well as for completely new knowledge to be created. This is all for the purpose of satisfying inner or outer needs.

There is a diverse range of needs that catalyse change in general, and knowledge change in particular, in the world of people. Such needs cover a variety of areas in people's lives such as the examples listed below, and these examples are not exhaustive.

Social needs

Humans are social animals. We all need to belong to someone, and we need to live somewhere. Typical of all animals, we are territorial in that we want to own the people that belong to us as well as the spaces we live in. Our social needs then, include such things as accommodation, health, demographics, communication to name a few. I will single out the need to communicate. In Africa in years gone by, the drum was a very important communication tool. With time we, like the rest of the world, moved to the fixed telephone. Right now, again, like the rest of the world, we have moved to such modes of communication as the mobile telephone, email and different teleconferencing platforms, to name a few. Our social networks have been expanded through such platforms as Facebook, LinkedIn, Twitter and Instagram, again to name a few. What a far cry from the drum! Guess what, the developments that we have experienced in the social arena are attributable to the creation and development of new knowledge and innovation from people who identified specific unmet or partially met needs.

Economic needs

Economic needs encompass various sub-sets such as agriculture, industry, tourism and other such.

Sometimes economic needs are exacerbated by world depressions, such as the Great Depression in Britain in the early 1930. This Great Depression had a far-reaching impact on most countries in the world, be they rich or poor. Personal incomes, tax revenues, levels of profitability and prices seriously nose-dived. International trade suffered a 50% reduction. The rate of unemployment rose to between 25% and 33% in various countries (Garraty, 1987).

Sometimes, a people's economic needs are interfered with or severely compromised as a result of a political dispensation and or governance challenges. Some vivid examples will be employed here. The first one is Nazi Germany under Hitler's dictatorship (1933–1945) (Turner, 1985), when the usual tell-tale signs of mal-management were evident – hyper-inflation, price controls, foreign exchange controls and other such measures. Basically, Germany during that period abandoned most known economic principles, such as the requirement to back banknotes with gold and foreign currency. In other words, money was simply printed. Fast forward to Zimbabwe during the late 1990s to 2008. The same mistakes were made. The rate of inflation went as high as 80 billion percent (Hanke & Kwok, 2009)! Again, this was as a result of a dictatorship, resulting in a nation that was cowed into non-resistance following some brutal encounters with the security forces.

When such things happen, innovation is needed in the way we recover from such, as well as on how we avoid such calamities in the future.

Environmental needs

Humans (and creation in general) have a right to a clean environment. Therefore, environmental needs, which include sanitation, forestry, land degradation and other such, are a trigger for the development, and even creation of new knowledge in that realm. In one example, History reminds us that during the medieval period in England, King John was killed by dysentery (Church, 1999). This disease caused a very violent diarrhea which resulted in bleeding and death. Now, while King John had his own short comings as a leader and ruler (such as causing a civil war, murder, being a sexual predator, cruelty, to name a few), the dysentery that caused his demise was a result of poor sanitation, specifically resulting in people consuming dirty water and food contaminated by human waste. This could have been avoided if King John, during his rule, had improved sanitation in England. Present-day England (and indeed the present-day world) has on the whole benefited from sanitation innovations including the processes of developing clean water as well as sewer reticulation systems enabling people to live in clean environments.

In 1596 John Harrington invented something that has made a significant impact on sanitation and health, something that in this modern age we take for granted, the flush toilet (Kilroy, 2009). His innovation has not only brought changes to the environment, but to health in general (Jørgensen, 2010).

Political needs

Political needs incorporate the way countries and nations are governed. If we were to focus on this, we would see a thread of development and change in national governance issues, probably ranging from monarchies, dictatorships and democratic rule, in many countries in the world. We would probably find countries that have historically gone through the full spectrum of such, and that may have now settled for democracy. We need to however understand that such nations are still open and subject to further change and development.

The issue to note is that the way a country is governed affects the lives of people. A more recent example of this is the situation in Zimbabwe where Robert Mugabe's thirty-seven-year rule seriously impoverished the Zimbabwean people. The so-called land reform program saw white people who were at the time more experienced in commercial farming activities having their farms forcibly taken from them with the result of reducing food productivity and increasing the rate of unemployment. This also negatively impacted food security in Zimbabwe. The point I am making here is not that the white farmers should not have been disturbed, but rather that there should have been a more robust strategy to manage the policy shift to mitigate the suffering of the people. Is this relevant to knowledge creation? Yes, it is, in more ways than one:

- First of all, the land reform program was as a result of a need. While white farmers had huge tracts of land in fertile areas where the rain pattern is favorable for successful farming, the generality of their black brothers and sisters had next to nothing. For those with any land to talk about, such land is in dry, arid parts of the country with inconsistent rainfall patterns. This knowledge can be of significant use to our neighbours in South Africa who at the time of writing this book, were talking about land expropriation without compensation. The knowledge about what happened in Zimbabwe could be used by South Africa so that in their own land redistribution exercise they correct the Zimbabwean mistakes and give their program a better chance to succeed.
- The knowledge of all this can help other nations to strategically restructure their own land ownership schemes to ensure that no specific sector of the populace sees itself as disadvantaged so that the "need" is addressed before it causes disruptions in society.
- More importantly, an analysis of such mistakes can be catalytic in terms of moving someone to innovate the treatment of land in various nations so that a blueprint that works is put in place.

Historical needs

History provides us with a glimpse of the past, some of which was good, some of it bad, some necessary, some unnecessary. It gives us lessons about things that are important in our lives today, and things to avoid going into the future. It gives us our identity and completes us, particularly if such history involves our lineage.

Regarding history then, we can learn from those who have gone before us who documented a lot of information that we benefit from today. The lesson for us is that we too take the trouble to somehow keep a record of what happens in our lives, our family, and so on, for posterity. Innovation and knowledge creation could be focused around how we can very easily record things as they happen and keep such information in a format that can easily be accessible in the future. In this digital age this should not be too difficult, particularly with innovations such as cloud services where one can store information in the so-called "cloud" platform. When we trace back writing as a skill, without going too far back in history, we find that things used to be written on a scroll which would be rolled up for safe keeping. Fast forward, there was the typewriter. Fast forward again there was the computer. Even with the computer there have been many changes and improvements. The first computer filled an entire room by itself. At the time of writing this book computers had become sleek, thin and light, yet with a lot more memory for storage of information. All these changes have been brought about by innovation and the creation of new knowledge.

From an indigenous knowledge perspective, we may find that as an African people (or any people for that matter) we may have abandoned knowledge in our history that is good and useful. It would be worth our while to dig back into such and see how it can be resuscitated and used again. A favourite example for me is the Chinyika story where, when the people were starving as a result of incessant droughts hunger, through a democratic process, the people revisited their indigenous knowledge by starting to grow a crop of their ancestors (rapoko/finger millet/rukweza), restoring Chinyika back to the land of plenty (Lessem, Muchineripi & Kada, 2012).

Intellectual needs

We all need mental stimulation. We naturally thirst for knowledge. I have a grandson who was four years old at the time of writing this book. He was going to nursery school, and would come back reciting new nursery rhymes that he has just learnt. He would recite to anyone who cared to listen. He would also start to count from one to five or six, showing off his new knowledge. Like this little boy we all have our intellectual needs, which are expressed through the questions that we ask and the gaps that we discover in the knowledge that we have already acquired.

The average person wants to learn so that they qualify for something and can find a job. There are however some people who thrive on knowledge itself, and on experimenting with the knowledge, resulting in new discoveries and new inventions.

Those of us who have raised kids will remember the stage when they ask a lot of questions. It is a natural instinct, designed to build their knowledge database. There have been many innovations that have helped us along in our quest for knowledge. I have a friend who lost her sight, and reads and writes in braille (a very useful innovation). Over and above the braille she has an entire library of audio books. It took someone's innovativeness to come up with this idea of audio books.

Educational needs

Education is the playground in which we learn to cope with the complexities of the world, including the developments that continuously enshrine this ever-changing environment. The United Nations Educational, Scientific and Cultural Organisation (UNESCO) believes that education is a human right for all throughout life and that access must be matched by quality. This organisation is the only United Nations agency with a mandate to cover all aspects of education. It has been entrusted to lead the Global Education 2030 Agenda through Sustainable Development Goal (SDG) Number 4. UNESCO believes that quality education is the ingredient that will help people break away from poverty by getting better jobs as well as reducing inequality, particularly between the genders. Many nations use UNESCO as their benchmark for the development of educational curricula.

Education then, is a fundamental need in this day and age – a need that affects the rich and poor, the intelligent and the not so gifted, male and female, and this need cuts across race, colour and creed. In its latest Handbook on Measuring Equity in Education (UNESCO Institute of Statistics, 2018), UNESCO provides guidance on access to education (or lack thereof) by disadvantaged groups. Organisations such as UNESCO therefore do all they can to come up with or encourage innovations and initiatives that make it possible for all people to access quality education.

By studying the Education Curricula throughout the world, and educational strategies adopted by different countries and nations, educators can come up with curricula that promote the type of education that positively impacts the lives of people.

I cannot resist here talking about the Da Vinci Institute (though later I will devote an entire chapter in this book to the Institute). In its programs, the Da Vinci Institute encourages students at various levels (Certificate, Degree, Master's Degree and PhD) to identify a need (work-based challenge) and to propose and develop solutions to address such. Some of these solutions are very innovative and have the potential to develop into cutting edge creations.

Spiritual needs

Spiritual needs include issues of religion, whatever we perceive it to be. We all need vital beliefs that give some sense of meaning and hope to our lives, in a world bedogged with losses, tragedies, and failures (Clinebell, 1995). We therefore all need spiritual resources to help heal the painful wounds of grief, guilt, resentment, unforgiveness, self-rejection and shame.

We live in a world where there are different religions. Even in the same religion we encounter different ways of worshipping. Being a Christian, I will draw on my Christian examples to illustrate this issue.

Before Jesus went to heaven, he instructed his disciples to stay in Jerusalem to wait for the Holy Spirit (Acts 1:4), which came as promised at Pentecost (Acts 2:4). After this, the disciples started to preach the word. There developed a fellowship of believers who dedicated themselves to the apostles' teaching and to fellowship (Acts 2:42). This was the first Christian church. However, this church has developed into different churches with time, all believing and living by the bible. The differences are in the way people worship. To use a simple example, in an English church a piano will most likely accompany the music while in an African service (Zulu, Shona, Chewa, Xhosa, Tswana, to name a few languages) traditional instruments may be used. An English church will use classical tunes for their music while music in an African church will be more robust with vernacular tunes and energetic dancing. Other differences will be liturgical, defining a Roman Catholic Church from a Methodist one. The long and short of it all is that groups of Christians with different cultures and different personality traits will find ways of worship that suit them, and may form their own church. One thing is for sure, a religious grouping will render mutual support and a sense of belonging to its members. In these religious groupings, the way things are done also changes as time moves to incorporate more "modern" practices. The long and the short of it is that such religious groupings generally fulfil the spiritual needs of their membership.

This list of needs is not at all exhaustive, for potential problem areas encountered by the human race cannot be conclusively named. There are more issues in existence now not listed here, as well as more yet to arise in the human space. The purpose of this book is not to come up with solutions to all these issues (for it would have to be an enormous volume to do that). Of interest is that there are new disciplines that arise as people apply their minds to the meeting of the needs, and to improving the way things are done.

The interesting features are that there are disciplines which arise as people apply their minds to solving the problems of humanity. As humanity has progressed from the days of early creation to pre-modern, modern and new information and digital age, much knowledge creation, production and innovation continues to happen, serving to satisfy the ever-increasing complexity of human needs.

Knowledge creation and the world of work

The world of work comes with many challenges. Knowledge Creation, Development and Innovation in companies can happen within people, machinery and systems, to name just three areas.

People innovation results through the way we shape our people to make them more creative, productive and innovative. Competition comes in all shapes and sizes, and companies often have to be innovative in one way or other to have an edge on the said competition. It has been said over and over again that companies compete through their people because it is the people who, if provided with the right environment and tools, can become innovators and create a competitive edge for the company. Companies may have great people, but until they see and treat such people as talent, they are just like any shop at the corner. Sandy Ogg, CEO Works founder (McKinsey Quarterly, March 2018) stresses the criticality of linking talent to value. Innovation then, must also involve the way we treat, perceive and develop people to enable companies to fully benefit from the talent within. This includes promoting the creativity of employees by allowing them to experiment and make mistakes here and there. This then becomes a culture issue. Google for example, believes in meritocracy, and this has the effect of making employees feel valued and empowered, resulting in higher levels of creativity and problem solving (Schmidt & Rosenberg, 2015). In such environments there is no culture of fear, and creativity is promoted. Sadly, many organisations are constrained by corporate politics and fear culture, which inhibit innovativeness. Therefore, apart from the usual things that organisations believe in, such as training and development, a culture of creative freedom is important. The Da Vinci Institute promotes such an innovative environment in their students, be they at Certificate, Bachelor's, Master's or PhD level, through their programs in the Management of Technology, Innovation, People, Systems (TIPS) and Business. Da Vinci integrates the TIPS framework by engaging students in aligning innovativeness by co-creating new workplace realities to solve work-based situations. The challenge I am sure, is for students to maintain the acquired level of innovativeness when they get back to their workplaces as there could be a variety of barriers, including organisational culture.

Machinery or equipment is another area that either promotes or hampers productivity. In a manufacturing company I worked in, there was huge, complex machinery manufactured in Germany. With the economic meltdown that happened in Zimbabwe around 2008, skills emigrated to more lucrative markets and it became a struggle to effectively maintain and repair the machines. This was clear evidence of poor knowledge sharing and transfer. This seriously negatively affected productivity. Over and above that, some components of the machinery either became damaged or exceeded their lifespan. There was no foreign currency to import spares as a consequence of a constrained economic environment. The first problem was resolved by negotiating with a former employee to take leave in his job elsewhere in the region and come to train the employees in the company on how to maintain and repair the machines. This was a slow and painful process. Productivity continued to be hampered during the learning curve. The solution to the second problem (no foreign currency to import spares) was interesting. Employees were empowered to find solutions, and they did. Some of the solutions involved welding off some outlets to close them off permanently. Did this work? Yes, it did. The challenge was then knowing where the modifications were for future reference. It became necessary to meticulously document any modifications to machines, and to share such knowledge with all employees who had the potential to do repair work or service on the machines in the future. So, employees, when given the opportunity, can come up with innovative ways of solving a company's problems.

The lesson here is that we need to appreciate that employees are a resource at our disposal. This resource, however, is different from other resources such as machines and money. This resource has feelings, and thinks. While the thinking part is acknowledged and appreciated, many leaders in organisations fail to acknowledge and appreciate that, to mobilise this resource, it is important to make individuals feel empowered and appreciated. I worked in a company where one of the executive employees was promoted into a higher position than his team mates. Sadly, instead of taking advantages of the strengths of his colleagues and harnessing their skill and wisdom, the senior employee started to micro-manage his colleagues. The result was rather unfortunate. There was a very high level of disengagement in the top team. Some team members started to look for jobs. Others observed their working hours and packed their bags and went home dead on five o'clock. As long as they were seen to have been at work, that was good enough. Good reports were given at management meetings, but these were not always a reflection of good performance. How we focus on the insignificant and miss opportunities to promote greatness!

Genealogical process

Through a genealogical process, human needs have become more complex due to a variety of factors, not least because of population increases. The needs for an expanding population require increasingly new knowledge to be developed and used. For example, according to the Bible, when Adam and Eve were in the Garden of Eden, they had everything they needed and could communicate with God (Genesis 2: 15–17). In today's world resources are scarce and many wars are fought over those meagre resources.

Because of the increased population in the world there are more social pressures. Governments are therefore faced with the challenges of coming up with creative methods of introducing and maintaining harmony in families, communities, societies, countries and the world at large, and of providing adequate resources such as energy, accommodation, food and clothes, to their citizens. All this calls for different forms of knowledge creation, development and innovation. In the quest to find solutions to some of these challenges, countries are developing genetically modified foods to feed the increased populations, for example.

Larger populations also result in more social pressures, hence effective governments try to be a step ahead in terms of ways of promoting harmony at all strata of society. This further reinforces the need to create new appropriate knowledge and systems to address social structures and conflict resolution strategies.

New systems also need to be created and developed in the world of work to cope with increased social demographics. The banking sector, for example, has introduced such facilities as internet and mobile banking as well as automated teller machines (ATM) to reduce human traffic in the banks and bring some kind of sanity to the socio-economic "battlefield". These are exciting developments, but the down side is that these smart systems take away people's jobs.

There is a diverse range of disciplines and sub-disciplines in this arena. This can be classified as follows:

- *The creation of totally new knowledge*
  When there is a need that has not been totally met before. Examples of this include John Harringdon's flush toilet described earlier, which has had an amazing impact with regard to clean environments and good health.
- *Innovation to create new, efficient ways of doing things*
  Edwards Deming, an American (Gitlow & Gitlow, 1987) introduced Total Quality Management (TQM) to the Japanese specifically, and to the world in general with his "formula".

$$QUALITY = \frac{RESULTS\ OF\ WORK\ EFFORTS}{TOTAL\ COSTS}$$

(and we give credit to the Japanese for TQM!). Many manufacturing companies in the world have utilised the essence of Total Quality Management, and it has brought about results.

Henry Gantt invented the Gantt Chart (named after him) to assist project managers by measuring activities by the time required to complete such activities, and to link such activities with other activities that should be completed before them, leading to an informed estimation of the time needed to complete a project (Gantt, 1919). The Gantt chart is still used today.

- *Innovation to produce new products and systems.*

There are so many new innovations that have been developed in this century alone, such as the mobile cellular phone which has brought about a lot of flexibility in voice communication. The Internet too has been another amazing innovation. This is the global system of interconnected computer networks that use the Internet protocol suite (TCP/IP) to link devices worldwide (Taylor, 2000). This was initially developed at the requirement of the US federal government in the 1960s to build robust, fault-tolerant communication with computer networks (the need). This has contributed immensely to the ease of getting access to information, as well as to written communication through such media as email. The Global Positioning System (GPS) is yet another recent innovation. It is described as a worldwide radio-navigation system formed from a constellation of twenty-four satellites and their ground stations. Without going too deeply into the technical aspects of this, GPS helps us to find the location of an address we are going to just by connecting to this on our mobile phones.

Contemporary Zimbabwean context

In this section I wish to revisit *Integral Green Zimbabwe: An African Phoenix Rising* (Mamukwa, Lessem & Schieffer, 2014).

This book was written when the chips were really down in Zimbabwe as a result of Robert Mugabe's dictatorship. Ndlovu-Gatsheni (in Mamukwa, Lessem and Schieffer, 2014) outlines the Zimbabwean political/economic journey, from coloniality (which he claims constrains "the people's genius, and their innovative spirit") (p. 22), *Chimurenga,* independence and neo-colonialism. He hints that Zimbabwe may be constrained and paralysed by coloniality. Mamukwa, in the same book explores options available to Zimbabweans in an environment where survival depended on one's innovativeness. We see in the book that innovation is not always about doing new things but is sometimes about revisiting the old.

Let me hasten to say that Integral Green Zimbabwe (2014) was primarily about a dream of things to come. It was also about people drawing deep into themselves to find solutions to the economic/political challenges obtaining. These solutions were not just directed at individuals and families but at communities as well, in the true *Ubuntu/Unhu* spirit. The Chinyika story is one such innovation where Dr Chidhara Muchineripi mobilised the community to brainstorm on solutions to starvation as a result of incessant drought in the area (Lessaem, Muchineripi & Kada, 2012). The result was a re-innovation, where the community decided to re-engineer an old agricultural crop and system, resulting in the near commercial scale growth of finger millet (*zviyo/rukweza*), following the footsteps of their forefathers. Chinyika today is the land of plenty as a result of that re-innovation.

There are more stories to be drawn from Integral Green Zimbabwe, stories which were a blessing to communities that were beneficiaries to such. One hopes that such innovations will continue to uplift the lives of people in Zimbabwe, and that the new political dispensation creates an enabling environment for many more such innovations. One further hopes that there will be opportunities for bigger, greater and far-reaching innovations as a result of a more enabling environment.

However, in order to come up with appropriate solutions and innovations, there is need to trace the problems to be solved to their logical origin, otherwise a wrong solution is developed.

Still on the Zimbabwean situation, I wish to share some economic innovations that are developed in the street. Semi-literate people work as money changers for profit. They are quick to develop a system which encompasses a profitable rate, and work with more knowledgeable people who dictate the rate. This may seem rather insignificant, but when one gets to understand the level of education of some of these people then one is amazed at their genius.

Why knowledge can never remain static

Heraclitus (date unknown) said, "The only thing that is constant is change". This is so true, as we experience in our lives on a daily basis. Sometimes we are excited about change because it is obviously to our benefit, and sometimes change is painful and uncomfortable for us. One thing is for sure though, change continues to raid our lives. With change then comes knowledge. When any change comes, we need to understand the new position and develop coping mechanisms. Quite often this requires new knowledge on the new ways of doing things, or sometimes we simply need to develop ways of managing the new situation.

As highlighted earlier, sometimes change is developmental – it brings new and exciting products, and new ways of doing things. Other times change is negative and takes us back in terms of development. However, we can benefit even in these apparently negative eras as they give us a push to find ways of survival and the need to improve our lot.

People do not have control over knowledge production in general. This is likely to happen anyway even without our input. What maybe within our power is to influence such change through research and development. This way we can influence the quality of the knowledge produced.

Consciousness to evolution: Knowing what you need to change

In order to innovate, we need to heed the call to innovation, the consciousness to a need or gap. Heeding such a call will result in a conscious effort to do something. Chinyuku (in Mamukwa, Lessem & Schieffer, 2014, p. 192) developed the Industrial Ecology model. Working in the paint manufacturing industry, his consciousness was raised about the difficulties faced by paint manufacturing companies as a result of the very difficult operating business environment, with next to no local raw material and high shipping costs for imported raw materials. The Industrial Ecology model was designed to promote synergies in companies with similar needs so that they work together in purchasing and logistics, and use their skilled manpower to compete. In the same book (p. 198), Savory displays his consciousness of land deterioration in Zimbabwe as a result of overgrazing. He shares his innovation which is the use of the same livestock to reverse the damage to the land. Mamukwa in the same book describes Mick Pearce's building design of Eastgate Shopping Mall in Harare, Zimbabwe, modelled on the termite mound. The motivation? The amount of electricity used on lighting and air-conditioning in conventional buildings is huge. By employing biomimicry, Pearce sought to come up with a design that reduced such energy consumption by at least 10%. He modelled Eastgate Mall on a termite mound, enabling him to create a structure which had natural ventilation and cooling.

These few examples demonstrate that consciousness of a problem or challenge is the starting point to innovation.

The importance of knowledge in any civilisation

If I have given the impression that knowledge creation is all about modernity, I have erred. Knowledge creation is relevant and appropriate in any civilisation, however backward or advanced. In whatever historical context, knowledge creation and development happened all the time. Even in the ancient philosophical era, the likes of Aristotle studied everything from Botany to Zoology, to formal logic, but there is no evidence that any of them paused to reflect on what they were doing in terms of creating new knowledge at the time.

Conclusion

In this chapter I addressed the various motivations for knowledge creation and development, ranging from survival to luxury issues. I also expressed that the creation of new knowledge happens anyway, even without our input. However, research helps us to create relevant and appropriate knowledge, and to change from old knowledge to new in an ordered and less chaotic manner. Research also helps society to deal with tried and tested knowledge. In life we often find ourselves having to deal with problems that have arisen from the solutions of the past. Testing then, hopefully addresses the possible future problems by, if not eliminating such, at least minimising and mitigating.

References

Barton, D., Carey, D. & Charan, R. (2018). *An Agenda for the Talent-first CEO*. Book Excerpt. San Francisco: McKinsey Quarterly.

Church, Stephen D. (1999). *The Household Knights of King John*. Cambridge: Cambridge University Press.

Clinebell, H. (1995). *Counselling for Spiritually Empowered Wholeness: A Hope-centred Approach*. New York and London: Routledge.

Gantt, Henry L. (1919). *Organizing for Work*. New Jersey: The Quinn and Roben Company (Reprinted by Hive Publishing Company, Easton, Maryland)

Garraty, J. A. (1987). *The Great Depression: An Inquiry into the Causes, Course, and Consequences of the Worldwide Depression of the Nineteen Thirties as Seen by Contemptor*. New York: Anchor.

Garraty, J. A. (1987). *The Great Depression: An Inquiry into the Causes, Course, and Consequences of the Worldwide Depression of the Nineteen Thirties as Seen by Contemptor*. New York: Anchor.

Gitlow, H. S. & Gitlow, S. J. (1987). *The Deming Guide to Quality and Competitive Position*. New York: Prentice Hall.

Hanke, Steve H. & Kwok, Alex. (2009). On the Measurement of Zimbabwe's Hyperinflation. *Cato Journal*, 29 (2). Available at SSRN: https://ssrn.com/abstract=2264895

Jørgensen, D. (2010) *"The Metamorphosis of Ajax, Jakes, and Early Modern Urban Sanitation"*. *Early English Studies*, 10.

Kilroy, G. (2009). *The Epigrams of Sir John Harington*. Farnham: Ashgate.

Kinghorn, J. (1986). A Privvie in Perfection: Sir John Harrington's Water Closet. *Bath History*, 1, 173–188.

Lessem, R., Muchineripi, P. C. & Kada, S. (2012). *Integral Community: Social Economy to Social Commons*. Surrey: Gower.

Mamukwa, E., Lessem, R. & Schieffer, A. (2014). *Integral Green Zimbabwe: An African Phoenix Rising*. Farnham, Surrey: Gower.

McKinsey & Co. (2018). McKinsey Quarterly Report 2018 Number 1: Overview and full issue. San Francisco.

Nonaka, I. (1990). *Management of Knowledge Creation*. Tokyo: Nihon Keizai Shinbun-sha.

Schmidt, E. & Rosenberg, J. (2015). *How Google Works*. London: John Murray.

Turner, H. A. (1985). *German Big Business and the Rise of Hitler*. New York: Oxford University Press.

UNESCO: Data for Sustainable Development Goals: uis.unesco.org, viewed 19 February 2019, <http://uis.unesco.org/sites/default/files/documents/quick-guide-education-indicators-sdg4-2018-en.pdf.>

Part II

The context

A background to knowledge creation

3 The philosophy of knowledge creation

Introduction

I will devote this entire chapter to philosophy as it relates to and influences knowledge creation and societal learning. My approach will be to try and understand firstly philosophy in general, then African philosophy specifically, in an attempt to appreciate and understand, among other issues, the African perspective on knowledge creation and societal learning. Hountondji (2002) contends that real history influences the philosophy of a people. If this is to be believed (which I strongly feel it is), it is therefore important, in the analysis of any aspect of a people, to understand such philosophy in the backdrop of the history of such a people. For example, it is important to note how dictatorship and the adoption of Marxism-Leninism by African governments might have had a negative bearing on independent thought and knowledge creation. Hountondji (2002) suggests that some of these ideologies could have been introduced by dictators as smokescreens to oppressiveness. These new ideologies were backed up by instilling fear in the masses, for the self-intentions of the oppressive leadership. "Once fear was internalised and the appropriate ideological environment was created, the tyrant could sleep peacefully". (Hountondji, 2002, p. 113). The questions that beg to be asked are: What was/ is the effect of that fear on the indigenous rhythms of a nation? What impact did this then have on the culture of freedom of thought and knowledge creation? How did/does this affect national focus on developmental issues? How then, can we leverage on this history to promote a culture of knowledge creation in Africa in general and the world at large? It is my contention that, if we are to make an impact on the Zimbabwean situation in particular, Africa in general and the world at large, we need to approach our proposition from a way of thinking – a philosophy.

On identifying literature for this thesis, my observation was that, some of the authors of the literary works on African philosophy are people who have been schooled in Europe and America. In my view, their literary lenses have therefore been colored by the origin of their schooling. On the other hand, this could also work in the opposite direction, that their exposure in the North and West will also render a certain level of objectivity to their opinion.

Hountondji (2002) contends that African philosophy is a European invention. European philosophers were the first to study and try to understand this, ahead of our own African philosophers. He goes on to say it was a "product of intellectual history at the intersection of the most diverse disciplines, notably anthropology, the psychology of peoples, missionological theory and a good many other concerns" (p. 124). This then, he counsels, needs to be read with critical vigilance. He goes further to highlight the need for African intellectuals to free themselves from a thought system that has been worked out in advance by geographically far removed people who have their own perspectives and agendas to consider.

Appiah (1992) proposes that, while it is true that in Africa there is oral culture manifesting in religion, mythology, poetry and narrative, it is not true that the people have held on to an indigenous national education leaving only the educated to become "children of two worlds". He contends that at the level of "popular culture" even the illiterate embrace symbols of cultural globalisation such as Michael Jackson and Jim Reeves. What this essentially implies is that we are no longer in control of the influences around us, with all the media at our exposure. We as an African people are not immune to the influences of the global world. Neither are we immune to the influences of our origin and history. Therefore, when we talk of African philosophy, we need to appreciate that the contemporary African has all these influences affecting his thought process, and traditional African philosophy in these circumstances maybe a myth.

Among other issues therefore, in this literature review I will seek to understand the different perspectives from different African philosophers and their views on what and in what ways, might have impacted the African philosophy (ethnophilosophy?), and how then this might have affected a culture (or absence thereof) of knowledge creation in the various African cultures.

To place the subject of philosophy into context, in this chapter, though focusing on African philosophy, particularly of its relevance to knowledge creation and societal learning, I will take the liberty to dwell briefly on philosophy and philosophers in general, starting with the ancient philosophers, proceeding to modern philosophers who do not necessarily fall into the category of African philosophers. Philosophy being a relatively new subject to me as an African academic, I felt the urge to do this in an effort to put things into perspective for myself and for other African students of philosophy who may read this book. This is in order to trace back the history of philosophy, hopefully bringing the subject of African philosophy into perspective. In addition, many African philosophers make reference to these early philosophers, indicating that they themselves were influenced in one way or other, by their critical thinking.

What is philosophy?

Philosophy can be described as the study of general and fundamental problems, such as those connected with reality, existence, knowledge, values, reason, mind and language (Grayling, 1998). It has many branches, including metaphysics, ontology and epistemology. In the interests of time and writing space, I will briefly deal with the three branches mentioned here.

Metaphysics

Metaphysics is the branch of philosophy that seeks to explain the fundamental nature of being, and the world. It seeks to answer such questions as, "What is there?" and "What is it like?" (Chalmers, Manley & Wasserman, 2009). It seeks to bring clarity to people's understanding of existence, objects and their properties, space and time, cause and effect and other such issues.

Ontology

Ontology is a central branch of metaphysics, which investigates the basic categories of being, existence or reality (Effingham, 2013). It is concerned with investigating what entities exist and how such entities relate – how they can be subdivided according to their similarities and differences.

Epistemology

Sometimes referred to as the theory of knowledge, epistemology is probably the branch of philosophy that is most relevant to the subject of knowledge. It is concerned with the nature and scope of knowledge, and seeks to answer such questions as "What is knowledge?", "How is knowledge acquired?" and "To what extent is it possible for a given subject or entity to be known?" (Fine, 2000).

The early philosophers

This summary on some of the early philosophers is done to set the scene and put things into perspective with regard to the origins of knowledge and knowledge creation.

Ancient philosophers

Confucius, Socrates, Plato and Aristotle come under the classification of *ancient philosophers*. **Confucius** (551–479 BC) was a Chinese philosopher whose main interests were moral philosophy, social philosophy and ethics. He was a teacher, editor, politician and philosopher, and his ideas were termed "Confucianism". As a politician he believed that the best government is the one that rules through people's natural morality rather than by using bribery and coercion (Chin, 2007).

Socrates (469–399 BC) is classified as one of the founders of Western philosophy who made lasting contributions to the field of Epistemology, according to Plato. Socrates did not write any philosophical tests, and what is written is a product of the writings of his students, especially Plato. He was killed by the Greek government for corrupting the youth with his ideas, for not believing in the Greek gods and for being what Plato termed "the gadfly" of Athens (by irritating the citizenry with talks of justice and the pursuit of goodness) (Kagan,1987). Sometimes there is a price to pay for being a pioneer in the areas of knowledge. The story of Socrates also shows that there could be philosophers, even in Africa, who have never put their thoughts into writing.

Plato (428–348 BC) was an ancient Greek philosopher whose areas of interest included rhetoric, art, literature, justice, virtue, politics, education, family and militarism. Plato was a student of Socrates, a mathematician and a writer of philosophical dialogues. He was the founder of the Academy in Athens (the first institute of higher learning in the Western world). His notable ideas were known as Platonic realism. (Fine, 2000).

Aristotle (384–322 BC) was a Greek philosopher and a polymath. He was a student of Plato and teacher of Alexander the Great. During his career he went to Asia Minor where he carried out research on botany and zoology on the Island of Lesbos. He studied almost every subject possible, and is considered to have been a *universal genius,* together with the likes of Avicenna, Goethe and Isaac Newton. He is credited with the earliest study of formal logic. (Ackrill, 1981).

The unique feature about the ancient Greek philosophers was that they learnt from one another. For example, Plato was a student of Socrates, and Aristotle was a student of Plato. This phenomenon must have given the philosophers a springboard for their critical thinking. This became part of Greek societal learning. These men, among others, were clearly the fathers of philosophy, and their influence on subsequent philosophers of all ages, colour or creed cannot be over-emphasised. This is where it may have all begun. Modern day "philosophers" can draw useful lessons from the ancient philosophers, from a coaching and mentoring perspective.

Modern philosophers

For the purpose of remaining in the size confines of this chapter I will omit the other group of medieval philosophers and go to modern philosophers.

Descartes, Milton, Hume, Kant and Hegel are some of the well-known "modern" philosophers.

Descartes, Milton, Hume, Kant and Hegel

René Descartes (1596–1650) is the one who coined the phrase, "I think therefore I am" in the process of discovering that "I exist" is real and cannot be disputed https://www.iep.utm.edu/descarte/. He was educated at a Jesuit college where he was taught Mathematics and Physics, among other disciplines and was introduced to Galileo's work. His family was Catholic, yet he fought in the Protestant Dutch Army in 1618. In 1619 he had three dreams that influenced his future, resulting in him seeking a new method for scientific inquiry and to envisage a unified science. He broke away from the philosophical thought of his time by seeking to replace the traditional Scholastic–Aristotelian philosophy of the time and focusing on a more mechanistic model of creating knowledge through reason, which gained him the name "Father of Modern Philosophy". Descartes confirmed the existence of God, and that God was not a deceiver.

The two fundamental ways that Descartes broke away from the early philosophy are;

a.   He rejected substantial forms as explanatory principles in physics, and argued for "clearer and more fruitful explanations" being obtained through deduction.
b.   He rejected the notion that all knowledge must come from sensation, as such sensations are not always reliable.

This is an indication of the progression in the conception and development of knowledge.

John Milton (1608–1674) was a civil servant for the Commonwealth of England. He was scholarly, and is best known for his poem *Paradise Lost* (Thorpe, 1983). Privately tutored, he resented the university curriculum which he considered to consist of "stilted formal debates on abstruse topics". He became a proponent of monism or animist materialism, the notion that a single material substance which is "animate, self-active and free" composes everything in the universe: from stones and trees and bodies to minds, souls, angels, and God. His political thought leaned towards republicanism. His approach to theology, particularly Christianity could be termed as mixed and confused. He rejected the Trinity and believed the Son was subordinate to the father. He disliked Catholicism, though he did not lose his personal Faith. Milton inspired later poets and authors such as T. S. Eliot, Thomas Hardy and Harold Bloom.

David Hume (1711–1776) was a Scottish philosopher, historian, economist and essayist (Mossner, 2001). He was best known for his philosophical empiricism and scepticism. Introducing *A Treatise of Human Nature* Hume wrote, "'Tis evident, that all the sciences have a relation with human nature …. even *Mathematics, Natural Philosophy, and Natural Religion,* are in some measure dependent on the science of Man". He believed that the science of Man was the only solid foundation for the other sciences, and that this science assumed experience and observation as foundations for logical arguments. He is classified as an empirist. Although Hume himself did not talk much about induction, his work has been closely identified with inductive inferences – reasoning from the observed behaviour of objects to their behaviour when unobserved. On the self, Hume held that this was a bundle of experiences linked by the relations of causation and resemblance. He also conceived moral and ethical sentiments to be sources of intrinsic motivation. Hume's attitude towards Africans was that, due to their blackness, they "are precluded from the realm of reason and civilisation" (Serequeberhan, 1991, p. 5).

Immanuel Kant *(1724–1804)*

Born in Russia (Prussia at the time) Kant never travelled more than ten miles from the town of his birth, and never married (Kuehn, 2001). In his early work he came up with the philosophy that time and space were not materially real, but merely a condition of our internal intuition. At age forty-six he went into what became known as a "silent decade", where he isolated himself. When he came out of this, he published what is now recognised as one of greatest works in history, *Critique of Pure Reason*. This has indeed been recognised as the most significant work of metaphysics and epistemology in modern philosophy. In his philosophical work, Kant tried to answer the question, "What is enlightenment?" He postulated that judgements are the preconditions for any thought. His moral philosophy was based on what he called "categorical imperatives" – principles that are intrinsically valid, which must be obeyed by all. He also wrote on the idea of freedom as well as aesthetic and political philosophies, among many other subjects. Like Hume, Kant believed black people were inferior to white, and is quoted to have remarked about a black man, "… this fellow was quite black from head to foot, a clear proof that he was quite stupid" (Serequeberhan, 1991, p. 6).

Georg Wilhelm Friedrich Hegel (1770–1831)

Some of Hegel's works include the *Phenomenology of Spirit*, *The Science of Logic* and the *Elements of the Philosophy of Right*. His thought was to an extent influenced by Plato and Kant. Together with several other thinkers, Hegel regarded freedom and self-determination as real and having ontological implications for soul and mind. On the subject of "Spirit" Hegel greatly admired and praised Aristotle's work. From a religious perspective, Hegel believed in Jesus Christ as the son of God, and as being both divine and human (Pinkard, 2000).

About Africa, Hegel contends that it "is no historical part of the world; it has no movement or development to exhibit" (Serequeberhan, 1991, p. 6). These sentiments by some early philosophers about Africa and its people must have influenced the attitude of colonial masters when they came to Africa, resulting in the classification of Africans as second-class citizens in the colonies. This might also have influenced the quality of education given to African people as the "less intelligent" of the human species, resulting in their lack of creativity and innovation. For all their serious philosophical thought, Kant, Hume and Hegel, among others, were willing to categorise the African people as inferior, less intelligent, even stupid, without any scientific evidence.

Husserl (1859–1938)

Husserl studied mathematics, physics, astronomy and philosophy, and in turn taught philosophy. One of the prominent African philosophers, Hountondji, must have been fascinated by Husserl as in one of his books (Hountondji, 2002) he devotes the first two chapters explaining more than criticising Husserl's philosophy. This is a clear illustration of the influence that Western philosophers have had on African philosophers.

Husserl gave lectures on *Phenomenological Method,* among other subjects, and during his life and after, he attracted philosophers to phenomenology (Hountondji, 2002). He asserted that "in order to study the structure of consciousness, one would have to distinguish between the act of consciousness and the phenomena at which it is directed". He also expressed clearly the difference between meaning and object. He believed that truth-in-itself has an ontological correlate – being-in-itself. He further identified logic as a formal theory of judgement, and mathematics as formal ontology. Husserl is known for his serious critique of psychologism, among other things.

Senghor (1906–2001)

Although he was an African philosopher, I decided to discuss Senghor together with Modern Western philosophers because of the time of his philosophical contribution, and his strong links to France, particularly during his tenure as president of Senegal. Born in Senegal, he sailed to France when he was aged twenty-two. He received his post-secondary education in France (Thiam, 2014). He became a teacher and was also a poet. He even fought in the French army in 1933 during the German invasion of France. Together with Aimé Césaire and Léon Damas, Senghor coined the concept of "négritude" as a reaction against the strong dominance of French culture in the colonies, and against the perception that Africa did not have a developed culture compared to that of Europe (Appiah, 1992). Negritude was not an anti-white racism but sought to emphasise dialogue and exchange among different cultures.

Between 1983 and 2001 he wrote several books including the *Liberté* series. He was the first African to be elected a member of *l'Académie francaise,* in 1983.

As President of Senegal (1960–1980 Senghor) avoided the Marxist anti-Western ideology followed by many African governments, but rather opted to maintain close ties with France. This may have contributed to Senegal's political stability. His tenure as president was characterised by the development of African socialism. This created an indigenous alternative to Marxism. He also drew heavily from the *négritude* philosophy during his rule. During his lifetime, he was awarded the Lifetime Achievement Award by the African Studies Association in recognition of his "outstanding scholarship in African studies and service to the Africanist community". Indeed, when he died in 2001, Jacques Chirac (French President, 1995–2007) said, "Poetry has lost one of its masters, Senegal a statesman, Africa a visionary and France a friend".

In Senghor therefore, we see an individual who was a product of both the indigenous and exogenous knowledge rhythms, and he maximised on both to come up with a workable hybrid of knowledge that was to benefit the people of Senegal.

Contemporary African philosophers

Serequeberhan (1991) classifies contemporary African philosophers into two:

a. Those that believe that philosophy is a "culture-neutral universalistic discipline", who reject the African traditional wisdom, arguing that African philosophy can only be a geographic orientation. These philosophers, according to Serequeberhan, include Bodunrin, Wiredu and Hountondji.
b. Those that critically engage the critique of ethnophilosophy, emphasizing, in their concept and approach to philosophy, the serious engagement of traditional, historical as well as the contemporary situation of the continent. Serequeberhan himself identifies with this group in which he includes Owomoyela, Towa, Okolo and Wamba-Dia-Wamba (Serequeberhan, 1991).

Early explorers and missionaries' views on Africa

Serequeberhan (1991) introduces the concept of racist and ethnocentric view of early explorers, missionaries and colonisers towards the African people. According to these new entrants into the "dark" continent, the African was black, bad and unintelligent. Marx and Engels articulate the converse Eurocentrism as a philosophical position of the colonisers. Conquest confirmed as metaphysical truth the lack of humanness of the colonised. Hegel (Knox, 1969) is quoted to have called the African people barbarians who were inferior to the civilised European nationalities.

Said (1994) points out that colonisation created "little Europes" in Africa and India. This in many ways resulted in the African internalising a lot of negative disposition towards his indigenousness. This also resulted in the stagnation of African culture and to a certain extent, African philosophy. With the advent of "civilisation" and education emerged a creation of "neo-colonial elites" who mimic the coloniser, resulting in a new form of "coloniser" (the Europeanised African). This has made it difficult to expel colonialism from post-colonial Africa. Kenneth Kaunda (1966) touched on this when he bemoaned the intentions of colonial masters when they "train" Africans;

> Take training in any field – wherever you send your people they will be indoctrinated, consciously or unconsciously. They will be taught, very vigorously, to look at problems from the aid-giving country's point of view. In most cases, we like to think in terms of getting aid from various sources – that is, from both east and west – hoping against hope that this will be a shield against interference from either. In fact we end up with a mixture of various explosive gases in one bottle, and inevitably, explosions follow.

This view is supported by Onyewuenyi (Serequeberhan, 1991) when he bemoans the absence of the study of African Philosophy in European, Asian and Western Universities. He adds that this is a result of the popular Western European and American conception of the African. This depicted a savage, lazy African who did nothing, developed nothing or created nothing historical. Onyewuenyi attributes this to a racist and propaganda angle brought through by Christian missionaries, learned historians, ethnographers and explorers. Indeed, Christian missionaries termed Africa the "dark continent". Instead, while there was some evidence of African civilisation in the pre-colonial era, this was deliberately hidden to champion the concept that the African was sub-human, partly to justify such acts as slavery and economic exploitation.

(On the other hand, in many African states then, the African governments have in many cases turned out to be more brutal to the African citizenry, and resulted in worse suffering than was imposed by the original colonisers.)

Herodotus, for example, (date unknown) clearly stated in his writings that most of the Greek culture was derived from the Nile kingdoms. However, in reality, the correct historical and documented views about the African past are not popularised, according to Onyewuenyi. Freeman (2012) highlights that the first civilisation was in Sumeria and early Egypt. He actually depicts the African continent at some stage being more civilised than Europe which he described as being the home of a lowly race of hunters and herdsmen. Count Constantin Volney who visited Egypt in 1787 acknowledged that the black people in Egypt were the origins of European arts, sciences and even the use of speech. Yet the same people would become the subject of contempt because of their "sable skin and woolly hair".

Grimal (1992) writes about Ptahhotep who was the city administrator and first minister during the reign of Pharaoh Djedkare Isesi in the Fifth Dynasty. Ptahhotep wrote about Egyptian wisdom and literature, and his work is dated roughly around 25 BC. This then proves that there was significant knowledge and literacy in Africa going back many centuries, before the colonialists came with their so called civilisation.

One then wonders what happened to Africa. Why is it that, having been one of the first civilisations we have lost our position and now look to the North and West for new knowledge? Why have we lost our confidence and innovativeness?

Tempel's (1959) contribution, for the benefit of Belgian colonisers, made a positive impact by bringing the realisation that the "Bantu/African is not a beast devoid of consciousness, but a human being whose conscious awareness of existence is grounded on certain foundational notions" (Serequeberhan, 1991). Tempel postulated that the African was desirous, among all things, to be recognised by the white man as a full human being, with dignity. The colonised Africans were like the proletariat in capitalism. The articulation of African philosophy, therefore, needs to take place with this background in mind.

Views and facts on Western philosophy

Macel et al. (1984), criticised Western philosophy as academic and dehumanised, and bases his criticism on the fact that Western philosophers aim at constructing a conceptual system, as he sees this as divorcing thought from life. Regrettably, it is this type of philosophy that has become popular in Europe and America. He also criticises the notion that if there are no academic philosophers in Africa, then there is no African philosophy. Onyewuenyi contends that there are many academic philosophers in Africa but their work was deliberately hidden from the world, e.g. Plotinus, an Egyptian who wrote books on philosophy and opened a school in Rome, and of course Ptahhotep. The first woman philosopher, Hypatia was from Alexandria, and was murdered by Christians. Hence, what is now known as Greek or Western philosophy was actually copied from indigenous African philosophy. Socrates's famous statement, "Man, know thyself" was inscribed on Egyptian temple doors before Socrates was even born. Aristotle received his education in Africa and took over an entire library belonging to the Egyptian Mystery system. Clearly then, Africa has made a great contribution to philosophy as the world understands it today, though no credit has been accorded to the "dark continent" for any of this.

James (1954) contends that Greek philosophers were apprenticed under Egyptian Mystery Priests.

African philosophy

Abraham (1962), talks about a Ghanaian philosopher, Amo Anton, who entered the University of Thalle in Holland in 1729 where he later became Master of Philosophy. He proceeded to produce a book on logic in 1738. There were philosophers in Timbuktu and Jene in West Africa, and African scholars in the Mali and Songhai empires around 1520 (Davidson, 1966). There is, therefore, a lot of evidence of documented works on African philosophy, which has been totally ignored. Philosophy therefore, is not totally new to Africa. Sadly, this philosophical progress may have been disrupted by colonisation. However, there is also evidence that the consciousness of African people to the field of philosophy, particularly in the modern and contemporary eras, begins when they are exposed in one way or other, to Western philosophy. Examples of this include Senghor who was educated and worked in France, Hountondji who was also educated in France, Appiah who had healthy doses of both indigenous and exogenous culture and education, to name a few.

Onyewuenyi (Serequeberhan, 1991) contends that a philosophy of a people has nothing to do with academic exponents, and insists that philosophising is a universal experience. Every culture has its worldview. He adds that philosophy seeks to establish order among various phenomena surrounding our world, therefore there is African philosophy. He contends that metaphysics is necessary for art, morality, religion, economics, and sociology. Studies have indicated that Africans have accepted their foundations as consisting of ancestral worship, animism, totenism and magic.

Oruka (Serequeberhan, 1991) contends that African philosophy today is still in the meta-philosophy stage where the questions are, "What is philosophy?"

and "What is African philosophy?" GyeKye (1995) adds that the absence of a written historical past and the indigenous output of African thinkers lends credence to the question, "Is there African philosophy?"

Oruka comes up with some trends in current African philosophy, including ethnophilosophy and philosophic sagacity. Oruka's ethnophilosophy implies that Africa is free from philosophic rational discourse and personalised philosophical activity, as philosophy is viewed as general communal activity. With philosophic sagacity he contends that the problem in Africa is not lack of logic, reason or scientific curiosity, as there is evidence of same. Instead, his argument is that in fact communal consensus cannot be a hindrance to individual critical reflection. Therefore, traditional African folk wisdoms and taboo left some room for real philosophic thought.

Philosophical sagacity is a reflection of a person who is a "sage" and a "thinker". A sage is versed in the wisdoms and traditions of his people. Sages could be simply moralists who are faithful to the tradition, or just historians. However, some sages can develop philosophic capacity. Thinkers, on the other hand, are rationally critical, and recommend only those beliefs and wisdoms which satisfy their rational scrutiny. Sages with philosophic inclination (thinkers) make a critical assessment of their culture and beliefs, thus producing a system within a system and order within order. The first order is that of the culture philosophy. The second order is that of philosophic sagacity – using reason to assess the first order.

Oruka argues that, the important issue is not to write, but consistency. He disagrees with the notion that Africa is having a late start (or continuation?) in philosophy. He adds, "Lack of knowledge of one's or people's philosophy is not proof of the non-existence of such philosophy".

Oruka further contends that there is now a new kind of philosophy, "professional" philosophy. It is professional because it has professionally trained philosophers as its managers. It employs techniques commonly associated with European or Western philosophy. While this is fundamentally a criticism of ethnophilosophy, it lacks a dominating subject matter of its own. It also lacks a history showing debate and available literature to authenticate it.

Bodunrin, on the other hand, argues that philosophic sagacity becomes a joint product of both sage and the interviewer (the trained philosopher). This interaction can promote philosophical provocation. There is a difference between people capable of serious philosophical discourse and African philosophers. While some African people can engage in philosophical discourse, this does not necessarily make them philosophers. He believes that there has not been organised, systematic philosophical reflections by the Africans themselves, and this is what has created the European denial of philosophy in Africa. He argues that some African philosophers have treated the traditional way of life as a starting point, but with urbanisation and sophistication in other areas, this starting point might have become irrelevant.

Bodunrin postulates that philosophy is a conscious creation – one cannot be said to have a philosophy unless one has consciously reflected on one's beliefs.

He further argues that without writing it is not possible to have a tradition of philosophical reflection. Bodunrin further adds that some philosophic thinkers tend to romanticise the African past, yet not everything about our past is good, otherwise it would not have been easy to be colonised by a few white people.

Mudimbe (1988) observes that colonisation of the African continent was not the worst thing that happened to Africa, and sees structured distortions of colonisation consisting of four main political propositions. These are, prioritisation of industrial revolution over agricultural revolution, the simultaneous promotion of all branches of industry with a preferential approach to heavy industry, the emphasis on tertiary and service activities and the preference of exports to the detriment of the total economic system.

The outcome was the capitalist world system in colonised states, the underdevelopment dependences in organisational structures, lack of the structural capacity for autonomy and sustained growth, the total reorganised and submission to a Western model (eurocentrism) as well as the development of paradigmatic oppositions: traditional vs modern, oral vs written and printed, agrarian and customary communities vs urban and industrialised civilisation, subsistence economies versus highly productive economies. In addition, there was a progressive destruction of traditional realms of agriculture and crafts, leading to social disintegration of African societies and the growth of the urban proletariat. The new order broke the culturally unified and religiously integrated structure of African traditions through the introduction of schools, churches, the press and audiovisual media. There was also the discovery of African art and the constitution of African studies – the invention of Africanism as a scientific discipline.

Mudimbe therefore sees a mixed bag of benefits, both negative and positive, in colonisation. The biggest disadvantage in my view, is the loss of indigenous knowledge and cultures.

Appiah has a very interesting background consisting of strong genetic links in the indigenous and exogenous. The product of a Ghanaian father and an English mother, Appiah was born in London and raised in Kumasi, Ghana, educated in Cambridge, worked in Ghana and attended several universities in the United States, including Cornell, Yale, Harvard and Princeton; a truly global, multi-cultured individual. His mother's side of the family was a titled family in England, his maternal grandfather was an English statesman. His father was a descendent of Osei Tutu, the warrior emperor of pre-colonial Ghana (Appiah, 1992). This makes him a most interesting and objective critique of African culture and philosophy. Coincidentally Appiah wrote the foreword to Hountondji's book, *The Struggle for Meaning* (Hountondji, 2002).

Appiah (1992) asserts that, post colonisation Africa has continued to use European languages because in the task of nation building we could not afford to use each other's (among other reasons). He notes that most Africans south of the Sahara are Europhones. He also believes that colonial authority sought to stigmatise traditional religious beliefs.

He highlights that some early philosophers argued that blacks were inferior to whites, e.g., Hume (1748): "I am apt to suspect the Negroes to be naturally inferior to the Whites. There scarcely ever was a civilised nation of that complexion, nor even any individual, eminent either in action or speculation" (in Appiah, 1992). This was an attempt to conceptualise race in biological terms, which Appiah does not endorse.

Appiah suggests that yes, Africa has a stronger oral culture than other continents, manifesting in various forms. However, modern Africa has become part of the global village, appreciating what people on other continents appreciate, be it music or other good things in life. This may raise the question of the tangibility of pure African culture as well as African philosophy. The question is, what, in this day and age can be termed "pure African" when the world has become a cocktail of various forms and levels of indigenous and exogenous.

Of reading, Appiah says,

> The African teacher of Literature teaches students who are, overwhelmingly the products of an educational system that enforces a system of values that ensures that, the realm of culture, the West in which they do not live is the term of value; the American teacher of literature, by contrast, has students for whom the very West is the term of value but from whom the West is, of course, fully conceived of as their own. He proceeds to say, While American students have largely internalised a system of values that prohibits them from seeing the cultures of Africa as sources of value for them – despite ritualised celebrations of the richness of the life of savages – they have also acquired a relativist rhetoric that allows them, at least in theory, to grant that, "for the Other", his or her world is a source of value. American students would thus expect African students to value African culture, because it is African, while African students, raised without relativism, expect Americans to value their own culture because it is, by some objective, superior.
>
> (p. 69)

He therefore notes, sadly, that Africans themselves have begun to believe that their own culture is inferior.

I will now discuss the thoughts of specific contemporary African philosophers, who, in my view, have stood out in their philosophical thought with regard to African philosophy.

Kwasi Wiredu (1980)

According to Wiredu, the study of African philosophy must involve interpreting, clarifying, analysing and, after a critical evaluation, assimilating and developing the resultant body of thought. He adds that Contemporary Africa is in the middle of a transition from a traditional to a modern society. Such change involves changes in the physical environment as well as in the mental outlook of the African peoples, manifested in beliefs, customs and ordinary daily habits and pursuits.

Wiredu contends that the test of a contemporary African philosopher's conception of African philosophy is whether it enables him to engage fruitfully in the activity of modern philosophising with an African conscience.

According to Wiredu, there is a traditional African philosophy, and there is an emerging modern African philosophy. The contemporary African philosopher can do this without ignoring his own background of traditional African thought as well as the resources of his indigenous language.

He identifies three complaints which can afflict society and interfere with requisite development as anachronism, authoritarianism and supernaturalism.

He observes also that traditional African culture generally is weak in areas of logic, mathematical, analytical, and experimental procedures and strong in intuition and emotional skills. This has resulted in weaknesses in traditional technology, warfare, architecture, medicine etc. These weaknesses or shortcomings have resulted in many hardships for the African people. In medicine for example, instead of seeking to sharpen their diagnostic skills traditional healers dip into witchcraft and necromancy. Due to poor pharmacology people die in droves because the prescriptions given are unresearched.

While all African nations have embraced modernisation through literacy, science and industrialisation, industrial activity is limited to repair and maintenance of machinery, and not design and development of new equipment. Wiredu gives the example of a Ghanaian mechanic who, when working for a white man will use the tools provided to ensure precision and accuracy, but on opening his own workshop, he reverts to estimating using his own eyes, resulting in substandard work. Wiredu suggests that this is a result of growing up in an environment that does not give importance to exact measurements.

Wiredu yearns for a cultural revolution where the mentality of the people is changed, where there is change in mental habits in the areas of traditional medicine, handling of machines and interpretations of ill fortunes, to name a few. This can be achieved over time through introducing a methodological component in our education, initiating children early into the discipline of formal and informal logic and into the methodology of rational thinking and developing minds that are eager to test claims and theories against observed facts and adjust beliefs accordingly.

Traditional life, according to Wiredu, is guided by philosophical concepts that are alive on a day-to-day existence. He postulates that the best philosophers are always conscious of the ultimate relevance of their thinking to the practical concerns of life. This generation is living in the transitional epoch in which our actions and habits are governed even unconsciously by inherited traditional concepts as well as global influences.

Wiredu proposes that it is a function of philosophy in any society to examine the intellectual foundations of its culture, through reasoned criticism and where possible, reconstruction. This is the way to philosophical progress. The importance attached to group life is one quality that we as Africans must keep. The sense of solidarity and fellowship is complemented by the extended family, spilling into the larger community. This works because of the sense of fellowship that extends sympathy to people beyond the immediate blood relatives.

Industrialism tends to be a threat to this solidarity and humaneness.

He further postulates that African philosophies as they are today are folk philosophies, consisting of what elders said or are said to have said. Traditional philosophies (African or otherwise) are pre-scientific. These consist of unwritten proverbs, maxims, usages, etc., passed down from generation to generation.

In the contemporary world science has brought many changes. In Africa, the introduction of science has been through colonisation. Industrialisation has brought changes to family life, resulting in the traditional ethic losing part of its hold on society, which includes the residence of knowledge and wisdom which used to be in the elders, extensive family and neighborhood connections which facilitated communal fellowship and responsibility and informal education through a person's upbringing, focused on moral outlook and traditional religion. With modernisation, technology and urbanisation, some of these factors have changed.

Scientific education conflicts with traditional religion and medicine. It also conflicts with Christianity. With the increase in scientific influence, through industrialisation, the issue of philosophy becomes a matter of individual responsibility. Wiredu believes that science is a critical factor in the transition from tradition to modernity, therefore the modern philosopher should take cognizance of this. He also assumes philosophy can be universal. When we learn a new language, we also learn a philosophy, mostly unconsciously. Therefore, with the advent of the English language, we have bought into the Western philosophy to varied levels.

Western societies too have passed through a stage where explanations of phenomena relied on the agency of spirits. Some less sophisticated sections of Western populations still do. Because traditional thought cannot match modern, science-oriented thought, some Western liberals conceive Africans as their intellectual inferiors.

Due to the influence of Western anthropology, and partly due to insufficient critical reflection, many contemporary Africans tend to identify African thought with traditional African thought. Being traditional is not synonymous with being non-literate. India has a long tradition of written literature, yet only recently did the scientific spirit have an impact on the Indian way of life.

However, a culture cannot be scientific and non-literate at the same time.

There is need to do an analysis to separate the backward aspects of our culture from those worth keeping.

According to Wiredu therefore, for true development to happen in Africa we need to develop habits of critical thought. The difference between Western

Philosophy and traditional African philosophy is that the Western philosopher argues for his thesis, clarifying his meaning and answering objections. African traditional thought should only be compared with Western folk thought. The contemporary African philosopher therefore cannot divorce himself from the philosophies of the West.

What can philosophy do for Africa?

It is Wiredu's view that, if the philosopher has a duty to combat ideology in the bad sense, he also has a duty to promote ideology in the good sense. Regrettably, in Africa it has been the politician rather than the philosopher who has tended to propound an ideology. As there have not been real impact upon thought habits, such ideologies have tended to degenerate into instruments of coercion.

Wiredu further says,

> We are engaged not only in social and economic reconstruction but also in cultural reconstruction. What we ought to do, what we are in any case compelled by modern developments to do, is to speed up that process. This implies the admission that our culture is less than ideal in some important respects and that we have to introduce new elements into it, elements that will sometimes derive from alien sources. This, if you consider the matter frankly, is what is meant by that modernisation which many people, high and low, say they want in Africa. **That our culture ... our traditional, indigenous culture – is not what it might be has always been an unpleasant thought, and very unwelcome to those engaged in the enterprise of trying to infuse a sense of racial self-respect in the African masses.** The thinker ... must rise above the common level of insight. It is in fact, only the African who is free of racial inferiority complex who can look critically at our culture and acknowledge its shortcomings.
>
> (p. 59)

He suggests that inferiority in our people was induced by colonisation, and was responsible for racial self-deprecation. However, for progress and development, it is important for us to understand that to borrow from another culture does not necessarily imply a belief in the over-all superiority of that culture. No culture in the world is perfect. Therefore, the culture from which another culture has made a borrowing may itself be in need of reformation in some other respects, e.g., Africa may need to borrow technology from the West, but it does not mean that generally our culture is inferior to the Western culture.

Wiredu goes further to say that the acquisition of knowledge does not automatically make a man wise, or an intellectual. The intellectual is one who, through education, has developed the mind to process facts and extracting their significance for human life. While wisdom is not the same thing as knowledge, knowledge precedes wisdom. Knowledge is indispensable to wisdom. A wise man is one who is skilled in turning knowledge to serve the purposes of human relations. This is what we need to achieve in Africa and other developing communities.

Kwame Gyekye (1995)

According to Gyekye (1995), the absence of a written African historical past and the indigenous output of African thinkers, gives credence to the question, "Is there African philosophy?" He contends that philosophical concepts, ideas and propositions can be found imbedded in African Proverbs, linguistic expressions, myths and folktales, religious beliefs and rituals, customs and traditions of the people, in their art symbols and in their socio-political institutions.

Gyekye believes that philosophy is a cultural phenomenon – philosophical thought is grounded in cultural experience. African philosophical thought, therefore, he suggests, is expressed both in the oral literature and in the thoughts and actions of the people. He points out that sometimes when a people are not very literate they tend to express themselves through artistic symbols. He quotes Busia (date unknown), who says "Akan drum language is full of riddles that conceal reflective thought and philosophy".

In his view, a philosophical doctrine does not have to be shared by all Africans for it to be African (there is no need for consensus); it need only be a product of the rational, reflective exertions of an African thinker, aimed at giving analytic attention or response to basic conceptual issues in African cultural experience.

Philosophies of some cultures have been written down for centuries, making it possible to interpret, elucidate, refine and extensively develop them both vertically and horizontally. Philosophies of other cultures, such as African cultures have remained part of the oral tradition. However, Gyekye suggests that the absence of written philosophical literature does not imply the absence of philosophical thinking or philosophical ideas. There is need though to draw a distinction between traditional African philosophy and modern African philosophy.

Gyekye too refers to Northern philosophers (e.g., Aristotle). He makes the point that Greek philosophy was a component of Hellenic culture. By deduction, so too is African philosophy. Furthermore, it is difficult to separate the philosophy of the individual thinker from that of his people and age.

He adds that language embodies a philosophical point of view and also influences philosophical thought.

Gyekye recognises as significant resolutions passed at the second Congress of Negro Writers (1959) by the Commission on Philosophy;

a. African philosophy can never consist of reducing the African reality to Western systems;
b. The Western philosophic approach is not the only possible one, therefore;
   i. The African philosopher should learn from the traditions, tales, myths and proverbs of his people, and
   ii. He must divest himself of a possible inferiority complex, which might prevent him from starting from his African being to judge the foreign contribution.

Gyekye also points out that philosophy responds at the conceptual level to the fundamental problems posed at any given time. For example, it would contribute in solving problems created by colonisation and reconstructing African societies in the post-colonial era, which will require profound investigation into fundamental ideas and general principles. This is where philosophy becomes relevant. To interpret this in a more local sense, what aspects of Zimbabwean philosophy can we depend on to help us propel ourselves to raise our phoenix? How do we respond to the circumstances of our society?

According to Gyekye, then, contemporary African philosophers must try to provide conceptual responses to the problems confronting modern African societies. It is important to study and understand the philosophical output of other cultures, for such study may help deepen the understanding of our own. However, focus of understanding our own should be placed on our own cultural, linguistic and historical background of African people. Philosophy is essentially a cultural phenomenon, according to Gyekye.

He places emphasis on the aspect of working together as a community to achieve more. He borrows from the Akan thought, which says that communalism is not a negation of individualism, but a recognition of the limited character of the possibilities of the individual, which limitations diminish the individual's self-sufficiency. This is articulated in the following Akan quote:

> One finger cannot lift up a thing.
> If one hand scraps the bark of a tree for medicine, the pieces fall down.
> The left arm washes the right arm and the right arm washes the left arm.

This is synonymous with "Harambe" in Swahili, and "nhimbe" or "humwe" in Shona culture. Emphasis is placed on the value of collective action, mutual aid and interdependence as necessary conditions not only for an individual's welfare, but for the successful achievement of even the most difficult undertakings (and for the benefit of the larger community).

The Akan social philosophy seeks to avoid the excesses of both communalism and individualism, "allowing for a meaningful, albeit uneasy interaction between the individual and society". Gyekye subscribes to this, and at the same time gives space to modern philosophy to address current societal problems.

Paulin Hountondji

According to Hountondji (2002) African philosophy can only be seen as such if produced by an African. He displays the live debate that gives reality to the different perspectives on African Philosophy by different philosophers. This shows a rhythmic development of African philosophy through debate, criticism and academic discourse. Hountondji (2002) shows how, for him, this happened through the likes of Robert Niamkey. Philosophy should however not mean one thing in Africa and another elsewhere.

Of science, Hountondji argues that, being both object and model of philosophical thought, science is also the ultimate end of thought and of human life in general, the infinite task that gives meaning to humanity's collective existence. Science is a lever of actual knowledge, and hence should offer an opportunity to a thinking subject to articulate the acts of knowing expressed through the corpus. Science, therefore, only finds realisation in actual knowledge. Science is a product of knowing resulting from the knowledge acts of numerous individuals, and has no other aim than to enable the reproduction of these same acts by other individuals. African philosophy then, is immediately at a disadvantage as science is not one of Africa's strongest points.

Language, on the other hand, according to Hountondji, is a phenomenology of logical and mental experiences. Thought is the silent form of language. Solitary thought is only an imaginary form of listening. Things speak by themselves. By so doing they establish a universe of meaning that is anterior to man, that human discourse aspires to find. Richer than human languages, the universe of meanings is richer and considered wider than the world of objects.

Hountondji contends that "… the inferiorization of black cultures should not be considered as the cause, but rather the result of colonization seen as economic, political, and military phenomenon". He adds that "… the myth of white superiority cannot be effectively combated by holding up against it a counter myth". In other words, both superiority of the white man and the inferiority of a black man are myths.

Hountondji does not subscribe to "primitive unanimity" where everyone is in agreement with everyone else. He instead sees the African field as "plural, like all fields, a virgin forest open to all possibilities, to all potentialities, a host to all contradictions and intellectual adventures".

According to Hountondji (2002), shutting ourselves into our cultural past as Africans is both an apologetic relation to our heritage and an act of responding in exactly the way that is expected of us. He points out that there are those with racist tendencies which make people see others' cultures as inferior and their own as superior. On the other hand, those people with "inferior" cultures may sometimes tend to go out of their ways to justify and critique their cultures instead of taking an objective look. While there are positives and negatives in every culture, negative attitudes towards different cultures may result in losing opportunities to learn from the diversity.

Hountondji's background lends a certain objectivity to the subject of African philosophy. As he says, even reading a book on a particular philosophy does not necessarily leave an individual unchanged. His European education did not leave him, as an African philosopher unchanged either. We see a philosopher who has probably leant to mix and adapt indigenous and exogenous rhythms to come up with a hybrid rhythm that speaks to the new global world. In this sense African philosophy has to take its place in a world where other philosophies remain relevant even to the African people, depending on their circumstances.

Hountondji therefore speaks even to the circumstances of industry in developing countries where workers are on the whole a product of a hybrid system of education (indigenous informal early education followed by exogenous formal education, followed by exogenous training at the workplace, in the general context of an indigenous lifestyle tempered with the exogenous influences to such lifestyles by the globalisation concept that has been heralded by the information age).

The subject of African philosophy is an on-going debate in which even the proponents themselves move and modify their positions as more information is released into the body of knowledge. Is philosophy therefore, dynamic like culture? Or is it static? He also subscribes to ethnophilosophy as a form of African philosophy.

Ethnophilosophy

There is need for us to fully understand what ethnophilosophy is, because a number of philosophers tend to hide behind this word when it comes to African philosophy.

Hountondji (2002) defines ethnophilosophy as the attempt to explore and systemise the conceptual world of traditional African cultures. It is based on myths, folk wisdom and the proverbs of the people. His analysis is that this can be inaccurate, hence we need to be careful how we put it to philosophical use. He comes up with two assumptions that relate to ethnophilosophy, (a) the assumption that there is a central body of ideas shared by all Africans (unionism), and (b) that there is value in the recovery of this tradition. Tempels, Senghor, Mbiti and Kagame are also proponents of ethnophilosophy. Towa and Wiredu (Serequeberhan, 1991) argue that there is no value in digging up information on ethnophilosophy. For Wiredu (1980), there are no African truths, but only truths, some of them about Africa. Appiah (1992) on the other hand believes that, while ethnophilosophy on its own has no value, it is a starting point of negotiating and understanding the conceptual lives of contemporary Africans. According to Mudimbe (1988), some professionals have expressed reservations that ethnophilosophy can lead to "intellectual heresies" by promoting ambiguous commentaries on primitive rationality.

Gyekye (1995) criticises Hountondji and Towa's explanation of ethnophilosophy as implying a 'monolithic' set of ideas and beliefs, leading to unionism. He adds that this further implies that there is lack of individuality in traditional philosophical thought, as if an entire tribe would think with one mind.

What seems to be prominent in the debate on ethnophilosophy is that it is relevant in as much as it sheds light on the background to African thought but cannot stand alone as a field of philosophy. Even Hountondji (2002) acknowledges that while it is useful to understand traditional African culture, this cannot be the be all and end all of African philosophy.

Professional contemporary African philosophers

It would not be proper or fair to complete this exposé without paying tribute to contemporary African philosophers, who, for all intends and purposes are breaking new ground in critical thought. This should be encouraged, as should the sharing and critiquing of this critical thought for continuous development in this fascinating field of knowledge. The debate on whether African culture can be classified as philosophy, and the discourse surrounding ethnophilosophy is important and necessary in the journey of knowledge. Ten or twenty years from now, I am sure there would have been a meeting of the minds where all this critical thought is concerned. Even if there is not, Africans specifically, and academe in general, will benefit from the myriad of different philosophical thoughts. The field of Knowledge Creation will benefit more.

Philosophy and knowledge creation

What bearing then, does all this have on knowledge creation and societal learning?

The ancient philosophers made massive contributions to knowledge creation by bringing to the fore some ground-breaking philosophical viewpoints which would influence philosophy for centuries to come. Socrates is credited with being one of the founders of philosophy, and he contributed to the field of ethics, among other areas. He believed in self-development, and mentored other great ancient philosophers. Plato wrote Socrates's philosophy, mentored Aristotle, is credited with the concept of epistemology, and contributed in developing further the subject of philosophy and science, among other achievements. He founded the Academy of Athens. Aristotle is credited with being the first to write on Western philosophy, he taught Alexander the Great, and was credited with the first formal development of logic, among other achievements. Three things keep recurring in the ancient philosophers; that is establishing new knowledge, teaching and mentoring others and, apart from Socrates, putting their discoveries and those of others into writing. This then becomes a very good model to follow on knowledge creation and societal learning.

To expand an appreciation of the effects of colonisation, I will dwell a little on the Zimbabwean (then Rhodesia) situation after colonisation. African people were forcibly moved from the land of their forefathers to less fertile land. When urbanisation developed, men were allowed to move to the then Salisbury (present day Harare) for the purpose of providing labour to white people. A "pass" system was introduced to keep track of the movement of Africans. Movement in certain areas was restricted (Yokushini, 2006). In the countryside, new laws were enacted to prescribe how many cattle individual families could keep, governing restrictions on hunting and other such. This gives credence to Fanon's postulations, when he summed it all up;

> Colonial domination, because it is total and tends to oversimplify, very soon manages to disrupt in spectacular fashion the cultural life of a conquered people. The cultural obliteration is made possible by the negation of national reality, by new legal relations introduced by the occupying

power, by banishment of the natives and their customs to outlying districts by colonial society, by expropriation, and by enslaving of men and women.

(Fanon, 1959)

What thought, if any – what creativity and innovation would come from the people described by Fanon? He goes further to describe the situation of a colonised nation, where every effort is made to make the colonised person admit and accept the inferiority of his culture and himself, and conversely the superiority of his oppressor. This is what has handicapped the Zimbabwean's mental capacity for the past couple of centuries. The available intellect is focused on acquiring the ways of the colonisers, and these people are rewarded with better jobs and better posts in life, which motivates more people to adopt the same ways. It becomes common cause to criticise one's own culture. Mbembe (2001), expresses similar thoughts when he says that colonial sovereignty was based on three rights, namely the right of conquest, the right of legitimation, and finally the right of maintenance, spread and permanence. The colonisers were here to stay, and things would be done their way. The colonised were the property and "thing" of power. This had serious handicaps on the individuality of the colonised, his creativity and innovativeness. Regrettably, Africans were at the mercy of the worldview of the colonisers. This may be the reason why companies and individuals struggle to be innovative.

Lessons learnt from philosophy

The lessons learnt from philosophy are many, and only a few will be highlighted here. The first one is probably that philosophy is the route to solving social woes in countries and the world. It is philosophers that come up with new thoughts and ideas for problem resolutions. The importance of mentoring and teaching others in knowledge creation and societal learning is also apparent, as demonstrated in the Hellenic philosophical community. It is also important to have a culture of continuous critical analysis of the said philosophies, which comes out even in the contemporary African community of philosophers. This has the effect of improving the thought process and challenging philosophical thought. This is a critical lesson, because philosophers, like in any field of study, may have some scientific blind spots, which can be highlighted and corrected by others.

Secondly, it is not right to put people into categories and to direct stigmas towards them, simply because we do not understand them enough. The likes of Hume, Kant and Hegel jumped to the conclusion that Africans, because they are black, are inferior, (another scientific blind spot?) and yet we read about very successful Africans such as Amo Anton (Abraham, 1964), Senghor, Nelson Mandela (Mandela, 2010) and Barack Obama (Woodward, 2010), to name a few. There is no culture that is necessarily superior to another, only different. Communities would benefit all round by keeping the good aspects of their indigenous culture and trade in the not so good ones with the good exogenous cultures they come across.

It is evident that colonisation had the result of turning Africans into repairers and maintainers of machinery rather than creators of such machinery. This was not only as a result of the education given to Africans but also the levels that they were placed in jobs (not too high levels). Radical approaches need to be adopted in organisations to turn people into champions of creations rather than just maintainers of other people's creations. The starting point would be somehow restoring people's confidence in themselves, to convince them that they are just as intelligent and capable as their Western and Eastern counterparts, but only differentiated by their exposure, and to create opportunities for such innovation. On the other hand, African people in general also need to work at recording the information they generate for posterity as well as training themselves in terms of improving precision and accuracy.

Africans may have been trail blazers in terms of philosophy and literacy, particularly Egypt. Somehow the ancient time Egyptians gave their knowledge away to Greece. They gave an entire library away. Now Egypt is just another country without the early start gains of the knowledge signified by their philosophy and literacy. The critical lesson is, hold on to your knowledge. Share it by all means, but do not lose it.

Finally, philosophy is a source of motivation and emancipation. It creates passion and strong belief in the proponent of any philosophical thought. Particularly in the early philosophers, even governments would turn against proponents of particular philosophical thought, to the extent of killing them for it. People were sometimes emancipated enough to die for what they believed in, for example, Socrates was tried and killed for "corrupting the minds of the youth and for impiety (not believing in the Greek gods)". Yet Socrates' work is revered to this day. Socrates could have fled, but he chose to stay and go through the trial and death because he was psychologically emancipated to the extent that he did not fear death. Confucius lived in exile for many years because the Chinese government of the day did not agree with his critical thought. Nelson Mandela stayed in prison for twenty-seven years for the same reason. African countries continue to suffer at the hands of dictators because there are few people emancipated enough in their minds to fight this, like Mandela did.

What then is knowledge?

Knowledge (and its definition) continues to be an issue of on-going debate among philosophers in the field of epistemology. Plato and others specify that for anything to be accepted as knowledge: "it must be justified, true, and believed". Cavell (2002) says that knowledge acquisition involves complex cognitive processes such as perception, communication, association and reason.

The next question is, why is the creation of new knowledge so important in organisations? Nonaka and Takeuchi (1995) argue that knowledge is perishable, therefore organisations cannot be complacent with today's knowledge, as different types of knowledge will be required as the competitive environment changes. Creating new knowledge will therefore become the source of competitiveness and experience has shown that lack of innovation, even in the way customers are treated, leads to loss of market share. Nonaka and Takeuchi define organisational knowledge creation as "the capability of a company as a whole to create new knowledge, disseminate it throughout the organisation, and embody it in products, services and systems". This is where we draw the line between individual inventions and innovations and organisational knowledge creation. Gumport (2002) postulates that there is a possibility that knowledge creation may grow into a legitimate and enduring academic field, like Sociology and Mathematics, and that this can only happen through faculty interest and intellectual content.

The link between philosophy and knowledge creation

Nonaka and Takeuchi (1995) dwell a lot on the definition of knowledge from the perspective of different philosophers.

Plato contends that the physical world is a mere shadow of the perfect world of "ideas". This comes through pure reason. Aristotle on the other hand says that form cannot be isolated from a physical object and does not exist independent of sensory perception. He stresses the importance of observation and the clear verification of individual sensory perception.

Descartes questioned all beliefs except the existence of the questioner in his famous statement, "I think therefore I am". He intimates that ultimate truth can only be deduced from the real existence of the thinking self. True knowledge about external things can be obtained by the mind, and not by the senses, he says.

Locke (the founder of British empiricism) criticised Descartes and contends that ideas come through two kinds of experience: sensation and reflection.

Kant, Hegel and Marx try to come up with a synthesis. Kant argues that knowledge begins with experience but does not all rise out of experience because the human mind plays an active role. His philosophy is called "transcendental idealism". His position is closer to rationalism than empiricism. Hegel on the other hand believed that knowledge begins with sensory perception, which becomes more subjective and rational through a dialectic purification of the senses, reaching the stage of self-knowledge of the "Absolute Spirit". This is the highest form of knowledge. Like Kant, his position is also closer to rationalism than to empiricism. Karl Marx came up with the belief that perception is an interaction between the knower (subject) and the known (object), with knowledge being obtained by handling things.

Contemporary philosophers have challenged the Cartesian split which says that the essence of the human being lies in the rational thinking, placing emphasis on the importance of some form of interaction between the self and the outside world in seeking knowledge:

- Edmund Husserl (a German philosopher) – focused on the relationship between the thinking self and the world. He built the foundation of phenomenology (human consciousness of self and other objects). "Pure consciousness" can be reached through "phenomenological reduction" – where all factual knowledge and reasoned assumptions about a phenomenon are set aside so that pure intuition of its essence may be analysed.
- Martin Heidegger (student of Husserl) contends that "our being in the world" (*Dasein*) is characterised by active relationships with other things in the world. He rejected the Cartesian dualism between the thinking subject and the objective world. He reckons *Dasein* is not a detached spectator like Descartes's thinking self, but someone who has a close relationship between knowledge and action.
- Jean-Paul Sartre – a French existentialist stated that "For human reality, to be is to act", and that the act must be defined by an *intention*. The intentional choice of the end reveals the world.
- Maurice Merleau-Ponty – a French phenomenologist who contended that perception is a bodily cognitive action aimed at something and that consciousness is "not a matter of 'I think that' but I 'can'". The body is subject as well as object, and through it we can perceive things and understand other people. The body subject contains knowledge of bodily habits as driving a car, typing and a blind man's use of a cane.
- Ludwig Wittgenstein, an Austrian proponent of "analytical philosophy" initially viewed language as a "picture" of reality that corresponds to logic. He rejected metaphysics as "nonsensical". Later he viewed language as a "game" played by multiple persons following rules.
- William James, (1907) a proponent of *Pragmatism,* argued that if an idea works, it is true; if it makes a difference to life in terms of cash value, it is meaningful.
- John Dewey, (1929) another proponent of *Pragmatism,* argued that "ideas are worthless except as they pass into actions which rearrange and reconstruct in some way, be it little or large, the world in which we live". This has attempted to develop an interactive relationship between human beings and the world by means of human action, experiment and experience (Nonaka & Takeuchi, 1995).

Challenges to the various definitions and understandings of the subject of knowledge will most likely continue, as long as the human race remains in existence. The interest of these different definitions of knowledge in this book is derived from the relevance of these definitions to understanding knowledge and knowledge creation.

Conclusion

The history of philosophy tells us that critical thought started in Africa (Egypt to be specific). The Hellenic philosophers such as Aristotle, were in a way products of the Egyptian education system (James, 1954). It is evident then, that colonisation disrupted the indigenous rhythms of the African peoples, resulting in the loss of self-confidence, innovativeness and creativity.

Sadly, although critical thought started in Africa, it was donated to the Hellenic communities who then became heroes in terms of making strides in the knowledge arena. Colonisation did not help Africa as Africans were subdued by their colonisers. They therefore lost the heart to develop critical thought and philosophy. This has put Africa back a lot in terms of knowledge creation and philosophy. It is through this that the innovation drive can be enhanced in Africa.

The race and colour issues sometimes interfere with progress as the issue of classifying some races as superior or inferior stands in the way of knowledge development and philosophical thought. People should focus on consolidating the good and useful integration of the indigenous and exogenous knowledge rhythms.

Nonaka and Takeuchi have done extensive work on the issue of knowledge sharing, transfer and development, and their starting point was philosophy, particularly ancient philosophy. This goes to show that this is a relay – we pick up from the giants that went before us, make our own contributions and leave it for the giants coming behind us to continue. It is a never-ending journey.

In the next chapter, I will turn onto the subject of "religion" and how it affects or influences knowledge and knowledge creation.

References

Abraham, W. (1962). *The Mind of Africa*. Chicago: University of Chicago Press.

Abraham, W. E. (1964). The Life and Times of Wilhelm Anton Amo. *Transactions of the Historical Society of Ghana*, 7, 60–81.

Acemoglu, D. & Robinson, J.A. (2012). *Why Nations Fail: The Origins of Power, Prosperity, and Poverty*. London: Profile Books.

Ackrill, J. L. (1981). *Aristotle the Philosopher*. Oxford and New York: Oxford University Press.

Appiah, K.A. (1992). *In My Father's House: Africa in the Philosophy of Culture*. New York: Oxford University Press.

Cavell, S. (2002). *Knowing and Acknowledging: Must We Mean What We Say?*. London: Cambridge University Press.

Chalmers, D., Manley, D. & Wasserman, R. (2009). *Metaphysics*. New York: Oxford University Press.

Chin, A. (2007). *The Authentic Confucius: A Life of Thought and Politics*. New York: Scribner.

Davidson, B. (1966). *History of a Continent*. London: Weidenfeld & Nicolsson.

Effingham, N. (2013). *An Introduction to Ontology*. New York: Wiley.

Fanon, F. (2008). *Black Skin, White Masks*. New York: Grove Press.

Fanon, F. (1959). (English Translation – 1965) *A Dying Colonisation*. New York: Grove Press.

Fine, G. (2000). *Plato 1: Metaphysics and Epistemology*. New York: Oxford University Press.

Freeman, H. (2012). *The Sumerians: A History from Beginning to End*. New York: Hourly History Limited.

Grimal, N. (1992). *A History of Ancient Egypt*. Boston: Blackwell Publishing.

Grayling, A. C. (1998). *Philosophy 1: A Guide through the Subject*. London: Oxford University Press.

Gumport, P. J. (2002). *Academic Pathfinders: Knowledge Creation and Feminist Scholarship*. Hartford: Greenwood Press.

Gyekye, K. (1995). *An Essay on African Philosophical Thought: The Akan Conceptual Scheme*. Revised Edition. Philadelphia: Temple University Press.

Gyekye, K. (1977). *Tradition and Modernity: Philosophical Reflections on the African Experience*. New York: Oxford University Press.

Hegel, G. W. F. (Author), Knox T. M. (Translator) & Pelczynski, Z. A. (Introduction). (1969). *Hegel's Political Writings*. Oxford: Clarendon Press.

Holland, H. (2008). *Dinner with Mugabe: The Untold Story of a Freedom Fighter Who Became a Tyrant*. Capetown: Penguin Books.

Hountondji, P. J. (Ed.) (1977). *Endogenous Knowledge: Research Trails*. Dakar: Senegal.

Hountondji, P. J. (2002). *The Struggle for Meaning: Reflections on Philosophy, Culture and Democracy in Africa*. Columbus: Ohio University Press.

James, G. G. M. (1954) Reprinted in 2015. *Stolen Legacy*. New York: Create Space Independent Publishers.

Kagan, D. (1987). *The fall of the Athenian empire*. Ithaca, NY: Cornell University Press.

Kaunda, K. (1966). *African Development and Foreign Aid Speech*. A Speech Delivered at the Opening of the University of Zambia.

Kuehn, M. (2001). *Kant: A biography*. Cambridge: Cambridge University Press.

Macel, G., Schilpp, P. A. & Hahn, L. E. (1984). *The Philosophy of Gabriesl Marcel*. Chicago: Open Court Publishing.

Mandela, N. R. (2010). *Nelson Mandela: Conversations with Myself*. Oxford: Macmillan.

Mbembe, A. (2001). *On the Postcolony*. Los Angeles: University of California Press.

Meredith, M. (1997). *Mandela: A Biography*. London: Simon & Schuster.

Meredith, M. (2002). *Robert Mugabe: Power, Plunder and Tyranny in Zimbabwe*. Johannesburg and Capetown: Jonathan Ball.

Meredith, M. (2005). *The State of Africa: A History of Fifty Years of Independence*. Johannesburg and Capetown: Jonathan Ball.

Mossner, E. C. (2001). *The Life of David Hume*. New York: Oxford University Press.

Muchineripi, C. (2012). *Baobab Tales: The Opening Tale (Integral Innovation at Chinyika in Zimbabwe: Finger Millet, the Mundoza Tree and the Four Worlds)*. BTD: Transform.

Mudimbe, V. Y. (1988). *The Invention of Africa: Gnosis, Philosophy and the Order of Knowledge*. Bloomington and Indianapolis: Indiana University Press.

Nonaka, I. & Takeuchi, H. (1995). *The Knowledge Creating Company: How Japanese Companies Create the Dynamics of Innovation*. New York: Oxford University Press.

Pinkard, T. (2000) *Hegel: A Biography*. Cambridge: Cambridge University Press.

Said, E. (1994). *Culture and Imperialism*. London: Vintage Books.

Serequeberhan, T. (1991). *African Philosophy: The Essential Readings*. Saint Paul, Minnesota: Paragon House.

Temple, P. (1959). *Bantu Philosophy*. Paris: Presence Africaine.

Thorpe, J. (1983). *John Milton: The Inner Life*. San Marino: Huntington Library.

Thiam, C. (2014). *Return to the Kingdom of Childhood: Re-envisioning the Legacy and Philosophical Relevance of Negritude*. Columbus: Ohio State University Press.

Wiredu, K. (1980). *Philosophy and an African Culture*. London: Cambridge University Press.

Wiredu, K. (1996). *Cultural Universals and Particulars: An African Perspective.* Bloomington and Indianapolis: Indiana University Press.

Wiredu, K. (2004). *A Companion to African Philosophy.* Boston: Blackwell Publishing.

Woodward, B. (2010). *Obama's Wars: The Inside Story.* London: Simon & Schuster.

Yokushini, T. (2006). *African Urban Experiences in Zimbabwe: A Social History of Harare Before 1925.* Harare: Weaver Press. Available at www.iep.utm.edu/descarte/ (access 17 June 2019).

Part III

Context

Knowledge consciousness in different societies and communities

4 Religion and the subject of knowledge

Introduction

In the previous chapter, a study was carried out on philosophy in general, and African philosophy in particular. Of specific interest was the link between colonisation in Africa and the apparent lack of innovativeness among the African people. The significance of this came from the fact that civilisation came from Africa, and it was the African people that mentored even the Hellenic philosophers. However, all these gains were lost after the colonisers came with strategies to conquer and subject the African people. As I now go deeper into the subject of knowledge creation, it raises my interest that the East has played a significant role in developing concepts and models in knowledge creation, and there was very little colonisation in the East. Where colonisation happened, such as Malaysia, India and Singapore, independence happened quite early on in the nineteenth century, (India in 1947, Malaysia in 1957, and Singapore 1963) unlike in Africa where Zimbabwe only became independent in 1980, and South Africa as late as 1994, as a case in point.

The purpose of this chapter then, is to examine the philosophical reasons for knowledge creation in the East. First, I will briefly look at what some prominent philosophers contributed to the knowledge creation arena. Included here will be the contributions of the likes of Descartes, Husserl, Heidegger, James and Dewey, among others. In addition, an analysis will be done of the role of religion in knowledge creation, by examining the philosophies of the five major religions, i.e. Christianity, Islam, Hindu, Chinese Folk Religion and Buddhism. I will conclude by examining Jaworski's "Source" (Jaworski, 2011), including the "U" process, a model he developed together with Scharmer and Kahane, (Senge et al., 2005).

One aspect that has always intrigued me is the possibility that there may be a link between knowledge creation and religion. In a limited way I will touch on this.

Religious influences on knowledge creation in the East

The logical place to begin here is to try and understand religion with regard to what it is and how it affects or influences knowledge creation.

What is religion?

In as much as philosophy has a bearing on the concept of knowledge creation, I will also look at religion and the possibility that it too, may play a role in knowledge creation and innovation. Religion is an organised collection of belief systems, cultural systems, and world views that relate humanity to spirituality and, sometimes, to moral values (Durkheim, 1964). Karl Marx said this about religion; "Religion is the sigh of the oppressed creature, the heart of a heartless world, and the soul of soulless conditions. It is the opium of the people". It is argued by others in academia that Marx was not necessarily condemning religion with this definition but acknowledging the effect that it has on people. Many religions have narratives, symbols, traditions and sacred histories that are intended to give meaning to life or to explain the origin of life or the Universe (Shouler, 2010). From their ideas about the cosmos and human nature, they tend to derive morality, ethics and religious laws or a preferred lifestyle. Some scholars classify religions as either *universal religions* that seek worldwide acceptance and actively look for new converts, or *ethnic religions* that are identified with a particular ethnic group and do not seek converts (Hinnels, 2005). Others believe there should be no distinction at all, pointing out that all religious practices, whatever their philosophical origin, are ethnic because they come from a particular culture (Masuzawa, 2005). It is estimated that there are at least forty (40) religions in the world, with an estimated membership of seven billion people.

The purpose of this definition of religion is not to distinguish one religion from another, but rather to unite the concept of religion with regard to how any religion shapes people's lives and determines their behaviors. There are five main religions in the world, namely Christianity, Islam, Hinduism, Chinese Folk Religion and Buddhism. A glance at all these religions confirms that they all believe that good must reign over evil, and that the human race must be kind to one another and to the environment. I will take a cursory glance at how these five religions (most of them steeped in the East), relate to knowledge and knowledge creation, if at all.

Below will be an interrogation of what specific religions say about knowledge and knowledge creation.

The Christian perspective

In the Bible, Proverbs is considered to be the book of wisdom, written by King Solomon who specifically asked God for the gift of wisdom. The following quotations from Proverbs are an indicator of how importantly the subject of knowledge is perceived in the Christian faith: "The fear of God is the beginning of knowledge, but fools despise wisdom and discipline" (1: 7); "Wise men store up knowledge, but the mouth of a fool invites ruin" (10:14); "Whoever loves discipline loves knowledge, but he who hates correction is stupid" (12:1); "Every prudent man acts out of knowledge, but a fool exposes his folly" (13:16); and "It is not good to have zeal without knowledge, nor to be hasty and miss the way" (19: 2). This seems to dwell on the importance and necessity of knowledge as a factor defining people's lives and actions, strongly castigating a life without knowledge with words such as "fools", "folly", "stupid" and "missing the way". Although there is no clear and straightforward formula on how to create knowledge, it is very clear in the Bible that the acquisition of knowledge, and actions based on a position of knowledge, should define a person's life. In any case, after God created Adam and Eve in the Garden of Eden, he said to them, "... rule over the fish of the sea and the birds in the air and over every living creature that moves on the ground. ... I give you every food bearing fruit on the face of the whole earth ..." (Genesis 1:28–30). God gave man dominion over the earth yet did not simplistically provide a manual for dealing with the resources he had created, though the Bible outlines how man must interact with man and with the environment. It was now up to man to experiment and develop knowledge for his meaningful interface with the world that was given as a gift to him. The Bible goes further and says knowledge is one of the gifts of the spirit (1 Corinthians 12 vs. 8). According to this then, some people are naturally more inclined towards knowledge because they have a gifting for it.

From the Christianity based countries (predominately the North and West) came a lot of inventors. The early inventors were not necessarily educated but were mostly mechanic type individuals who had gone through some kind of apprenticeship. However, there were some with a university education. Werner von Siemens (1816–1892) founded the electrical industry. Henry Ford introduced the innovation of mass production of cars. Kettering, who was head of General Motors for thirty years, helped invent the automobile electric starter. Emile Berliner contributed to phonograph technology as well as designing the earliest helicopter models (Drucker, 1970). There are many others.

The Islamic perspective

The Arabic word for knowledge is "ilm", which generally refers to Islamic knowledge. However, while some Qur'an verses refer to Islamic knowledge, their use and interpretation refer to knowledge in general terms (www. islamweb.net). Muslims rose, in four decades, "to the zenith of civilisation ... based on Islam's emphasis on learning" (www.islamawareness.net). The Qur'an upholds the acquisition of knowledge. I will select a few verses that speak directly to the subject of knowledge: "Are those who have knowledge and those who have no knowledge alike? Only the men of understanding are mindful" (Qur'an 39:9); the Qur'an encourages people towards scientific research – "And those who so bring the truth and believes therein, such are dutiful" (Qur'an, 39:33); indeed, every Muslim man and every Muslim woman's prayer should be, "My Lord! Enrich me with knowledge ..." (Qur'an, 20:114).

Some traditions and sayings of the Prophet Mohamed supplement the Qur'an: "The acquisition of knowledge is compulsory for every Muslim, whether male or female"; "The ink of the scholar is more sacred than the blood of the martyr"; "The best form of worship is the pursuit of knowledge"; "Scholars should endeavour to spread knowledge and provide education to people who have been deprived of it. For where knowledge is hidden, it disappears"; "To listen to the words of the learned and to instil unto others the lessons of science is better than religious exercises" http://islamawareness.net.

Al-Jayyousi (2012) reminds us that, though Islam is sometimes viewed as a challenge and risk to the West, in fact, the celebration of cultural diversity is a key component in Islamic values. He talks about wisdom (hikma), justice for all (adl), public interest (maslaha) and innovation (ijtihad) as tools for sustainable development. He goes further to stipulate the underlying principles in Islam as natural state (fitra) which strives for high performance and productivity, the account for the ecosystem services (mizan) which employs a comprehensive concept of wealth, respect for all communities of life (umam), which promotes the role of trustee, and understanding the union of life. Excellence (ihason) and family and community values (arham) are part of the underlying principles. Emphasis is also placed on limiting mischief and corruption (fasad). Al-Jayyousi (2012) contends that from an Islamic perspective, the attainment of knowledge (ilm) is obligatory at both individual and societal level, with the Qur'an encouraging believers to read. He believes that to educate people holistically is to let people know, understand and respect the interdependence of all things and the equality of all species in sustaining their lives on earth.

It is evident therefore, that the subject of knowledge acquisition and the discovery of new knowledge in scientific research for instance, is a very prominent feature of the Islam religion.

There are many known Islamic inventions, including the game of chess, which was developed in Persia; Abbas ibn Firnas attempted to construct a flying machine before the Wright brothers; soap as we know it today, was first developed by the Arabs; in 800 A D Jabir ibn Hayyan invented liquefication, crystallisation, distillation, purification, oxidation, evaporation and filtration; al-Jazari created the crank–shaft, the use of valves and pistons, and the combination lock (Vallely, 2006).

The Hindu perspective

Hindu scriptures recognize two types of knowledge: lower and higher, described by Gurdjieff, the Hindi teacher, as objective and subjective (Ouspensky, 2001). Knowledge of the rites and rituals and scholarly study of scripture is considered lower knowledge; higher knowledge is the knowledge of atman and Brahman gained through personal experience or self-realisation. Of the two, higher knowledge is true, because it liberates the individual from the cycles of births and deaths. Scientific knowledge is of the lower kind (subjective, according to Gurdjieff).

The relationship between Hinduism and science is not easy to describe. Since Hinduism does not have a central ecclesiastical authority, as the Catholic Church does for example, it is difficult to get any official verdict on any position that might be controversial, such as evolution, capital punishment, abortion, stem-cell research, birth control, or human cloning. However, Gurgjieff (Ouspensky, 2001, p. 65) explains that, "if knowledge gets far ahead of being, it becomes theoretical and abstract and inapplicable to life". The implication seems to be that we should only obtain knowledge that is useful to us in the here and now, and not carry out experiments for their sake, and not for use by people. This was confirmed when the Hindu spiritual leaders offered their unanimous opinion on human cloning to former president Bill Clinton:

> It is our wish to inform the President that Hinduism neither condones nor condemns the march of science. If done with divine intent and consciousness, it may benefit and if done in the service of selfishness, greed and power, it may bring severe negative karmic consequence. The simple rule is this: cause no injury to others and let dharma – the law of good conduct and harmony with the universe and its many forces and creatures – be the guide for all such explorations. It is a sin to tinker with God's work.
>
> (www.networkplaces.com/hinduism)

On knowledge transmission, Gurgjieff believed that it was more advantageous to keep large quantities of knowledge in a small group of people rather than distributing knowledge to vast groups (contrary to Nonaka and Takeuchi's concepts, as we shall see). The implication of this is that tacit knowledge would be left in a few people and not be converted to explicit knowledge, and this would not be a positive stance for organisations (more about this later). For corporate organisations for instance, the challenge is often that not enough people in the organisation are in possession of certain knowledge, and the solution that is sought is to have more people "knowing".

The Hindu religion is also a source of significant inventions, despite the apparent conservative approach towards research, experiments and knowledge. Indians, (where the Hindu religion originated) invented buttons for ornamental purposes; calico and muslin material, rocket artillery, rulers, and the snakes and larders game. Discoveries made in India include cashmere wool, indigo dye, and sugar refinement, among other things. Mathematics and the number system are said to have originated in India. Eye cataract surgery is also said to have started in India.

The Chinese folk religion perspective

China has a collection of ethnic religious traditions which have historically comprised the predominant belief system in China and among Han Chinese ethnic groups up to the present day. Shénism describes Chinese mythology and includes the worship of shéns (shén; "deities", "spirits", "awarenesses", "consciousnesses", "archetypes") which can be nature deities, Taizu or clan deities, city deities, national deities, cultural heroes and demigods, dragons and ancestors (Chamberlain, 2009).

Chinese folk religion is sometimes categorized with Taoism, since over the centuries institutional Taoism has been attempting to assimilate or administrate local religions. More accurately, Taoism can be defined as a branch of Shénism, since it sprang out of folk religion and Chinese philosophy. Chinese folk religion is sometimes seen as a constituent part of Chinese traditional religion, but more often, the two are regarded as synonymous. With around 454 million adherents, or about 6.6% of the world population, Chinese folk religion is one of the major religious traditions in the world. In China more than 30% of the population adheres to Shénism or Taoism (Yang, 1970).

With so many religions, it has been difficult to establish the Chinese position on knowledge creation, if any, except many critical inventions came from China, even during ancient times. Active religions in China, in addition to the folk religions which have a share of 30% of the population, include Buddhism, Christianity, and Islam. However, outside of religion, the mores and morals of Chinese society were deeply influenced by Confucianism. Some of Confucius's quotes on knowledge are as follows;

> "I hear and I forget. I see and I remember. I do and I understand"; "I am not one who was born in the possession of knowledge; I am one who is fond of antiquity, and earnest in seeking it there"; "The essence of knowledge is, having it, to apply it; not having it, to confess your ignorance"; "Learn as though you would never be able to master it; hold it as though you would be in fear of losing it"; "By three methods we may learn wisdom: First, by reflection, which is noblest, second, by imitation, which is easiest; and third by experience, which is the bitterest"; "He who learns but does not think, is lost! He who thinks but does not learn is in great danger"; "Even when walking in the company of two other men, I am bound to be able to learn from them. The good points of the one I copy; the bad points of the other I correct in myself"; "The scholar who cherishes the love of comfort is not fit to be deemed a scholar"; "Those who do not study are only cattle dressed up in men's clothes"; "The determined scholar and the man of virtue will not seek to live at the expense of injuring their virtue. They will even sacrifice their lives to preserve their virtue complete".
>
> (Lan, 2005)

It is amazing that, though recorded so many years ago (Confucius lived between 551 and 479 BC), these quotations sound very relevant to the current age of human existence. From these quotes, it is clear that knowledge acquisition was a very important aspect of Confucius's philosophy. He was clear on learning from experience and from others while at the same time reflecting on the new knowledge. He believed that, the beginning of knowledge was the understanding of the extent of one's ignorance as well as one's knowledge. One wonders how much of the teachings of this great man have had a bearing on knowledge creation in China. Extending Confucius's belief to modern organisations, it makes sense that, in order to create new knowledge, one has to understand the gaps in the organisation in order to productively focus the knowledge-creation process in the area where it is needed the most and where it is most likely to bear fruit.

Inventions from Ancient China include the compass, iron ploughs, deep drilling rigs, ship's radar, harness for horses, porcelain and toilet paper, to mention a few.

The Buddhist perspective

Buddhism is originally from the Indian continent, though no longer confined to it.

The Buddhist emperor Asoka carved the following statement in rock:

> One should not honour only one's own religion and condemn the religions of others, but one should honour other religions. … So doing, one helps one's own religion to grow and renders service to the religions of others too. In acting otherwise, one digs the grave of one's own religion and also does harm to other religions.
>
> (Nairn, 2009)

As religions are a source of knowledge, the emperor could be implying that it is wise to share the knowledge steeped in the different religions, rather than remain narrow minded and deprive ourselves of other forms of knowledge that exist in other religions.

The Dalai Lama explains the fourth noble truth as "a spiritual path that leads to the pure happiness of liberation and enlightenment" (Jacobs, 2011). The use the word "enlightenment" in this context could be referring to knowledge acquisition. However, of the five most popular religions in the world, Buddhism is the one that does not appear to have a deep focus on the issue of knowledge creation.

It is not clear which inventions were by Buddhists. Suffice to say Buddhism has always been alive in China and India, and as we have seen, many inventions originated from these two countries.

The fundamental difference between all the inventions and innovations highlighted here and what we want to aspire for in organisations is that, these inventions are individual and not organisational or societal.

Religion in Japan

Japan is one country that has made immense contributions to the subject of knowledge creation, particularly in the backdrop of Nonaka, Takeuchi and others. Similar contributions have been made in the field of improving the manufacturing process, such as **Kaizen** or "improvement", or "change for the better", the philosophy or practices that focus upon continuous improvement of processes in manufacturing, engineering, and business management,

(Laraia, Moody & Hall, 1999), and **lean manufacturing, lean enterprise,** or **lean production**, often simply known as "**Lean**", (Bowen & Spear, 1999). I will however not focus on this in this book. It is therefore pertinent that we examine the religious context in Japan and see if this could have a bearing in this innovativeness in the context of knowledge creation.

Most Japanese do not follow a single religion; rather, they incorporate elements of various religions in a syncretic fashion known as *Shinbutsu shūgō*. Shinto and Japanese Buddhism are therefore not practiced as two completely separate and competing faiths, but rather as a single, rather complex religious system (Whelan, 1995).

Japan practices full religious freedom and minority religions such as Christianity, Islam, Hinduism and Sikhism are in existence. About 70% of Japanese people, however, profess no religious membership, (Johnstone, 1975, p. 323) and 84% of the Japanese claim no personal religion. In census questionnaires, less than 15% reported any formal religious affiliation by 2000, 65% do not believe in God, 55% do not believe in Buddha and some 70–80% of the Japanese regularly tell pollsters they do not consider themselves believers in any religion.

Could this spiritual freedom have a bearing on the fact that the Japanese seem to "think outside the box" with regard to knowledge creation?

Nonaka and Takeuchi (1995) define an intellectual tradition of the Japanese people, where they place emphasis on the "whole personality", in contrast to the Western approach where knowledge is separated from "human physiological and epistemological development". Thus, the Western approach appears to value the physical experience over intellect.

Japan has been responsible for some high technology modern inventions such as the floppy disk, the video cassette, the camcorder, the pocket calculator and the compact disc. Of course, the Japanese have always been known for their martial arts too!

The Japanese approach integrates Buddhism, Confucianism and major Western philosophical thoughts (Nonaka & Takeuchi, 1995).

The philosophy has advocated a oneness of humanity and nature, with the sympathy to nature being depicted in the *Manyohshu,* the notion of "the beauty of change and transition" (*mono no aware*), the delicate sentiment conveyed by the *kokin-wakashu* and the stylish (*iki*) lifestyle and art in the urban culture of eighteenth- and nineteenth-century Yedo (old name for Tokyo). This was dubbed "emotional naturalism" by Yujiro Namakura (1969), a contemporary Japanese philosopher.

While Japanese epistemology has nurtured a delicate and sophisticated sensitivity towards nature, it has prevented the objectification of nature and the development of "sound scepticism". Namakura viewed this as failure to build up rational thought of clear universality, because of failure to separate and objectify self and nature.

Tsujimura (1996) a Japanese linguist, contends that physical and concrete objects are indispensable for Japanese expression. Epistemologically, Japanese people think visually and manipulate tangible images.

The Japanese language reveals a unique view of time and space. The Japanese see time as a continuous flow of a permanently updated "present". In contrast, Westerners have a sequential view of time and grasp the present and forecast the future in a historical retrospection of the past. The Japanese leave their existence to the flow of time, placing emphasis on being flexible in accordance with the flux and transition of the world. Their view of space is also free from a fixed perspective. They believe in the oneness of human and nature (Nonaka & Takeuchi, 1995).

The question that needs to be asked therefore is, what bearing does all this have on knowledge creation in Japan?

Jaworski's "Source"

Jaworski (2011), an American with a very heavy Eastern influence, also makes his contribution to the knowledge debate. On religion, Jaworski contends that "The spiritual rhythm of adult life charts the milestones humans pass through from adolescence to old age, milestones that are universal in nature". He talks about the "Source", which could be a religious or spiritual "Ba" and contends that humans can learn to draw from infinite potential of the Source by choosing to follow a disciplined path toward self-realisation and love, the most powerful energy in the universe.

He claims that scientific studies have shown that deliberate practices such as meditation, qigong, aikido, tai chi and yoga, performed over time, can produce changes in the brain and central nervous system, making possible new levels of awareness. To him a disciplined path involves a shift from resignation to possibility – seeing the world as open and full of possibility, engaging in contemplative practices (concentration and mindfulness) and energy practices such as qigong, spending time in nature to enable access to the Source, and the courage to act in an instant. When you are operating from Source, he argues, there is no doubt. You know what to do and you just do it. There is rightness to it.

One of Jaworski's associates, Scharmer (2007) developed a model that he coined the U-Process, because of its U shape.

The journey through Scharmer's U develops seven essential leadership capacities, as follows.

Holding the space of listening

The foundational capacity of the U is listening: listening to others, listening to oneself, and listening to what emerges from the collective. Effective listening requires the creation of open space in which others can contribute to the whole. In the development of knowledge, keeping eyes and ears open to what

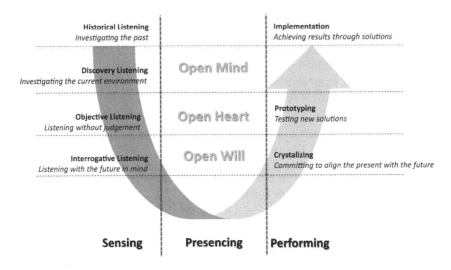

Figure 4.1 Scharmer's U Process.
Source: Jaworski, J., 2011 *(Adaptation and Design Elizabeth Mamukwa, 2019).*

is already in existence and incorporating it into one's thought process can save a lot of time and cost.

Observing

Observation is the second capacity. Scharmer (2007) contends that the capacity to suspend the "voice of judgment" is key to moving from projection to true observation. The moment one starts to judge, the observation ceases to be objective, and the danger is that one might begin to see what one wants to see.

Sensing

According to Scharmer (2007), the preparation for the experience at the bottom of the U – presencing – requires the tuning and bringing "together" of three instruments: the open mind, the open heart, and the open will. This opening process is not passive but an active "sensing" together as a group. While an open heart allows us to see a situation from the whole, the open will enables us to begin to act from the emerging whole. This openness facilitates in knowledge creators the benefit of existing knowledge regardless of its source. Once one starts judging, opportunities to benefit from what others have already done might be missed or lost.

Presencing

Scharmer further contends that the capacity to connect to the deepest source of self and will allows the future to emerge from the whole rather than from a smaller part or special interest group. This brings with it a flavour of spirituality.

Crystallising

When a small group of key persons commits itself to the purpose and outcomes of a project, Scharmer argues, the power of their intention creates an energy field that attracts people, opportunities, and resources that make things happen. This core group functions as a vehicle for the whole to manifest.

Prototyping

According to Scharmer, moving down the left side of the U requires the group to open up and deal with the resistance of thought, emotion, and will; on the other hand, moving up the right side of the U requires the integration of thinking, feeling, and will in the context of practical applications and learning by doing (Scharmer, 2007), which is the essence of prototyping.

Performing

Scharmer (2007) contends that organisations need to perform at a macro level: they need to convene the right sets of players (frontline people who are connected through the same value chain) and to engage a social technology that allows a multi-stakeholder gathering to shift from debating to co-creating the new. This part is the real action of the process, where, in the case of knowledge creation, new knowledge is created. Theory U therefore encourages one to step into the emerging future.

Brian Arthur (Jaworski, 2011) modifies Scharmer's U-Process, and uses it as a model for decision making. He postulates that, "… for the big decisions in life, you need to reach a deeper region of consciousness. Making decisions then becomes not so much about 'deciding' as about "letting the *inner wisdom* emerge".

Arthur highlights three stages of the decision-making process, namely;

a. Observe
b. Reflect and retreat
c. Act swiftly, with a natural flow.

Jaworski (2011) and his associates encourage one to go to a place of deeper meaning. They imply that the development of a new cognitive capability – the capacity to sense and realise emerging futures, constitutes a new form of knowledge creation. Michael Polanyi shares that "human beings create breakthrough knowledge through 'indwelling' resulting in sudden illumination", and John Milton says "…give your deepest appreciation to nature, and you will be amazed what she will teach you" (Jaworski, 2011). This may be why organisations generally go away on a retreat for strategy formulation and other activities that involve defining a critical way forward,

The role of the facilitator, or what Nonaka and Takeuchi would term "the knowledge officer", and the state of the facilitator's consciousness, is critically important for enabling creative discovery in the team while using the U-Process. Jaworski believes that

> Knowledge is a function of being. When there is a change in the being of the Knower, there is a corresponding change in the nature and amount of knowing … what we know depends on what, as moral beings, we choose to make ourselves.
>
> (Aldous Huxley, 1946)

This theory makes religion relevant and active in knowledge creation. The critical elements of knowledge include integrity – dedication to the truth – (keeping your conscience clean), assumption of responsibility and discharge of one's obligation and duty, self-discipline and the delay of gratification. He contends that love and the community are critical components of all this, as there is enormous power in comradeship as well as bonds of mutual trust and love for one another. You are your brother's keeper.

Jaworski (2011) highlights that leaders have a critical role in the development of knowledge. He comes up with four categories of leaders:

Stage I – Self-centric leaders, displaying undeveloped spirituality, as in young people and 20% of adults. These are generally incapable of loving others.

Stage II – Achieving leaders, mature to the point of valuing others, e.g., family, peers, organisations, faith groups or nations. They conform to established rules of the church, company etc.

Stage III – Servant leaders. This group consists of leaders who embrace all people regardless of race, gender, class, or creed. They use their power and influence to serve and develop others. While they have a high need for achievement, this is not done at the cost of others.

Stage IV – Renewing leaders, who have the values of servant leaders and more. They have tacit knowledge that can be used for breakthrough thinking, strategy formation, operational excellence and innovation. They believe that there is an underlying universe that is capable of guiding us and preparing us for the futures we must create. It is these leaders that influence the creation and development of knowledge. I would place the likes of Plato, Aristotle, Confucius and other early philosophers, and even the likes of Nonaka and Takeuchi, in this category.

Although he does not specifically advocate any particular religion, Jaworski's (2011) contribution has a very heavy dose of spirituality. His "Source" sounds like a religious entity, but he is careful not to define it as such, leaving it to the reader to define it in terms of his own religious and spiritual background. However, he makes it clear that one's connection with this "Source" determines one's creativity and innovation.

Conclusion

The subject of knowledge was formally started with the advent of the very first philosopher and has been sustained throughout philosophic history. The philosophical thought of the ancient philosophers started the whole debate about knowledge. The relay was passed on to the modern philosophers who added their own DNA to the subject. Nonaka and Takeuchi (1995) dwell on the likes of Descartes with his emphasis on the thinking self, Locke on his belief that ideas come from sensations and reflections, and Kant with his "transcendental idealism", to mention only a few. Even contemporary philosophers have their own world views about knowledge. The point to make is that like any subject, the subject of knowledge and knowledge creation will continue to be debated long after we are gone, and new perspectives brought to the fore. In the diversity of ideas and beliefs we will continue to venture into new territories of knowledge, which will be viewed in the backdrop of the old knowledge. It will remain important to remain open-minded and embrace new theories and thoughts with critical minds, in the continued quest for knowledge. Even as I work through this book, it remains important for me, and for the knowledge-creation perspective, that we continue to thirst for new knowledge and theories which can positively impact knowledge creation in the different organisations and the world at large. Indeed, it would be relevant and appropriate to also contribute to the body of knowledge.

Religion is one aspect that touches the majority of people in the world (even though a high number of Japanese people think they are not religious). However, as religion sets the tone on how people live, how they act and what their moral fabric becomes, it is safe to conclude that religion influences the creativity and innovation of people, and ultimately their susceptibility to knowledge creation. It is significant that where the specific religion does not encourage innovation, such as Buddhism, the innovations that come out of there may be limited. This is not about being a devout believer in a particular religion. It is more about the fact that religion influences language, mental models and culture.

However, Jaworski (2011) and his associates see this differently, as defined in the U-Process. They believe that there are aspects to do with the spiritual self in knowledge creation that some aspects are beyond the control of the individual but are determined by the "source".

The puzzle however, remains the Japanese who, even though professing to not being religious, come up with some ground-breaking innovations, such as the Matsushita bread maker, Honda's energy efficient engine prior to the oil shocks, Canon's AE-1, the first single-lens reflex camera with a built in electronic brain, to name just a few. I guess it is the spirit of competition, and the realisation that if there are no new innovations there is no survival. This may explain why Japan, the same geographic size as France and Germany has a stronger economy than both countries in terms of GDP (in 2012 Japan had the fourth highest GDP ahead of Germany and France, behind the European Union, United States of America and China).

In the next chapter I now focus on knowledge creation in the East, specifically concentrating on the works of Nonaka and Takeuchi. My particular interest will be how their model can be applied to knowledge creation in a different way to make it friendlier to other cultures.

References

Al-Jayyousi, O. (2012). *Islam and Sustainable Development*. Farnham: Gower.

Bowen, H.K. & Spear, S. (1999). Decoding the DNA of the Toyota Production System. *Harvard Business Review*, viewed 21 March 2018, <https://hbr.org/1999/09/decoding-the-dna-of-the-toyota-production-system>

Cavell, S. (2002). *Knowing and Acknowledging: Must We Mean What We Say?* London: Cambridge University Press.

Chamberlain, J. (2009). *Chinese Gods: An Introduction to Chinese Folk Religion*. Hong Kong: Blacksmith Books.

Drucker, P. F. (1970). *Technology, Management and Society: Essays* (6th Ed.). New York: Harper and Row.

Durkheim, E. (1964). *The Elementary Forms of the Religious Life*. London: George Allen & Unwin Limited.

Hinnels, J. R. (2005). *The Routledge Companion to the Study of Religion*. New York: Routledge.

Huxley, A. (1946). *The Perennial Philosophy* (1st Ed.). London: Chatto and Windus.

Jacobs, A. (2011). *His Holiness the Dalai Lama: Infinite Compassion for an Imperfect World*. London: Watkins Publishing.

Jaworski, J. (2011). *Source: The Inner Path of Knowledge Creation*. San Francisco: Berret-Koehler Publishers.

Johnstone, R. L. (1975). *Religion and Society in Interaction*. Englewood Cliffs: Prentice Hall.

Lan, D. C. (trans.) (2005). *Confucius: The First Ten Books*. New York: Penguin Books.

Laraia, A. C., Moody, P. E. & Hall, R. W. (1999). *The Kaizen Blitz: Accelerating Breakthroughs in Productivity and Performance*. New York: John Wiley and Sons.

Lockard, C. A. (2010). *Societies, Networks, and Transitions since 1450* (2nd Ed.). New York: Cengage Learning.

Masuzawa, T. (2005). *The Invention of World Religions, or, How European Universalism Was Preserved in the Language of Pluralism*. Chicago: Chicago University Press.

Nairn, R. (2009). *Tranquil Mind: An Introduction to Buddhism and Meditation*. Boston: Shambalala Press.

Namakura, H. (1969). *History of Japanese Thought: Japanese Philosophy before Western Culture Entered Japan*. London: Kegan Page

Nonaka, I. & Nishiguchi, T. (2001). *Knowledge Emergence: Social, Technical, and Evolutionary Dimensions of Knowledge Creation*. New York: Oxford University Press.

Nonaka, I. & Takeuchi, H. (1995). *The Knowledge Creating Company: How Japanese Companies Create the Dynamics of Innovation.* New York: Oxford University Press.

Ouspensky, P. D. (2001). *In Search of the Miraculous: Fragments of an Unknown Teaching.* New York: Harcourt.

Scharmer, O. (2007). *Leading from the Future as it Emerges.* San Francisco: Berrett-Koehler Publishers.

Senge, P. et al. (2005). *Presence: An Exploration of Profound Change in People, Organisations and Society.* New York: Doubleday.

Shouler, K. (2010). *The Everything World's Religion Book: Explore the Beliefs, Traditions and Cultures of Ancient and Modern Religions.* New York: Adam's Media.

The Holy Bible, New International Version. (1996) Oklahoma: Rainbow Studies.

Tsujimura, N. (1996). *An Introduction to Japanese Linguistics.* Cambridge: Blackwell Publishers.

Vallely, P. (2006). *How Islamic Inventors Changed The World.* Manchester: The Independent.

Whelan, C. (13 May 1995). *"Japan's 'New Religion' – Millions Disenchanted with Buddhism, Shinto Find Spiritual Options".* *The Seattle Times.* Retrieved 24 June 2010. <http://community.worldheritage.org/articles/eng/Religion_in_Japan>

Yang, C. K. (1970) *Religion in Chinese Society.* San Francisco: California University Press

Zuckerman, P. (2007). *"Atheism: Contemporary Rates and Patterns".* In Martin, Michael (Ed.). *Cambridge Companion to Atheism.* San Francisco: University of Cambridge Press.

5 Knowledge creation and societal learning in the East

The SECI model

Introduction

In the previous chapters the discussion encompassed the role of philosophy and religion in knowledge creation. The understanding was that philosophy was the starting point in terms of knowledge creation and will continue to come up with different perspectives on different subjects, including knowledge creation, as it has done in the past. It is important for us to embrace critically any new thoughts and theories arising in the future. The issue of religion and spirituality too has a bearing on knowledge creation, both from a culture and values perspective as well as from the angle of strong religious belief. We note that there have been many creations and innovations from people of various religious backgrounds. However, these creations have on the whole started off as individual projects where knowledge was mostly tacit. What then probably made the knowledge explicit is when the creation or discovery has become popular and more people are curious. The issue of patents was in fact introduced to protect knowledge, so that once created, other people would not claim ownership of such creations.

Of note was the fact that the Japanese, with all their exciting innovations, generally state that they are not really religious. Perhaps the influence of religion on the Japanese is more of a culture and values one as opposed to a spiritual influence. Now we turn to the subject of knowledge creation in the East, specifically in Japan.

It is not possible to think of knowledge creation in the East without thinking of knowledge creation in Japan. It is equally not possible to think of knowledge creation at all without thinking of Nonaka and Takeuchi. Though of Japanese origin, these two gentlemen have made an outstanding contribution in the field of knowledge in the world, to the extent that they are attached to international universities. In the previous chapter we saw that there were many inventions coming from a cross-section of countries and religions. However, the knowledge created in the process was not organisational knowledge, but more individual. This is where Nonaka and Takeuchi make a difference. In this chapter therefore I will focus a lot on their works, which have been picked up and developed further by other contributors, as we shall see.

Creating knowledge – an Eastern perspective

In this section, I will dwell on knowledge creation in Japanese companies, drawing mostly on the works of Nonaka and Takeuchi and their compatriots, which work has had a ground-breaking effect in the knowledge creation arena.

Organisational knowledge creation is the key to the distinctive ways that Japanese companies innovate. They have historically turned to knowledge creation as a means of breaking away from the past and moving into new and untried territories of opportunity. Coping with uncertainty was a matter of life and death for organisations, seen by the examples given below:

- Honda developed an energy efficient engine prior to the oil shocks.
- Canon rested its future on AE-1, the first single-lens reflex camera with a built-in electronic brain.
- Sony saved its life by an aggressive export strategy at the right time.
- Competing with strong brands such as IBM, General Motors, or Sears Roebuck, Japanese companies learnt not to be complacent and arrogant.

Japanese companies bring about continuous innovation by looking outside into the future, anticipating changes in the market, technology, competition or product. They understand that continuous innovation leads to competitive advantage. In this chapter, some examples will be given of Japanese companies and the innovations that they carried out.

Nonaka and Takeuchi's theory of organisational knowledge creation

Nonaka and Takeuchi (1995) write,

> When organisations innovate, they do not simply process information, from the outside in, in order to solve existing problems and adapt to a changing environment. They actually create new knowledge and information, from inside out, in order to redefine both problems and solutions and, in the process, to re-create their environment.

In a way, this statement summarises their theory on Organisational Knowledge Creation.

The two critical components of the development of knowledge in this theory are "tacit knowledge" and "explicit knowledge". The four modes of knowledge creation, namely Socialisation, Externalisation, Combination and Internalisation, are, in short, the different stages that knowledge creators go through in the conversion of tacit knowledge, to explicit knowledge, to tacit knowledge.

Tacit knowledge is defined as knowledge of experience (body), which is simultaneous (here and now) and analogous (obtained from practice) (Nonaka and Takeuchi, 1995). It is highly personal and difficult to formalise, making it difficult to communicate and share with others (Nonaka and Nishiguchi, 2001). Explicit knowledge, on the other hand, is defined as the knowledge of rationality (mind), sequential (there and then) and can be digital (theory). This is extended further by Nonaka, Konno and Toyama (Nonaka and Nishiguchi, 2001) who add that explicit knowledge can be expressed in words and numbers, and can be shared in the form of data, scientific formula, specifications and manuals, and can be readily transmitted across individuals.

The four modes of knowledge conversion

According to Nonaka and Takeuchi (1995) knowledge conversion happens through the four modes as described here.

SOCIALISATION: FROM TACIT TO TACIT

This involves sharing experiences in the form of mental models and technical skills. An individual can acquire tacit knowledge directly from others without using language, e.g. apprentices (through observation, imitation and practice). On-the-job training is another way of socialisation. The key to acquiring tacit knowledge is through experience. On its own, socialisation is a limited form of knowledge creation. Shared knowledge therefore has to become explicit for the organisation to benefit.

Examples

1. **Honda** set up "brainstorming camps" (tama dashi kai) – informal meetings for detailed discussion to solve difficult problems in development projects. Meetings were held off-site under informal circumstances. One of the rules was that there should be no criticism without constructive suggestions (based on the premise that making criticism is ten times easier than coming up with a constructive alternative)
2. In the case of **Matsushita Electric Industrial Company** managers apprenticed themselves to a hotel to learn how bread is kneaded while in the process of developing a bread-making machine.

EXTERNALISATION: FROM TACIT TO EXPLICIT

This is a process of articulating tacit knowledge into explicit concepts. Writing is useful for converting tacit knowledge into articulable knowledge, combining deduction and induction. This process is often driven by metaphor and/or analogy to create commitment to the creative process e.g. Hiroo Watanabe used the metaphor of "Automobile evolution" in developing a car for Honda, the "Honda City" (Nonaka and Takeuchi, 1995).

Examples

1. **Mazda** combined deduction and induction to create a sports car concept –
    RX7. This was deduced from the corporate slogan "create new values and
    present joyful driving pleasures". Concepts were induced from "concept
    trips" experienced by the development team and "concept clinics" where
    opinions were gathered from customers and car experts.
2. In developing **Canon's Mini Copier,** the challenge was that of producing
    a low-cost disposable cartridge.

Half the job is to create a product concept. Externalisation holds the key
to knowledge creation because it creates new explicit concepts from tacit
knowledge.

COMBINATION: FROM EXPLICIT TO EXPLICIT

Combination is a process of systemising concepts into a knowledge system.
It involves combining different bodies of explicit knowledge, through such
media as documents, meetings, telephone conversations or computerised communication networks. It also involves the reconfiguring of existing information
through sorting, adding, combining and categorising of explicit knowledge, e.g.
in formal education and training at schools especially such training as MBA.
  Middle managers play a critical role in creating new concepts.

Examples

1. Kraft General Foods carried out data analysis to pinpoint who shops where
    and how. Kraft successfully manages product sales through supermarkets by
    controlling four elements, namely consumer and category dynamics, space
    management, merchandising management, and pricing management.
2. Asahi Breweries adopted a new concept and dubbed it "live Asahi for live
    people". They enquired into what makes beer appealing and proceeded to
    develop a new product concept of "richness and sharpness".

At top management level, a combination mode is realised when mode-range
concepts (such as product concepts) are combined with and integrated into
grand concepts (such as corporate vision).

INTERNALISATION: FROM EXPLICIT TO TACIT

This is a process of changing explicit knowledge into tacit knowledge, and is
closely related to learning by doing. Internalisation occurs when experiences
through socialisation, externalisation and combination are internalised into the
individuals' tacit knowledge bases in the form of shared mental models or technical know-how.

For organisational knowledge creation to take place, tacit knowledge needs to be socialised with other members of the organisation.

Explicit knowledge becomes tacit through verbalisation, diagrams, documents, manuals or oral stories. Documents and manuals facilitate the transfer of explicit knowledge to others.

Examples

1. General Electric (GE) documents all customer complaints and inquiries in a database at its Answer Centre in Louisville, Kentucky, for use by members of a new product development team. People from new product development are also sent to the Answer centre to answer customer inquiries, thereby "re-experiencing" their experiences.
2. Internalisation can happen without "re-experience" when people read or listen to success stories. In Japan freelance writers or former employees write and publish books and articles about companies and their leaders.
3. Matsushita launched a companywide policy in 1993 to reduce yearly working time to 1800 hours, not to cut costs, but to extend innovation (Mind and Management Innovation Toward 1993 – MMIT'93). Internalisation was exercised through a one-month trial period.

Lessem and Schieffer (2009) aptly link the four modes of knowledge conversion with the four worlds as follows;

Socialisation is linked with Southern world of humanism (local–local), externalisation with the Eastern world of holism (local–global), combination with the Northern world of rationalism (global–global) and internalisation with the Western world of pragmatism (global local). They summarise this by adding that knowledge is socialised in the indigenous (in what we know and understand), in externalisation we link the indigenous and the exogenous, moving to the exogenous realm in combination and moving back to the familiar indigenous with the new exogenous knowledge in internalisation.

The knowledge spiral

When tacit and explicit knowledge interact, as in the Matsushita case, an innovation emerges. The socialisation mode usually starts with building a "field" of interaction. This facilitates the sharing of members' experiences and mental models, which yields "sympathised knowledge" such as mental models and technical skills. The externalisation mode is triggered by meaningful dialogue or collective reflection, using metaphor and or analogy where possible. The output is "conceptual knowledge". The combination mode is triggered by "networking" newly created knowledge and existing knowledge from other sections of the organization and crystallising them into a new product, service or managerial system. This gives rise to "systemic knowledge" e.g. a prototype and new component technologies (such as the micro-merchandising program in Kraft General Foods). "Learning by doing" triggers internalisation. Internalisation produces "operational knowledge" about project management, the production process, new product usage, and policy implementation, e.g. working 150 hours a month in Matsushita (Nonaka and Takeuchi, 1995).

An organisation cannot create knowledge on its own. The tacit knowledge of individuals is the basis of organisational knowledge creation. The mobilisation of tacit knowledge is organisationally carried out through the four modes of knowledge conversion, dubbed the "knowledge spiral" (above) by Nonaka and Takeuchi, (1995).

Organisational knowledge starts at individual level, moving up to expanding communities of interaction, crossing sectional, departmental, divisional and organisational boundaries.

Ideally a Research and Development (R&D) team should consist of a mixture of skills; the R&D people, someone from production, someone from marketing, etc., so that they bring different perspectives to the table. When I look at the R&D teams' composition in organisations that I have worked with, I see that such teams consist of the production and marketing people, to the exclusion of other specialists who may have something to contribute, even if it is from the perspective of being consumers of such products.

Ba: Platform for knowledge creation

Nonaka, Konno and Toyama (Nonaka & Nishiguchi, 2001) postulate that, to exploit and create knowledge effectively and efficiently, it is necessary to concentrate knowledge at a certain time and space. This is known as "Ba". The knowledge-creating process is also the process for creating Ba. They describe four types of Ba, as follows.

Originating Ba is where individuals share feelings, emotions experiences and mental models. It involves care, love, trust, commitment, freedom. Physical face-to-face experience helps to convert tacit knowledge into explicit knowledge. This is associated with socialisation.

Dialoguing Ba is consciously constructed by selecting people with the right mix of specific knowledge and capabilities for a project team, taskforce etc. Individuals' mental models and skills are converted to common terms and concepts. Here tacit knowledge is made explicit. This is associated with externalisation.

Systemising Ba refers to a place of interaction in a virtual world instead of sharing time and space in reality. This is associated with the combination phase, and the use of information technology can play a special role here.

Exercising Ba supports internalisation by facilitating the conversion of explicit knowledge to tacit knowledge. Interaction is on-the-site.

To manage knowledge creation, leaders must manage Ba by providing knowledge vision and by building and energising Ba. This can be done by providing a knowledge vision which defines what kind of knowledge the company must create as well as defines the value system that evaluates, justifies and determines the quality of knowledge the company creates. This must be articulated by top management.

By building and energising Ba, leaders can facilitate knowledge creation by providing physical space such as meeting rooms, or cyberspace such as a computer networks. Fostering love, care, trust and commitment among organisational members forms the foundation of knowledge creation. Language has also been thought to be an important instrument of knowledge creation.

Enabling conditions for organisational knowledge creation

Nonaka and Takeuchi, (1995) suggest five conditions required at organisational level to promote the knowledge spiral, and these are outlined below.

INTENTION

The knowledge spiral is driven by organisational intention, defined through its aspirations and goals. The essence of strategy is to develop the organisation's capacity to acquire, create, accumulate and exploit knowledge (emanating from a vision).

AUTONOMY

At individual level an employee should act autonomously, so that they can motivate themselves to create new knowledge. Ideas originally emanate from autonomous individuals before they are diffused within the team and then become organisational ideas. When the knowledge-creation process escalates to a team level, such a team should also be given full autonomy.

Hiroo Watinabe the former President of R&D, Honda North America, said,

> ...our work is not a relay race in which my work starts here and yours there. Everyone should run all the way from start to finish. Like rugby, all of us should run together, pass the ball left and right, and reach the goal as a united body.
>
> (Nonaka & Takeuchi, 1995)

There are different approaches to dealing with innovative development:

Type A – the relay approach where each phase of the development process is clearly separated and the baton is passed on from one group to another;

Type B is called the "sashimi system" because it looks like sliced raw fish (sashimi) served on a plate with one piece overlapping another (Fuji Xerox); and

Type C – the rugby approach, where people gang together to deal with an innovation process.

FLUCTUATION AND CREATIVE CHAOS

Fluctuation stimulates the interaction between the organisation and the external environment. An environmental fluctuation often triggers a breakdown within the organisation, out of which new knowledge can be created. This is also known as creating "order out of noise" or "order out of chaos".

Chaos results when the organisation faces a real crisis, for example the rapid decline of performance due to market changes or structure of competition. Management can deliberately create chaos by building tension in the team, which focuses the attention of the team on defining the problem and resolving the crisis.

Kobayashi, former chairman of Fujitsu (Yeh & Yeh, 2004) put this into perspective when he said,

> Relaxed in a comfortable place, one can hardly think sharply. Wisdom is squeezed out of someone who is standing on a cliff and is struggling to survive … without such struggles, we would have never been able to catch up with IBM.

REDUNDANCY

This is the existence of information that goes beyond the immediate operational requirements of organisational members. A concept created by an individual or a group needs to be shared by other individuals who may not need the concept immediately. Sharing redundant information promotes the sharing of tacit knowledge, because individuals can sense what others are trying to articulate. In this sense therefore, redundancy speeds up the knowledge-creation process.

Redundancy is critical at the concept development stage, while articulating images rooted in tacit knowledge. It enables individuals to invade each other's functional boundaries and offer advice or provide new information from different perspectives.

Ways of building redundancy in an organisation include overlapping "rugby-style" approach product development in which different functional departments work together, "Strategic Rotation" of personnel, helping members understand the business from multiple perspectives, making organisational knowledge more fluid, and holding frequent meetings on both regular or irregular basis, e.g. Honda's brainstorming camp and informal communication networks such as drinking sessions after work – these facilitate the sharing of both tacit and explicit knowledge.

There is need for balance between the creation and processing of information to avoid information overload and decreased operational efficiency.

REQUISITE VARIETY

An organisation's internal diversity must match the variety and complexity of the environment in order to deal with challenges posed by the environment. Everyone in the organisation must be assured of the fastest access to the broadest variety of necessary information. Information differential within the organisation will hinder interaction on equal terms. This is an aspect that needs to be corrected in many organisations.

The five-phase model for organisational knowledge-creation process

Nonaka and Takeuchi (1995) then proceed to articulate the phases that they see involved in the organisational knowledge-creation process.

SHARING TACIT KNOWLEDGE

Tacit knowledge held by individuals is the basis of organisational knowledge creation. This also applies to tacit traditional knowledge of a tribe, community or society. The Starting point is the sharing of emotions and feelings to build trust. Appropriate platforms for sharing that trust include multi-functional self-organising teams (variety of team members/skills). This corresponds to socialisation. It helps if Management sets challenging goals as to what should be achieved in this regard.

CREATING CONCEPTS

This involves an intensive interaction between tacit and explicit knowledge, where people share mental models. Deduction, induction and abduction are used to convert tacit knowledge into explicit knowledge. Abduction employs metaphors and analogies. Concepts are created cooperatively through dialogue.

JUSTIFYING CONCEPTS

Justification is a process of determining if the newly created concepts are worthwhile to the organisation. Justification criteria include cost, profit margin and degree to which a product can contribute to the firm's growth. Justification criteria can be both quantitative and qualitative. More abstract criteria can include value premises such as adventure, romanticism and aesthetics. Top management creates justification through organisational intent (vision, mission), while middle management exercises justification through mid-range concepts

BUILDING AN ARCHETYPE

Here, the justified concept is converted into something tangible or concrete. It is built by combining newly created explicit knowledge with existing explicit knowledge. This is a model or "mock up" before starting the real thing. People with different expertise are brought together to build this prototype, to come up with something that meets everyone's approval. This team is responsible for developing the blueprint as well as actually building the real thing. This is a complex phase that requires cooperation from various departments.

At this stage the new concept which has been created, justified and modelled moves on to an interactive process which takes place both intra-organisationally and inter-organisationally. Intra-organisationally, knowledge made real can trigger a new cycle of knowledge creation, expanding horizontally and vertically across the organisation. Inter-organisationally, knowledge created by the organisation can mobilise knowledge of affiliated companies, customers, suppliers, competitors and others outside the company, through dynamic interaction. For this to work, each organisational unit should have the autonomy to take the knowledge developed somewhere else and apply it freely across different levels and boundaries. Internal fluctuations such as frequent staff-rotation will facilitate knowledge transfer.

The impact of care in knowledge development

Von Krogh (Nonaka & Nishiguchi, 2001) brings into the fray a concept that may have been initially missed by Nonaka and Takeuchi (1995), to the extent that they did not focus on it. He identifies a distinction between high care and low care as factors that impact knowledge development. He contends that high care characterises relationships where there is greater propensity to help, high accessibility of individuals, an extensive attentive inquiry, and high lenience. Care is a shared value among organisational members. Low care, on the other hand, characterises relationships where there is a low propensity for help. Organisational members do not make themselves accessible to one another, attentive inquiry is limited, and members exhibit impatience and lack of leniency towards others. Care is not a shared value in the organisation. In organisations, although "genuinely caring" for our employees maybe one of the corporate values, sometimes people fall into the trap of poor accessibility to one another, frustrating the knowledge-creation process within the organisation.

Seizing knowledge under conditions of low care

This is a type of individual knowledge development where an employee feels there is no propensity to help him – there is reduced accessibility to those who should care, and attentive inquiry is lacking; he therefore has to find his own way.

There are no shared organisational values to direct proactive helping behaviour, and no assistance from colleagues. Knowledge development is sought toward effective task performance, and about getting a maximum grip of the situation so that the employee can effectively execute the given tasks.

In the process of seizing, the understanding and maximum grip on the situation is very much personal. He will use established rules to solve existing and new tasks and will experiment with new rules to master existing situations more effectively. In the absence of attentive inquiry, there are few requirements for thematization and effective sharing of the end result.

In this situation, knowledge development becomes egoistic opposed to altruistic, expected to serve the individual rather than the collective, and will be a means to gain power and influence organisational relationships. The individual knowledge therefore remains tacit.

Transacting knowledge under conditions of low care

Transacting knowledge is the type of social knowledge development that takes place under conditions of low care. There is little interest in the particulars of individual knowledge beyond what is of value to social knowledge and the task performance of the group. If help is offered, the helper will expect favours.

In the process of transacting knowledge, little or no time is allowed to explore new individual ideas. Low accessibility among members means that time pressure is critical in knowledge development. Knowledge that can be developed fast is of high value. Personal relationships are substituted by bureaucratic rules and procedures, driven by "specialists without spirit" (Nonaka & Nishiguchi, 2001). Experts transact knowledge because they feel they ought to, and expertise is about fast task execution and clear unambiguous claims about knowledge. Access to organisational members is limited to the prescriptions by organisational procedures.

Social knowledge is predominately explicit. There is no time for socialisation (tacit to explicit). The "expert" simply makes his claims explicit.

Groups of experts will keep secrets by protecting explicit knowledge from other groups in order to keep their power. They may however be forced to reveal what they know in order to reconfirm their status of expertise when challenged in a new situation. Social knowledge resulting from transacting has to be agreed among members on rules for task execution rather that an understanding of how to follow the rules, which are contested and negotiated. The rules form explicit expectation of behaviour.

Bestowing knowledge under conditions of high care

Unlike seizing, bestowing characterises individual knowledge development where organisational members make themselves mutually accessible and relate to each other in lenient, helpful and attentive ways. The individual is not left alone to develop knowledge on problem solving but enjoys the support of a social network of organisational members (Pagel, Erdly & Baker, 1987).

Here, shared values of care direct helping behaviour towards those who need it. Where a task cannot be performed, the individual task performer and other organisational members are expected to work together to develop knowledge on new solutions. Interest and leniency are directed to those who ask for help. Organisational members also ask if help is needed in order to improve task performance. While individual knowledge development is a personal journey, it is however accompanied by helpful colleagues. Positive and negative emotions such as satisfaction with a completed task and uncertainty with a future task can be expressed freely so that they are appreciated by other members of the organisation.

Care in organisations allows a vocabulary for expressing emotive activities and subjective experiences. Furthermore, in bestowing, the individual develops personal understanding of the task at hand and possible task solutions. Established rules will be used to solve existing and new tasks. Individuals will also experiment with new rules to master existing situations effectively. However, the individual is not necessarily captured by these rules. Attentive inquiry is very much alive. The individual can thematise his own experiences. Individual knowledge is both of tacit and explicit nature.

Indwelling knowledge under conditions of high care

Indwelling allows for inventing new words, displaying insecurity, conveying hunches, drawing on humour, laughing, playing, etc. Errors are accepted, allowing for repeated attempts. The effective functioning of organisational relationships substitutes for bureaucracy. Personal helping behaviour becomes a virtue to the organisation, leading to passionate expertise, eager to find opportunities to help others. There is an agreement on rules and how to follow and make use of them. Organisational members assume tutorship functions and help others learn how to practise rules of effective task execution. The social knowledge that results from indwelling is both explicit and tacit.

Limits to care

Von Krogh (Nonaka & Nishiguchi, 2001) accepts that there are limits to care. He agrees that it is not easy to consistently pursue knowledge development using the concept of care. It is difficult to diligently give colleagues attentive inquiry as people tend to get immersed into their own work. It is therefore important to include the concept of care into values to constantly remind people. Furthermore, care can push for agreements and remove the healthy conflict that is needed in organisations for the right things to happen. For example, in corporate organisations it would be undesirable if Finance and Marketing agreed all the time because that might result in Marketing selling to the wrong customers, resulting in a large, poorly performing debtors' book. Nor would it be profitable to have the Human Resource department agreeing with all departments all the time, as this may result in increased manpower levels and under-utilisation of staff. Healthy conflict is therefore important, and should be given space, even in conditions of high care.

Why organisational relationship matter

Von Krogh makes interesting observations about the need for organisational relationship. He argues that organisational knowledge development starts with individuals, so unless there are functional relationships, the sharing of that knowledge may fail to happen effectively. Individuals must discover the sources of innovation that they might develop, and organisational members must respect the individual experiences of their colleagues (including withholding negative value judgements).

Management styles for knowledge creation

Top-down management

Nonaka and Takeuchi (1995) contend that all organisations can create knowledge, but in most organisations the process is haphazard and unpredictable. The knowledge-creating company does this systematically.

Top-down management is classic and hierarchical, rooted in Max Weber and Frederick Taylor. This style conceives knowledge creation within the confines of the information-processing perspective. Selected information is passed up to top management, having been processed through the division of labour. Top management creates basic concepts for implementation by lower members. Top management concepts become the operational conditions for middle management, who will decide on the means to realise them. The decisions of middle managers constitute the operational conditions for front-line employees. Execution here becomes routine. The top-down organisation is shaped like a pyramid, the assumption being that only top managers are able and allowed to create knowledge. The danger of this approach lies in aligning the fate of a few top managers with that of the organisation. If the top managers are good, things can work out. However, if they are not, the company suffers. This approach is what is prevalent in many organisations. The result, regrettably, is that many a company may end up closing its doors. A good example of Top-down management is General Electric (GE) under Jack Welch. He was the lynch-pin of all that happened at GE. He introduced (and implemented) the "fix/sell/close" concept for businesses that were not doing well. The authority that resided with front-line employees was only what he allowed them. He introduced other business concepts such as integrated diversity which encouraged operating independence of businesses while the operators remained part of a greater team, and "boundarylessness" which signalled the breakdown of barriers such as hierarchy, geography and function. These concepts were probably good, and worked, but the fact of the matter is that their originator was Jack Welch, and not anyone else. Even he will never know the opportunities that may have been missed because other people were not given the opportunity and space to contribute to the GE business concepts and strategy.

Bottom–up management

This is a mirror image of top-down management. Instead of hierarchy and division of labour, there is autonomy. Knowledge is created at and controlled by the bottom. A bottom–up organisation has a flat and horizontal shape. Few orders and instructions are given by top managers, who serve as sponsors of entrepreneurially minded front-line employees. Knowledge is created by independent employees who prefer to work alone. The preeminence and autonomy given to an individual can make knowledge creation much more time consuming.

3M is a typical example of an organisation where this approach is used. The guiding principles here are autonomy and entrepreneurship, which are translated into the flow of ideas from below, acceptance of mistakes as normal, minimum interference from above, and the maintenance of a small and flat organisational structure. Top management act as mentors, with the role to look out for natural innovators and encourage them. Indeed, 25% of the remuneration of top management was derived from sales from new products, to try and force them to promote the development of new ideas.

Both of these management systems are not very good for knowledge conversion. In the top-down there is partial conversion focused on combination (explicit to explicit) and internalisation (explicit to tacit). In the bottom-up there is partial conversion focused on socialisation (tacit to tacit) and externalisation (tacit to explicit). Both models fail to recognise and give relevance to middle managers.

Middle–up–down management

In this management style, middle managers are the strategic knot that binds top management with front-line managers. They orient the chaotic situation found in front-line workers when they are faced with change situations into purposeful knowledge creation, and they provide their subordinates with conceptual frameworks that help them make sense of their own experiences. They try to solve the contradictions between what top management hopes for and the realities on the ground. Top management creates a grand theory while middle management tries to create a mid-range theory that can be empirically tested. This is the approach used at Canon.

In the structure of the knowledge-creating crew, front-line employees are the knowledge practitioners or knowledge operators who interface with tacit knowledge e.g. test drivers and salespeople.

Knowledge specialists interface primarily with explicit knowledge e.g. scientists in R&D, design engineers, software engineers, sales engineers, strategic planners, and specialists in Finance, HR, Legal and Marketing Research. They need to have high intellectual standards, a strong sense of commitment to re-create the world according to their own perspective, a variety of experiences both inside and outside of the company, skills in carrying out a dialogue with customers as well as colleagues within the company, and the need to carry out candid discussions as well as debate with others.

Middle managers are the knowledge engineers responsible for converting tacit knowledge into explicit knowledge and vice versa. They facilitate the four modes of knowledge creation and serve as a bridge between the visionary ideals of the top and the chaotic market reality of those on the front-line of the business. They have the critical role in facilitating the knowledge spiral along the epistemological dimension, across the different modes of knowledge conversion, and facilitating another spiral along the ontological dimension, across different organisation levels.

Knowledge created at individual level can move up to the group level, then to the organisation level and sometimes to the inter-organisational level.

In middle-top-down management the division of labour is such that top management are the knowledge officers who articulate and communicate the knowledge vision. They can even go to the extent of creating chaos to stimulate creativity, and they should have the capability to direct and manage the total process of knowledge creation. Middle managers are the knowledge engineers who should possess serious capabilities in project coordination and management. They should be able to employ metaphors to help others generate and articulate their imagination. They should possess the capacity to integrate various methodologies for knowledge creation, to engender trust among team members and to envision the future course of action based on an understanding of the past.

Front-line employees are the knowledge practitioners. They consist of the knowledge operators who interface with tacit knowledge e.g. test drivers, sales people. Knowledge specialists who interface primarily with explicit knowledge e.g. scientists in R&D, design engineers, software engineers, sales engineers, strategic planners, and specialists in Finance, HR, Legal and marketing research, are also part of the knowledge-creating crew.

Knowledge specialists need to have high intellectual standards, a strong sense of commitment to re-create the world according to their own perspective, a variety of experiences both inside and outside of the company, skills in carrying out a dialogue with customers as well as colleagues within the company, and the need to carry out candid discussions as well as debate with others.

Organisational structures and knowledge creation

Nonaka and Takeuchi (1995), carry out a critique of organisational structures. They contend that bureaucratic structures, which tend to be highly formalised, specialised and centralised, work under stable conditions, and in knowledge creation, are effective for combination and internalisation through the exploitation and accumulation of knowledge. Bureaucratic structures tend to be dysfunctional in periods of uncertainty where quick decision making becomes critical. This was evident when Zimbabwe went through the hyper-inflationary era, where money lost its value by the second. Suddenly, without any formalisation, effective organisations moved from bureaucratic to task force structures.

Nonaka and Takeuchi (1995) emphasise the importance of knowing when to use a particular structure. No structure is always good or always bad, but its relevance is determined by particular circumstances faced by an organisation at any given time. They cite Japan that lost World War Two because they stuck to bureaucracy, while America employed a more flexible structure which led it to victory. Businesses therefore need to employ a synthesis of non-hierarchical, self-organising structures in tandem with their hierarchical formal structure, hence benefiting from corporate level efficiency and local flexibility at the same time.

Nonaka and Takeuchi (1995) introduce the hypertext organisation, consisting of three totally different layers or contexts co-existing within the same organisation, namely the business-system context, the project team context and the knowledge base constitutes the other context. This should not be confused with the matrix structure where a member belongs and reports to two structures at the same time; in the hypertext structure, a member reports to one structure at a given time. There is an easy flow of organisational knowledge in the hypertext organisation, whereas the matrix structure is not oriented towards knowledge conversion. In a hypertext organisation, knowledge contents are combined more flexibly across layers and over time, and energy is used in a more concentrated manner. The hypertext organisation fosters middle-up-down management and has the capability to convert knowledge from outside the organisation.

A Case Study is given of Kao, Japan's leading household and chemical products maker which successfully utilises three different layers; the Business Systems Layer where a Division System is employed with fluidity; the Project-Team Layer, where horizontal, cross-divisional project teams are used; and explicit and tacit knowledge bases where knowledge-creating activities are captured and re-contextualised in the corporate-wide knowledge base.

Global interactions in knowledge creation

Nonaka and Takeuchi (1995) discuss successful projects where the East and West, or the East and North successfully partnered with each other to come up with best-selling products. One such example is the development of the Nissan Primera, which is a Japanese product developed with European partners, with 80% of its components emanating from Europe. The journey through this project was long and difficult, involving gaining tacit knowledge of European vehicle tastes and habits, as well as the socialisation of Japanese people into the European context.

Another example was the Shin Caterpillar Mitsubishi's REGA Project, where Caterpillar and Mitsubishi entered into a joint venture to manufacture hydraulic shovels. In the course of this project clashes were experienced due to differences in product development approaches. In Japan cost was considered the overriding factor with the question, "what is the best quality we can achieve within the allocated cost?" In America, safety and performance were considered more important. In America, such a product would be led by marketing department. In Japan a technology-led model was the norm, with R&D department taking the initiative. At Mitsubishi Heavy Industries, it was the Engineering Department's planning section that determined the specifications.

REGA was developed largely utilising Japanese methods of product development. However, American engineers added detailed written descriptions to the assembly procedure files which helped with externalisation. Mitsubishi learnt the importance of externalisation and the value of manuals became apparent in the replacement of engineers.

This case is an example of what can happen when Japanese and American engineers are placed on an equal footing to develop a global product. It represents a synthesis of US and Japanese approaches to organisational knowledge creation – a synergy of Japanese and American strengths.

Japanese strengths included socialisation (inter-plant meetings) and self-organising teams (the rugby style of product development). American strengths on the other hand included externalisation (asking the question "why?"), more specified design drawings, and standardised operation manuals, and combination (e.g. the cost-monitoring system).

Co-evolution and co-opetition

A case for co-evolution

Nishiguchi (Nonaka & Nishiguchi, 2001) develops an argument for co-evolution, using the metaphor of ecological species such as insects, basing this on Parsons' classical systems theory (1951). He develops the theme in such ecological relationships, arguing that such relationships begin with exploitation, where one species gains while the other suffers. This moves a step up to competition, where two existing species hamper each other from proliferation. Finally, there is symbiosis, where co-existent species help each other's proliferation.

Parsons (2015) argues that it would not be entirely unreasonable to try and interpret social evolution as an extension of ecological evolution, despite substantive differences in the mechanisms of development. Both types of evolution can be understood in terms of "evolutionary universals". In the organic world, vision is a good example of an evolutionary universal, while in human society, language is a good example, followed by religion, kinship and technology.

Social evolution can be interpreted as a process of progressive differentiation of social institutions.

Co-evolution is a process of parallel and relational evolution between ecologically complementary or independent species e.g. insect pollinated plants and pollinating insects. Co-evolution is caused by the selection of pressures that each exerts on the other. What are the examples of co-evolution between companies and their customers? What pressures do customer companies put on supplier companies that result in co-evolution? Health? Environmental demands? Technological? Prime contractor vs subcontractor? What are the benefits or disadvantages of the prime contractor (the predator) killing off or sparing the subcontractor (the prey)? These are some of the questions that must define knowledge creation and business strategy going into the future. Seneca said two thousand years ago, "Nature created us to be related to one another" (Nonaka & Nishiguchi, 2001).

Cooperation and knowledge creation

De Michelis (Nonaka & Nishiguchi, 2001) argues for cooperation within the knowledge-creation processes. A group of people engaged in a common performance is not an organisational structure, but a social aggregate cooperating in a work process, participating in a cooperative process, he contends (De Michelis, 1996).

A cooperative process can be characterised by the communicative relations binding its participants to each other and the actions they are performing.

The customers (those who have a condition to be satisfied) and the performers (those who can satisfy the condition) reach an agreement on the actions to be performed and share the evaluation of their execution. Accordingly, knowledge creation therefore can be a journey that involves the customers and the performers (suppliers). Together they can create knowledge that results in the development of a product, to the satisfaction of both suppliers and customers.

De Michelis further postulates that emphasis is not on knowledge, but on the process through which knowledge is continuously created, modified and updated: on the practice through which the members of a work group (or of a whole organisation) increase their ability to perform individually and collectively.

Attention is focused on pragmatic knowledge, on knowledge for action, both when it is embodied in the capabilities of the group members (tacit knowledge) and when it is described in documents and information databases (explicit knowledge). Knowledge creation is performed through knowledge transformation.

He argues that tacit customers do not exist! A customer makes their requests known in an explicit manner, through a document or through words that can be formalised in a document. If such information remained tacit, no one would know what the customer needs are.

Externalisation and internalisation both occur within a customer-performer relationship, for successful cooperation to have occurred. If externalisation is missing, the performers do not get any value from the performance of the performers; if internalisation is missing, then the performers cannot understand the conditions of satisfaction to be met.

Through socialisation the performers maintain their capability to cooperate smoothly and effectively; through combination the customers get and maintain their agreement on the request they make to the performers.

Participation in knowledge creation is more than access to documents (explicit knowledge), but through direct participation as much as possible.

Knowledge sharing is always partial between different organisations, since their identities are characterised by their different knowledge creation capabilities (competences, past experiences, work habits, objectives and rules and procedures). In addition, any organisation participating in a cooperative process may want to separate its internal knowledge-creation processes with respect to those involving other organisations in order to make an asset of part of the knowledge it creates. This does not necessarily mean separating the knowledge that is created within them, as there is need at some stage for an interchange of information and knowledge between customers and performers.

Co-opetition

Caspary and Nishiguchi (Nonaka & Nishiguchi, 2001) highlight the gains that can be derived from co-opetition. Cooperation with other global companies helped Japan to upgrade their knowledge and skill in the aircraft manufacturing processes, and in technology and marketing. Japanese companies gained recognition as interesting partners in international co-development programs for their contribution of experience in project and production management. They have enjoyed spin-on effects by the transfer of intra-firm knowledge in cost-saving management and production technologies from other commercial areas.

Without the collaboration of other companies, an individual Japanese company was too weak to carry out a large-scale development project in aircraft or engine development on its own. Over time Japanese companies managed to increase their work share in international development programs. Co-opetition stimulated communication and exchange among industries, in and out of Japan.

This resulted in three levels of knowledge creation:

- Inter-firm knowledge creation, which encompasses the transfer of aircraft and engine-related technology into other areas and the reciprocal transfer of know-how in production and management practices.
- Intra-firm knowledge creation, resulting in the necessity for cooperation as a consequence of the modest sizes of companies in the industry. Co-opetition stimulated communication and exchange of skills and knowledge among industries.
- Knowledge creation within semi-governmental organisations.

From a knowledge development perspective, the Japanese aircraft industry was able to learn together with competing global firms, which worked for it.

The synthesis of subjectivity and objectivity in knowledge creation

Ichijo and Nonaka (2007) remind us that humans are inherently subjective. They highlight that knowledge includes values and ideals. Human values are subjective, and the concept of truth depends on values, ideals and contexts. "Truth" becomes such through social interaction. To create organisational knowledge, subjective "tacit" individual knowledge has to be externalised into objective "explicit" knowledge shared within the organisation. This in turn is used and embodied by individuals to enrich their subjective tacit knowledge. This is what makes knowledge creation dynamic.

The knowledge-creation process is an ongoing process of validating the truth. Knowledge is socially created through a synthesis of different views held by different people. An organisation therefore needs to promote social interaction on the knowledge-creation platform to enable this process of synthesis, so that new knowledge is created as an ongoing process. Tentative and partial knowledge created out of an individual's values and experience is shared and justified by other members of the organisation to create new knowledge.

Implications of Nonaka and Takeuchi's knowledge-creation Model (SECI)

The interaction of tacit and explicit knowledge (knowledge conversion) gave rise to four modes: socialisation (from tacit to tacit), externalisation (from tacit to explicit), combination (from explicit to explicit), and internalisation (from explicit to tacit), now known as the SECI model.

Nonaka and Takeuchi outline the following implications of the SECI model. The interaction between tacit and explicit knowledge takes place at individual level and cannot be done by the organisation itself. The organisation therefore cannot create knowledge devoid of individuals. However, if knowledge cannot be shared by others, then it does not spiral itself organisationally. Socialisation starts by building a team whose members share their experience and mental models. Externalisation is triggered by successive rounds of meaningful dialogue. Metaphors and analogies enable team members to articulate their own perspectives and reveal hidden tacit knowledge. Combination is facilitated when the concept formed by the team is combined with existing data as well as with knowledge that resides outside the team. Internalisation is induced when team members begin to internalise the new explicit knowledge that is shared throughout the organisation.

Organisational knowledge-creation processes take place at group level, with the organisation providing the necessary enabling conditions. Five conditions required at organisational level to promote the knowledge spiral are; intention, autonomy, fluctuation and creative chaos, redundancy, and requisite variety.

The process by which organisational knowledge creation takes place is non-linear and interactive. The five-phase model of the process consists of sharing of tacit knowledge, concept creation, concept justification, archetype building, and cross-levelling of knowledge. This process moves cyclically and across levels. The first four phases move horizontally but the fifth moves vertically. The process can also take place inter-organisationally e.g. the Matsushita bread maker project.

Neither the top-down model of management nor the bottom-up model is best suited to promote dynamic interaction between tacit and explicit knowledge. The middle-up-down model integrates the benefits of top-down and bottom-up models and is therefore the best in class for bringing about organisational knowledge creation.

Both the formal hierarchy and the flexible task force have limitations with regard to knowledge creation. Nonaka and Takeuchi propose a hypertext organisational structure, which is most appropriate.

Neither the Japanese nor the Western methodology of knowledge creation can be viewed as the best. There is need to integrate the merits of both the Japanese and the Western methodologies to develop a universal model of organisational knowledge creation. The Nissan Primera case proved that the indigenous and the exogenous can work together to produce superior results.

The practical guidelines to follow in knowledge include creating a knowledge vision, developing a knowledge crew, building a high-density field of interaction at the front line, and piggy-backing on a new product development process. In addition, companies must maintain a highly adaptive and flexible approach to new product development, in a non-linear and dynamic manner, adopt middle-up-down management, and switch to a hypertext organisation. This makes life for the crew members easier because they only have to be in one layer at a time. Companies also need to construct a knowledge network with the outside world.

Creating knowledge involves tapping the mental maps of outside stakeholders, e.g. customers. Most customer needs are tacit, therefore they cannot always tell explicitly what they need or want (contrary to the earlier comment about tacit customers not existing). Sometimes customers do not quite know what they want, but a creative supplier can tell the customer what he wants (e.g. Apple's iPad).

In theoretical terms the knowledge-creation process is dynamic, producing two different kinds of knowledge spirals:

- The one takes place at the epistemological dimension across the four modes of knowledge conversion, i.e. socialisation, externalisation, combination and internalisation.
- The other takes place at the ontological dimension, where knowledge developed at individual level is transformed into knowledge at group and organisational levels.

The truly dynamic nature of this theory is the interaction of the two knowledge spirals over time, which interaction results in innovation.

The seven dichotomies that Nonaka and Takeuchi highlight in this model are;

- Tacit/explicit

Something new is created by getting tacit and explicit knowledge to interact. Socialisation brings about "sympathised knowledge, externalisation conceptual knowledge, combination systemic knowledge and internalisation operational knowledge".

- Body/mind

While Western epistemology, in the Cartesian split, separates body and mind, the Japanese place emphasis on bodily experience. Learning by doing therefore promotes internalisation.

- Individual/organisation

As knowledge is created by individuals, it is important for the organisation to support and stimulate the knowledge-creating activities of individuals and crystallise these at group level through dialogue, discussion, experience sharing and observation.

The individual and the organisation are not at opposing ends of the dichotomy. The individual is the "creator" of knowledge and the organisation is the "amplifier" of knowledge. Conversion of knowledge takes place at group or team level. Therefore, the dynamic integration of individuals (A) and the organisation (B) creates a synthesis in the form of a self-organising team (C), which plays a central role in the knowledge-creation process.

- Top-down/bottom-up

In top-down knowledge-creation structures, only top managers are able and allowed to create knowledge. This knowledge exists to be processed or implemented, suitable for dealing with explicit knowledge and focused on combination and internalisation.

In bottom-up structures, knowledge is created by entrepreneurially minded front-line employees, with very few orders and instructions from top management. This is suitable for dealing with tacit knowledge through socialisation and externalisation.

For both, middle managers are neglected.

The middle-top-down model provides a synthesis of the two. Knowledge is created by middle managers, who are leaders of teams or task forces, in a process involving a spiral interaction between the top and front-line employees. Knowledge is created neither through A or B, but through C, which synthesises the best of both sides.

- Bureaucracy/task force

Bureaucracy consists of highly formalised, specialised and centralised structures which work well in conducting routine work efficiently. Bureaucracy accumulates new knowledge through internalisation and combination.

The task force structure is flexible, adaptive, dynamic and participative, effective for carrying out a well-defined task that needs to be completed within a given time frame. Such a structure is indispensable for generating new knowledge through socialisation and externalisation.

Neither of the two is best suited for fostering organisational knowledge creation.

A hypertext structure, which is a synthesis of bureaucracy and task force, benefits from both. It contains a third organisational layer called the knowledge base, incorporating the corporate vision, organisational culture and/or technology.

- Relay/rugby

The relay approach in new product development is sequential, from phase to phase – concept development, feasibility testing, product design, development process, pilot production and final production. Functions are specialised and segmented. This results in longer lead times but has the advantage of enabling the pursuit of perfection.

The rugby approach involves the constant interaction of a multidisciplinary team whose members work together from start to finish. It encourages challenging the status quo, implementation of trial and error, and stimulates new kinds of learning.

The "American football" approach is a combination of both relay and rugby.

- East/West

It is possible to create a synthesis of East and West, but both sides must realise that differences do exist, and that both sides have their weaknesses and their strengths and should be willing to learn from each other.

Epistemologically, Western companies should start paying more attention to the less formal and systematic side of knowledge and begin to focus on highly subjective insights, intuitions and hunches gained through experience or the use of metaphors or pictures. **Ontologically,** Western companies need to learn to amplify or crystallise knowledge at group level through dialogue, discussion, experience sharing and observation.

The Japanese need to make better use of advanced information technology, software capabilities and computerised management systems to accumulate, store and disseminate explicit knowledge throughout the organisation. **Ontologically** they need to learn how to build stronger capabilities at individual level, throughout the organisation. Zimbabwean companies will have the benefits of both East and West and more, as it is steeped in the South.

Implications of the SECI model on a Zimbabwean Manufacturing company

There are many lessons to be learnt from Nonaka and Takeuchi's (1995) SECI model:

- The process of knowledge creation begins with acknowledging that individuals have tacit knowledge in them, which has to be shared by others. When shared, this tacit knowledge becomes explicit knowledge which other people now know. For the explicit knowledge to be internalised for use later, it has to be converted once again into tacit knowledge, albeit in different people, who may at a later stage have to share that tacit knowledge with others. As this process continues, it becomes a knowledge spiral because it should ideally be a continuous process.
- Ba has to be created to allow this knowledge conversion to happen, by creating space for individuals to share feelings, emotions, experiences and mental models. In knowledge creation, leaders must manage Ba by providing a knowledge vision and by building and energising Ba.
- The right levels of care promote knowledge creation in organisations.
- The correct management style is critical. Nonaka and Takeuchi advocate the "Middle-Up-Down" style, which gives middle managers a critical role to play in knowledge creation. The issue of structure is also important. While Nonaka and Takeuchi have nothing against bureaucratic and task force structures, which have their rightful places in running businesses, they introduce the hypertext structure as being more effective for knowledge-creation situations. They further suggest that the hypertext structure can co-exist with the bureaucratic and taskforce structures. It then becomes a case of when it is necessary to use which one.
- Nonaka and Takeuchi cite real life situations where success has been derived from dealing with innovation and knowledge creation at a global level. Even at local level, there is a distinct encouragement to engage other players such as customers and suppliers, and even competitors in the quest to create new knowledge.

These lessons, and more, will have to be embraced in the process of creating new knowledge in organisations.

Conclusion

When one looks at the innovativeness (or lack thereof) of a particular geographic or cultural group of people, it only follows logic that there are inherent factors in the geographic location, cultural set up, or even religion. Why, for example, are Japanese people more innovative than say, Sri Lankans, as an example? Both countries have a heavy dose of Buddhism. This is a whole new area of possible future research I think, which could yield very interesting results. Suffice to say, at this stage it is not very clear whether religion has a strong influence on innovation and knowledge creation. If anything, we have seen that while most Japanese people subscribe to certain religions, deep inside, they do not consider themselves as believers in any religion. Therefore, for them religion then is possibly a vehicle for social interaction. On the other hand, we have seen that most of the major religions indeed promote knowledge acquisition. However, Jaworski specifically links knowledge and decision making to some form of spiritualism.

Furthermore, there is a very strong link between philosophy and knowledge. To be precise, knowledge creation is steeped in philosophy, which is the starting point. Philosophy is itself a product of knowledge creation, where the philosophers of the day shared their tacit knowledge to make it explicit. Even in the case of Socrates who did not commit his works to writing, he somehow made his knowledge explicit through his students, such as Plato. The basic concepts of knowledge, such as empiricism and pragmatism, are products of philosophy.

What becomes very clear in this literature is that the future belongs to companies that take the best of East, West, North and South to start building a universal model. This is in tandem with Lessem and Schieffer's Four Worlds model. A lot has been said about the Japanese approach to knowledge creation versus the American approach.

Furthermore, companies should more and more exploit synergies with other companies in the search of new knowledge. The example of the benefits derived by the Japanese after partnering with organisations from the North and West in the manufacturing of aircraft engines, is landmark. This can only give credence to Lessem and Schieffer's (2009) four worlds perspective, and their emphasis that linking the local and global is important for transcultural co-creation. This says that, yes we may be different, but there are different strengths in our differences, and collectively we can achieve more.

As I move on in my integral research, I will now focus on the exploration of the Know-How of my research to innovation journey, using such tools as the GENE (Grounding, Emerging, Navigating, Effecting); the OFET (Origination, Foundation, Emancipation and Transformation); the Da Vinci Institute's TIPS Competitive Model; the Trans4m philosophy, Kolb's Learning Styles, to name a few.

I used the fundamental concepts of the SECI model in an effort to maximise on the tacit knowledge in the Turnall team, converting this to explicit knowledge, then into tacit knowledge, then into tacit knowledge, and so on. I really wanted to see the knowledge spiral working at Turnall (in conjunction with other tools), so that at the end of the day corporate knowledge loss would become a thing of the past. At the same time, I also observed the process to see whether there were any peculiarities that showed themselves in the implementation of the SECI model, and carried out an analysis of the said peculiarities, so that I could contribute to improving the model. At the end of the day, my aim was to come up with a company/industry/country specific model on knowledge creation. Cooperative inquiry was used at Turnall to explore this, leveraging on Heron (1996) and Reason and Bradbury (2008) for the process.

References

Bathelt, H., Feldman, M. P. & Kogler, F. (2011). Beyond Territory: Dynamic Geographies of Knowledge Creation, Diffusion and Innovation. New York: Routledge.

Benson J. (2004). *The Inner Nature of Colour: Studies on the Philosophy of the Four Elements.* Hendon, VA: Steiner Books.

Benton, C. F., Richter, F-J. & Takai, T. (2004). *Meso-Organisations and the Creation of Knowledge: Yoshiya Teramoto and His Work on Organisation and Industry Collaborations.* New York: Praeger Publishers.

De Michelis (1996). Work Processes, Organisational Structure and Co-operation Supports: Managing Complexity, in: Proceedings of the 5th IFAC Symposium on Automated Systems Based on Human Skills – Joint Design of Technology and Organisations. Berlin: Elsevier International.

Drucker, P. (1970). *Technology Management and Society.* London: Heinemann.

Gumport, P. J. (2002). *Academic Pathfinders: Knowledge Creation and Feminist Scholarship.* Hartford: Greenwood Press.

Heron, J. (1996). *Co-operative Inquiry: Research into the Human Condition.* London: Sage.

Ichijo, K. & Nonaka, I. (2007). *Knowledge Creation and Management: New Challenges for Managers.* New York: Oxford.

Kotter, J. P. & Cohen, D. S. (2002). *The Heart of Change: Real Life Stories of How People Change Their Organisations.* Boston: Harvard Business Press.

Lessem, R. & Schieffer A. (2009). *Transformation Management: Towards an Integral Enterprise.* Farnham, England: Gower.

Martin, B. R. & Etzkowitz, H. (2000). *The Origin and Evolution of the University Species.* New York: SPRU.

Marx, K. (1995). *Capital – Abridged Edition* (Edited by David McLlellan). Oxford: Oxford University Press.

Nonaka, I. & Nishiguchi, T. (2001). Knowledge *Emergence: Social, Technical, and Evolutionary Dimensions of Knowledge Creation.* New York: Oxford University Press.

Nonaka, I. & Takeuchi, H. (1995). *The Knowledge Creating Company: How Japanese Companies Create the Dynamics of Innovation.* New York: Oxford University Press.

Page, M. D., Erdly, W. W. & Baker, J. (1987). Social Networks: We Get by (and in Spite of) a Little Help from Our Friends. *Journal of Personality and Social Psychology*, 53, 793–804.

Parsons, T. (2015). *The Social System. (Classic Reprint).* London: Forgotten Books.

Reason, P. & Bradbury, H. (2008). *The Sage Handbook of Action Research: Participatory Inquiry and Practice.* (2nd Ed.). London: Sage.

Spear, S. & Kent B. H. (September 1999). *"Decoding the DNA of the Toyota Production System".* Harvard Business Review, viewed 21 March 2018, <https://hbr.org/1999/09/decoding-the-dna-of-the-toyota-production-system>.

Stacey, R. D. (2001). *Organisations: Learning and Knowledge Creation.* New York: Routledge.

Yeh, R. T. & Yeh, S. H. (2004). *The Art of Business: In the Footsteps of Giants.* Olathe: Zero Time Publishing.

6 Knowledge creation and societal learning in the North and West

Introduction

Peter Senge writes, *"Today's problems come from yesterday's solutions"* (Senge, 2006, p. 57).

In the preceding chapter I have dwelt significantly with knowledge creation in the East, focusing mostly on the works of Nonaka and Takeuchi and other like-minded innovators. What was of significant interest is that, Japanese institutions, private and public, resorted to innovative partnerships with the North and the West, and these partnerships generally brought together strengths from the East and the other worlds. In as much as the Japanese in particular have been known for some ground-breaking approaches to knowledge creation as well as to business philosophy, examples being the lean manufacturing systems, kaizen and others, they too have learnt using strategies from the North and West. In fact, Deming made an astronomical contribution to some of the systems that the Japanese are credited with today (Deming 1986), as we shall see later.

The purpose of this chapter is to carry out an analysis of traditional knowledge creation systems in the West, and further compare this with Eastern, and where appropriate Southern systems. Kidd and Richter (in Gramshaw, 2011) contend that the contrast between a Westerner and an Easterner has to do with the disposition of the two, where a Westerner appears to be more arrogant where an Easterner might appear more humble, though this does not necessarily reflect shrewdness (or lack thereof) or for that matter, level of knowledge or ignorance. It is just a disposition stemming from cultural and religious backgrounds. If an Easterner lives in America for a long time, it is possible that he too, to an extent, may borrow the ways of the American, and vice versa.

Due to historical considerations, some things that happen in the West most likely emanated from the North. A lot of the practices in the United States of America for instance, will have been a legacy of Europe. There will therefore be some similarities in what happens in the North and the West. Lessem and Schieffer (2009), define the North as being embodied in Rationalism, with high levels of conceptual strength. The West however tends to be more pragmatic, with a more practical treatment of things. The West, according to the (same authors), places emphasis on practical application, with the truth being tested by practical consequences. This chapter therefore sets out to highlight these peculiarities of the West with regard to knowledge creation, and where possible, to compare these with those of the other worlds.

Barthelt, Feldman and Kogler (2011) highlight two types of innovation, namely Science, Technology and Innovation (STI), and Doing, Using and Interacting (DUI). However, I choose to classify this into Scientific Innovation, Practical Innovation where certain inventions are created to solve specific societal problems, and Systems Thinking Innovation, where innovators come up with theories and models as tools for solving societal problems and achieving specific objectives. I will use examples, later in this chapter, to illustrate this.

The impact of the Smithsonian Institution on knowledge development in North America

Quite often limitations on knowledge creation and development are a result of lack of resources. This is why the Smithsonian Institution caught my attention. The background to this institution was that, when the English chemist and mineralogist, James Smithson, died in 1829, he left a will stating that if his nephew and sole heir died without heirs, his estate should go to the United States of America "to found at Washington, under the name of the Smithsonian Institution, an establishment for the increase and diffusion of knowledge among men" (Ewing, 2007). When his nephew died in 1835, indeed the United States Government was notified of this bequest. After all the necessary formalities, the estate of James Smithson was delivered to the United States in 1838, valued at just over half a million dollars, which must have been a lot of money at the time.

The terms of reference of this institution were rather vague and therefore open to a multitude of interpretations. Each of the different secretaries of the Institution over the years therefore applied a different focus to the institution, depending on his interpretation and his own area of specialisation or special interest. The areas of research covered have included increasing knowledge through scientific research, and diffusing knowledge through publication of the *Smithsonian Contribution to Knowledge* and through international exchange of publications, during Joseph Henry's tenure as Secretary; Spencer Fullerton Baird (1823–1887), focused his tenure from 1878 to 1887, on creating a great national museum. Baird's goal was a comprehensive collection of all the natural resources of the continent in the United States National Museum. Based on his knowledge of the natural resources of Russian-America, in 1867 Baird persuaded Congress to purchase Alaska.

During Baird's tenure, in 1879, the Bureau of American Ethnology was added to the Smithsonian's programs as well as research on the fishing industry that later led to the creation of the National Marine Fisheries Service.

Yet another secretary, Samuel Langley, attempted (unsuccessfully) to design the first flying machine (something that was successfully achieved by the Wright Brothers at Kitty Hawk, North Carolina, in 1903).

Alexander Wetmore set up a research station in the Panama Canal to facilitate research on the tropics. Other initiatives carried out by the institution included looking at primary and secondary education, putting up museums to cover various areas of research and interest, building observatories and setting up research centres (e.g. the Mpala Research Station in Kenya in 1992) (Ewing, 2007).

Major achievements of the Smithsonian Institution include the purchase of Alaska, research into a number of areas including tropical environments, fishing industry and solar phenomena, and building many museums to preserve knowledge about many aspects of scientific and other research. The institute also provided the military with information about little known areas of the world, such as the Pacific, particularly during World War II. This all bears testimony to the fact that the combination of resources and the freedom to pursue any forms of research can have surprising results. The Smithsonian Institution, thanks to the vague vision of an English man, has contributed immensely to the creation of new knowledge in America. Therefore, knowledge creation in America in this case, has been impacted by sources outside the United States – a case of the north impacting the west!

The indigenous and exogenous impact of knowledge creation in the United States of America

When we look at the American history, we see that there were the indigenous Americans (Indians), then a vast number of colonisers of America, ranging from the British, the Spanish, the French, the Dutch, the Portuguese, and so on. The sad thing is that the relic of the indigenous spirit appears to have been overwhelmed by the exogenous one. There is little significant evidence of the indigenous American spirit in the American society today. However, there are those who claim that some innovations credited to American immigrants actually emanated from Native American systems. For example, Scotsman Alexander Wood is credited with inventing the syringe in 1853. However, in pre-Columbian times South American Indians used a type of syringe made from sharpened hollow bird bones attached to small bladders to inject medicine, irrigate wounds or even clean ears. Additionally, indigenous healers also used larger and similar instruments for enemas (https://newsmaven.io/indiancountrytoday/ archive/10-native-inventions-and-innovations-that-changed-the-world-M0ZwDx1Ku0mQvn4Jn0KP4Q/ Retrieved 17 July 2017). It is anyone's guess how much more innovativeness by Native Americans could have become a reality if encouragement and recognition had been accorded to them.

The United States of America, while primarily colonised by the British, soon became a melting pot of cultures. What we call "Americans" today ranges from the indigenous Americans, the African Americans who ended up in America through Slave Trade, the colonisers of various nationalities, and those from the north, South, East and West who scrambled for America, viewing it as the land of opportunities (Hamby, 2010). We have seen from the Smithsonian story that even the funders of knowledge creation and development in America may have been from outside of America itself.

Therefore, the innovation culture of the United States will also tend to be a hybrid of the indigenous and exogenous. In fact, it becomes hypothetical to talk of indigenous and exogenous in America, as only the Native Americans (American Indians) can be truly termed indigenous. However, many non-indigenous Americans have started seeing themselves as Americans, to the extent that a man of Kenyan descent became the American President in 2009 (Woodward, 2010). Another example is, the president of the United States of America at the time of writing this book was himself a product of German and Scottish parentage, though born in America. Many professors from Africa, the North, the middle and the Far East end up in American universities, making a huge impact to both America and the world.

It can therefore be expected that the American knowledge creation philosophy is a hybrid philosophy, emanating from this melting pot of cultures. In other words, the exogenous rhythms drowned the indigenous and may have taken their place.

Traditional Mode 1 knowledge production

It would not be meaningful to discuss knowledge creation and not dwell on the concept of universities. The West inherited the traditional university concept from the North. Martin and Etzkowitz (2000), in their analysis of the history and evolution of the university species, describe the primary purpose of the medieval university as being twofold; the first was for teaching priests, public servants, lawyers, etcetera. The second purpose was for scholarship in a variety of disciplines such as biblical, medical, philosophy and classical. It was critical at that time that the teaching developed the full potential of the student as well as to teach students the knowledge and skills that were needed in society. With time, scholarship was, through research, broadened to incorporate the creation of new knowledge. This new knowledge was further classified to distinguish knowledge for its own sake as opposed to knowledge useful for meeting the needs of society.

The medieval university was with time transformed into the Humboldt university model in Germany, the Cardinal Newman University in Britain and the "Ivy League" university in America.

With time, in Europe a new type of university emerged, namely the institute of technology, or the polytechnic, and this was soon transferred to America and Japan as the "technical university". In America, the "land grant" university was later set up to meet initially the need for agricultural skills, but later to cater for industrial needs as well. In the United States, hybrids soon developed. For example, Cornell University started off as a compromise between the Ivy League and the land grant universities (Martin & Etzkowitz, 2000). Thus, even in the traditional university set up, universities evolved to meet the changing needs of society.

Gibbons et al. (1994) make the observation that the methods of knowledge production are changing. Society has been used to the traditional knowledge production concept, now known as Mode 1. This is traditionally the regular university set up, (or other academic institutions) where the new knowledge is produced for the sake of knowledge itself, within specific disciplines. There is little link with the needs of society. When the new knowledge is produced, it is not of prime importance whether users pick it up and use it. It goes into libraries with the hope that one day someone will have reason to use it.

Threats to the traditional university as the hub of learning and knowledge production are coming through electronic distance learning, as a case in point. More pressures are coming through the need for institutions of higher learning to address the needs of society. Globalisation, as well the high technology knowledge platform, tends to also produce a student with higher expectations from the Mode 1 universities. Such a student expects continuous learning, and from a variety of sources. The traditional university is now under pressure to meet the expectations of this modern student. In addition, universities are under pressure to teach skills relevant to the needs of the job market, which pressure can result in less emphasis on research, through which new knowledge is discovered.

Gumport (2002) contends, "New knowledge is created on multiple levels: through personal reflection on life experiences, in disciplinary legacies and local organisational contexts, and within historically specific societal conditions". She goes further to say that anyone who aspires to create knowledge "must in her or his own way become a pathfinder, engaged in an ongoing process of discovering a way through or into unexplored regions". In this statement, Gumport appears to be open to knowledge creation, in whatever mode it comes. In support of Mode 1 universities, she states that knowledge creating activities are highlighted through transmission (teaching different levels of students), production (research), and transfer (dissemination and application). She further argues that departmentalisation at universities, which led to specialisation, facilitated enhanced knowledge creation.

It can be argued that there will always be a role for Mode 1 universities to play in the creation of new knowledge, even though there will be other options which render flexibility to the learning situation (Martin & Etzkowitz, 2000). The issue at hand is therefore not to criticise the Mode 1 system, but to appreciate it for the role it plays in the production of scientific and academic knowledge. The issue is to acknowledge that there are options in knowledge production, which come with different emphases to the knowledge creation arena. This is where the Mode 2 University system comes in.

The Mode 2 system

Gibbons et al. (1994) contend that there is a definite shift from Mode 1 to the Mode 2 system of knowledge creation. They describe Mode 2 knowledge production as "socially distributed knowledge". For a start, the Mode 2 system involves multi-disciplinary research carried out in a variety of institutions. In the Da Vinci/Trans4M PhD program colleagues are carrying out research through such institutions as the Confederation of Zimbabwe Industries, private companies and specific industries such as tourism and manufacturing. This is far removed from the laboratories found in Mode 1 universities. The emphasis of knowledge production in this context is its application. The knowledge produced must be useful in the community that it is produced, and beyond, resulting in "the social distribution of Knowledge" (Nowotny, Scott & Gibbons, 2001). Gumport (2002) buttresses this by saying that social conditions in part determine what is possible for individual interest – what type of knowledge is created. Knowledge development is therefore an ongoing social process that takes place at cognitive and social levels through various patterns of communicating ideas, sharing common research interests and varied rhythms.

According to Nowotny, Scott and Gibbons (2001, 2003), in the Mode 2 system, knowledge is primarily generated in the context of application. It is trans-disciplinary in character, as it mobilises both theoretical perspectives and practical methodologies to solve societal problems. Hence, the Mode 1 system is still relevant to Mode 2. Discoveries made in the Mode 1 system can be (but not necessarily all the time) the starting point in the development and implementation of a Mode 2 concept.

In addition, Mode 2 knowledge is characterised by greater diversity of the areas where knowledge is produced. These include management consultants, think tanks and activist groups, to name only a few. Mode 2 knowledge also tends to be highly reflexive as it encourages and promotes multiple views. Quality control in its original form of "peer reviews", reductionist forms of quality control and clear and unchallengeable scientific criteria become problematic. It therefore becomes necessary to redefine quality to reduce discrimination and selectivity.

Huff (1999) proposes that Mode 2 arose out of unmet needs and opportunities. He says Mode 1 is too slow and inward looking, giving priorities to "pedigrees". On the other hand, he contends that, even though Mode 2 offers improved methods of knowledge production, it has its own limitations, as it moves away from science and technology into management. He proposes Mode 1.5, which is not in existence yet, but has the potential to be. He argues that the Mode 1.5 would have the following assumptions;

- Disciplinary knowledge and theoretical models would continue to constitute a useful knowledge base where Mode 2 experimentation is neither desirable nor possible.
- Research institutions that by some miracle are shielded from the need to make money from their knowledge production can produce what Huff terms "public goods" that companies and consultants cannot credibly produce.
- Business schools could also offer a desirable neutral ground for new knowledge to be generated through the interaction of people with diverse business background.

Clearly, for now Mode 1.5 will most probably remain a myth.

The nature of research in Mode 2 knowledge production

Nowotny, Scott and Gibbons (2001) contend that the nature of the research process is being transformed. They cite the elements of such transformation as the "steering" of research priorities, the commercialisation of research, and the accountability of science.

a) The steering of research priorities

The first element in the transformation of research is the increasing desire to influence research priorities. This happens at three levels, namely;

- At the supranational level (e.g. the European Union) attempts have been made to shape research priorities and build research capacity to meet identified social and economic needs (Nowotny, Scott & Gibbons, 2001).

    Barthelt, Feldman and Kogler (2011), contend that nations and states have re-organised themselves into supranational, national, regional and trans-local entities in the process of initiating research interest in different disciplines.
- At national levels, where government ministries (such as ministries of health, defence, or agriculture) have funded specific research programs sometimes for the dichotomous reasons of meeting both short-term political agendas and long-term research capacities.
- At the system levels in many countries, where Research Councils have increasingly adopted "more pro-active (or top-down) research priorities in place of essentially reactive (or bottom-up) policies", whereby the best research proposals, as identified by peer review, are funded. These programs are quite often a compromise between "political" goals, promising science, and available research capacity. Universities too have started to manage their research priorities more aggressively, instead of simply providing a support environment.

b) The commercialisation of research

According to Nowotny, Scott and Gibbons (2001) this has taken two main forms. First, as funding of research by public institutions has become more constrained, researchers have increasingly turned to alternative sources of funding. This has resulted in the formation of public-private partnerships, which the authors see as having the potential to reduce diversity and creativity. Second, institutions have awakened to the value of the "intellectual property" generated by their research. With public expenditure on higher education and research having generally failed to keep pace with costs, and universities having been encouraged to develop alternative sources of income; with the emergence of a Knowledge Society, knowledge "products", many of which are derived from university research, are increasingly valued, not in terms of their long-term potential, but in terms of immediate market value. In 1787 the issue of intel-lectual property rights became enshrined in the United States Constitution (Fenning, 1929). In 1790, President George Washington signed the Patent Act (1 Stat. 109) into law which proclaimed that patents were to be authorized for "any useful art, manufacture, engine, machine, or device, or any improvement therein not before known or used" (Ellis, 2005).

There are however some important consequences of seeking to exploit intel-lectual property. First, the exploitation of intellectual property transforms the organisational character of the university or institution. Secondly, it challenges the ideal of science as a public good. One pertinent issue becomes commer-cial confidentiality. If "intellectual property" is valuable, it cannot be given away "freely" by open publication in peer-reviewed journals, or at scientific conferences open to all. As the quality of science is largely determined by its exposure to refutation and counter-argument, this quality peer review is ser-iously compromised (Etzkowitz & Leydesdorff, 2000).

c) The accountability of science

Nowotny, Scott and Gibbons (2001) contend that the third element in the trans-formation of research is the growing emphasis placed upon the management of research – and, in particular, upon efforts to evaluate its effectiveness and assess its quality. They cite the example of the Research Assessment Exercise (RAE) conducted by the higher education funding councils of England, Scotland, and Wales, in 2001. While no attempt is made to influence the kind of research that is done in RAE, in terms of its themes, concepts, or methodologies, in practice, of course, the notions of international and national "significance" upon which the RAE relies as a measurement criterion, are not value-free. It was noted that, no matter how objective and neutral researchers try to be, the influence of the RAE on the behaviour of individual researchers, research groups, departments, subjects, as well as institutions has been inevitable.

The central idea of Mode 2

The central idea of Mode 2 therefore includes enhanced geographical prox-imity as potentially there could be many sites. Institutional proximity is increased through reduced differences between universities and industry. Knowledge flows more easily across disciplinary boundaries, and organisational research is more open and flexible. Preference is given to collaborative rather than individual performance. Excellence is judged by the ability of individuals to come up with sustained contribution in open, flexible organisations (Gibbons et al., 1994).

A comparison of Mode 1 and Mode 2

The basis of Mode 1 is cognitive proximity through a particular discipline, whereas Mode 2 is based on cognitive distance through a more trans-disciplinary

basis. The organisational proximity in Mode 1 is within a university department, compared to organisational distance in Mode 2 which operates
across organisations, e.g. Trans4M/Da Vinci Institute/Business Training &
Development. Mode one tends to have social proximity based on personal
networks. Mode 2, on the other hand, can operate within social distances by
utilising temporary open networks.

Mode 1 operates under strict academic norms, while Mode 2 can function
within institutional distances where there is even potentially conflicting goals.
In addition, Mode 1 research happens in some kind of laboratory. Mode 2
however thrives in geographical distance, even crossing national borders. The
typical example given above demonstrates this, where a Mode 2 in Geneva
(Trans4m), co-founded and co-managed by two professors living in England
and France, works with DaVinci Institute in South Africa to work with students
in Zimbabwe, Egypt, UK, Nigeria, Jordan, Pakistan, to name a few countries..
What a relevant example of a local/global perspective. The competitive edge
that Mode 2 enjoys therefore is flexibility created by cognitive, organisational,
social, institutional and geographical distances. In the process, Mode 2 is more
likely to be alive to issues of indigenous and exogenous rhythms.

The triple helix model

Etzkowitz and Leydesdorff (2000) have put forward an alternative but related
characterisation of the changing nature of knowledge production and of universities. They suggest that the increasingly close links between universities,
government and industry can be envisioned in terms of a "triple helix" model,
where universities are seen as taking on a new third mission (in addition to
the two traditional missions of teaching and research) of contributing to the
economy. According to Etzkowitz and Leydesdorff (2000), the taking up of
this third mission represents the "second academic revolution" (the first having
been when primarily teaching institutions took on the role of research [Jencks
& Riesman, 1968]). The result is the emergence of the "entrepreneurial university" which combines teaching, research and contributing to the economy
(Etzkowitz & Leydesdorff, 2000). This can be made sense of in view of research
carried out by PhD students through the DaVinci Institute, Transform and
BTD (except that the government arm is missing). This is also a good example
of this concept of entrepreneurial university, as the majority of these students
are seeking, through their various research projects, to improve the economic situation of their countries and by improving the performance of their
organisations. Questions have however been raised as to the issue of whether a
"third mission" or the entrepreneurial university represents a specialised phenomenon in knowledge production. Time will tell.

Driving forces behind universities

Some external drivers behind influencing the nature of universities moving
from the "pure" to the "instrumental" view of the university include the end

of the cold war, which resulted in the reduced need for research in physical sciences and engineering fields, as well as a diminished interest in nuclear energy (Martin & Etzkowitz, 2000). In addition, new technologies, such as information, communication and biotechnology have given rise to the concept of knowledge-based economies and have influenced universities to focus on these fields.

Furthermore, globalisation has resulted in increased competition in the field of knowledge. Science and technology have become strategic disciplines in terms of the competitiveness of nations. As if this is not enough, universities are having to contend with new entrants to the knowledge industry in the form of training institutions set up by companies. Examples are Unipart and British Aerospace University in Britain. In Zimbabwe there are companies such as the Delta group, and before that the Anglo American Corporation, which set up formidable training institutions of their own, to address specific skills that would normally be taught at universities, such as marketing, finance and human resources.

The limitation of resources has resulted in the assessment of the research and teaching quality of universities becoming more pronounced in the quest for increased accountability of government spending.

Companies are more and more basing their competitiveness on knowledge and skills, therefore if they do not find a desirable fit between what the universities offer and what they need, soon start their own training institutions. Business Training and Development (BTD) started as a training department of the Astra group of companies in Zimbabwe.

Internal drivers include interdisciplinary research which may have weakened the link between research and teaching. Lack of adequate investment and funding has resulted in poor infrastructure in the universities. Furthermore, while there is a higher demand of teaching due to the increased numbers of students, academic salaries are relatively low, affecting the morale of academic staff. For this reason, universities sometimes lose their good teachers to the private sector, and this obviously affects the quality of knowledge produced at the said universities. (Martin & Etzkowitz 2000).

Practical innovation

While in the West there have been many innovations that have emerged through different universities and institutions of learning, there have been also innovations that have come through the practical route. Many were to answer a specific need in the communities they were created.

In 1752 Dr Benjamin Franklin invented the flexible catheter when his brother John suffered from bladder stones. Dr Franklin's flexible catheter was made of metal with segments hinged together in order for a wire enclosed inside to increase rigidity during insertion. A polymath, politician and scientist, among other things, Dr Franklin was educated at St Andrews. He also invented the lightning rod, bifocals and the Franklin stove, among others. Looking at Benjamin Franklin's work, he was what might be known as the professional inventor, as he invented many useful things to be used in medicine, libraries, in the streets, and so on (Brands, 2000).

Another American inventor was Eli Whitney. Educated at Yale University, Whitney invented the cotton gin in 1793, which was to become one of the key inventions of the Industrial Revolution. This invention revolutionised the way cotton was harvested. Later he invented the concept of mass production which allowed for a boom in American industry, and eventually provided employment for thousands of workers (Lakwete, 2014).

In 1834 Hiram Moore invented the combine harvester, or combine, or thresher. This is a machine that combines the tasks of harvesting, threshing, and cleaning grain crops (Constable & Somerville, 2003).

Orville and Wilbur Wright were two American brothers, inventors, and aviation pioneers who invented and built the world's first successful aeroplane and made the first controlled, powered and sustained human flight, on 17 December 1903. From 1905 to 1907, the brothers developed their flying machine into the first practical fixed-wing aircraft. Although not the first to build and fly experimental aircraft, the Wright brothers were the first to invent aircraft controls that made fixed-wing powered flight possible (Ash, 1974).

Their critical breakthrough was their invention of three-axis control, which enabled the pilot to steer the aircraft effectively and to maintain its equilibrium. Right on the outset the Wright brothers focused on developing a reliable method of pilot control as the key to solving "the flying problem".

> The Wright Brothers were not highly educated. They never had the opportunity for university education, hence they were products of neither Mode 1 nor Mode 2. Wilbur went through high school but never received his diploma (which was then awarded posthumously on his 127th birthday). Orville dropped out of school to start a printing business. They gained the mechanical skills essential for their success by working for years in their shop with printing presses, bicycles, motors, and other machinery. Their work with bicycles in particular influenced their belief that an unstable vehicle like a flying machine could be controlled and balanced with practice. From 1900 until their first powered flights in late 1903, they carried out glider tests that also developed their skills as pilots. Their bicycle shop employee, Charlie Taylor, became an important part of the team, building their first aircraft engine in close collaboration with the brothers.
>
> (Ash, 1974)

This is a very negligible list of American inventions. There have been many, many other inventions over the years, ranging from the salt shaker, to the space rocket. Many of these were invented by individuals with particular qualifications, many of them having obtained some university training. Others were invented by people who were not very highly educated, such as the Wright brothers. Lessem and Schieffer (2009) describe the Western world as "pragmatic". The

Western world is therefore known for its practical and pragmatic solutions to the needs of society, which is evident in these inventions that are of practical use to society.

William Edwards Deming

Deming was an American statistician, professor, author, lecturer and consultant. He developed the "Plan-Do-Check-Act" cycle which was then popularly named after him (The Deming Cycle). From 1950 onwards, he taught top management in Japan how to improve design and by inference, service, product quality, testing, and sales through various methods, including the application of statistical methods (Gitlow & Gitlow, 1987).

Deming greatly contributed to Japan's reputation for innovative high-quality products and its economic power. He is regarded as having had more impact upon Japanese manufacturing and business than any other individual who is not of Japanese heritage. It is ironic that the Japanese are getting credit for what Deming created and shared. So, it is not the Japanese who developed these concepts, but Deming. The Japanese should however be credited for being good learners and recognising the value addition that Deming brought to them. In contrast, the Americans only began to recognise the value of Deming's contribution towards the end of his life. Deming was considered a hero in Japan, though he was only just beginning to win widespread recognition in the United States at the time of his death.

Deming was involved in the early planning for the 1951 Japanese Census. As the allied powers were occupying Japan, he was asked by the United States Department of the Army to assist with the census. He became involved in Japanese society, and as a result of his expertise in quality issues the Japanese Union of Scientists and Engineers (JUSE) invited him to work with them.

Many Japanese manufacturers applied the techniques that Deming recommended and taught them, and they experienced high levels of quality and productivity which they had not seen before. The improved quality resulted in lowered cost, and this created new international demand for Japanese products.

Deming would not accept royalties from the transcripts of his 1950 lectures, so JUSE's board of directors established the Deming Prize (December 1950) to repay him for his friendship and kindness, and this has continued to be a source of considerable influence on the disciplines of quality control and quality management.

Back home Deming continued to run his own consultancy business in the United States (Mode 2?). He worked with Ford Motor Company (among others) in 1981, when Ford's sales were falling. Between 1979 and 1982, Ford had incurred $3 billion in losses. In his intervention he told Ford that management actions were responsible for 85% of all problems in developing better cars. Under his tutelage, by 1986, Ford had become the most profitable American auto company, out-earning General Motors (Gitlow & Gitlow, 1987).

The philosophy of W. Edwards Deming has been summarized by his Japanese proponents as follows:

> *Dr. W. Edwards Deming taught that by adopting appropriate principles of management, organizations can increase quality and simultaneously reduce costs (by reducing waste, rework, staff attrition and litigation while increasing customer loyalty). The key is to practice continual improvement and think of manufacturing as a system, not as bits and pieces.*
>
> (Deming, *2000*)

In the 1970s, Deming's philosophy was summarized by some of his Japanese colleagues with the following "a"-versus-"b" comparison:

$$\text{QUALITY} = \frac{\text{RESULTS OF WORK EFFORTS}}{\text{TOTAL COSTS}}$$

Apparently, Deming was the creator of Total Quality Management, which the Japanese are now credited for.

Deming believed that when people and organisations focus primarily on quality, quality tends to improve and costs fall over time. However, he contends that when people and organisations focus primarily on *costs*, costs tend to rise and quality declines over time (Deming, 1986). The moral of this story is, you achieve more by not focusing on costs but on quality.

Deming further advocated that all managers need to have what he termed a System of Profound Knowledge, consisting of four parts:

1. *Appreciation of a system*: understanding the overall processes involving suppliers, producers, and customers (or recipients) of goods and services;
2. *Knowledge of variation*: the range and causes of variation in quality, and use of statistical sampling in measurements;
3. *Theory of knowledge*: the concepts explaining knowledge and the limits of what can be known (Gitlow & Gitlow, 1987).

Deming's story is a typical case of exogenous rhythms becoming indigenous.

Peter Senge

Senge (2006, p. 4) says

> It is no longer sufficient to have one person learning for the organisation, a Ford or a Sloan or a Watson or a Gates. It's just not possible any longer to figure out from the top and have everyone else following the orders of the "grand strategist". The organisations that will truly excel in the future will

be the organisations that discover how to tap people's commitment and capacity to learn at all levels in an organisation.

Born and bred in California, Peter Senge is the epitome of a Western opinion maker on issues of organisational learning and knowledge development.

He therefore promotes the notion of learning organisations, which happens through systems thinking (the fifth discipline). He contends that businesses and other human activities are systems that are bound by invisible connections on inter-related actions, which connections affect one another. He postulates that systems thinking is a fusion of four disciplines, namely Personal Mastery, Mental Models, Building a Shared Vision and Team Learning.

Personal Mastery involves a special level of proficiency. It is the discipline of continuously clarifying and deepening our personal vision, of focusing our energies, of developing patience and of seeing reality objectively. It is the cornerstone of the learning organisation. We cannot all be specialists in everything, even within the same department. However, if every single member of the team specialises in at least one area, we are all the better for it.

Senge shares the opinion that few organisations really encourage the growth of their people through personal mastery. As a result, people who enter the organisation as bright, well-educated, high-energy people, full of a desire to make a difference, soon "put in their time" so that they can do what matters to them at the weekend. The commitment is lost, as is the sense of mission, as well as the excitement they had when they started their careers. In the end the business gets very little of their energy, and very little of their spirit.

Mental Models, according to Senge, are deeply engrained assumptions, generalisations, and even pictures or images that influence the way we understand the world and how we react to it.

Building a Shared Vision is unearthing shared "pictures of the future" that foster genuine commitment and enrolment rather than compliance. Members of the team must believe in the vision so much that they are motivated to implement strategies that are instrumental in realising the vision. It would be interesting to carry out an analysis of how many managers in any organisation really believe in the company vision.

About Team Learning Senge contends that it "... is vital because teams, not individuals, are the fundamental learning unit in modern organisations. This is where the rubber meets the road; unless teams can learn, the organisation cannot learn". Even in Nonaka and Takeuchi's SECI model, though it is acknowledged that knowledge resides in individuals, unless there is a team strategy to turn individual tacit knowledge into team explicit knowledge, the model does not have a chance.

A learning organisation therefore is an organisation that is continually expanding its capacity to create its future. However, for an organisation to become a learning organisation, it should clear itself of learning disabilities. These include people who outlive their organisations by refusing to be retrained for new jobs, fragmenting manufacturing and other business process (Japanese car manufacturers have the same engineers for designing mounting for entire engine while American ones have different ones dealing with each component, resulting in slow and expensive process) and finding other people to blame for things that go wrong.

The illusion of taking charge, according to Senge (reactiveness in disguise) usually results in trying to solve a problem by increasing numbers and consequently increasing costs. A Management Team fighting for turf is also cited as a symptom of learning disabilities in an organisation.

According to Senge (2006) therefore, systems thinking is the cornerstone of the learning organisation. It is a discipline of seeing wholes and interrelationships. It is based on two types of giving feedback, i.e. reinforcing or amplifying feedback processes which promote growth, and balancing (or stabilising) feedback which operates whenever there is goal oriented behaviour, which is important for strategy implementation.

Senge's view on leadership is that leaders are designers, stewards and teachers, whose role is to build organisations where people expand their capacity to understand complexity, clarify vision, and improve shared mental models.

I see a close relationship, albeit with different areas of emphasis, between Senge and Kolb, the main differences being that Kolb focuses on learning individuals, while Senge focuses on learning organisations. However, even Senge admits that organisations learn through individuals. Furthermore, organisational learning only becomes useful and value adding in as much as it results in positive change in the organisations concerned.

Ram Charan

Ram Charan (2007) brings a slightly different focus to the debate by highlighting specific skills needed by leaders in order to get results. Among these is the issue of positioning the business to ensure that the needs of customers are met, for this is how money is made. He also places emphasis on influencing the way people work together thus leading to the social systems of the business and understanding your people. He adds that when high-energy, high-powered and high-ego people are moulded into a team, they will equal more than the sum of their parts. He postulates that a leader must know his destination and have very clear priorities that become the road map for meeting the goals of the business. Like Senge, Charan also believes in team learning for sustainable functionality of businesses.

With his colleagues, Drotter and Noel, Charan (2001) also developed the Leadership Pipeline as a tool for unclogging an organisation's leadership system and for developing leaders in the organisation. Over time organisations that have used this system claim that it is a useful tool for talent management. They came up with six turns in the pipeline which represent significant passages that cannot be mastered in a short time.

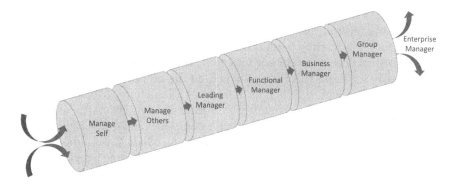

Figure 6.1 The Leadership Pipeline.
Source: Charan, Drotter and Noel 2001(Adaptation and Design: Elizabeth Mamukwa, 2019).

While not everyone will go through all six turns, (for there are issues of talent, capacity and opportunity), those who do will be all the better leaders for having systematically gone through all the turns. However, there may be a cost if individual managers are fast tracked through the pipeline and miss some turns while going up the corporate ladder. Managers need to have a comprehensive appreciation of the knowledge that is relevant in the lower level areas so that they fully appreciate what the individuals that they supervise may be going through.

While Charan was born in India, he worked in Australia and is an alumna of Harvard. Now based in America, Charan was named "the most influential consultant alive" by Fortune Magazine.

Conclusion

What has become clear in the quest to understand knowledge creation in the West is that the so-called West is a melting pot of all four worlds. The knowledge creation culture, therefore, is similarly coloured by all worlds. Moreover, while it is true that the West tends to be more pragmatic, the other worlds have equally shared knowledge creation tenets.

This discussion has highlighted that there are three types of knowledge creation in the West, and possibly elsewhere:

- Knowledge creation through research in either Mode 1 or Mode 2.
- Through practical inventions such as aeroplanes or combine harvesters.
- Through the development of models and tools through which to develop new knowledge and people, such as Kolb's Learning Styles Inventory, and Ram Charan's leadership pipeline.

All types of knowledge creation have roles to play in the lives of people in this world. Mode 1 university is now found almost in every corner of the world, and the contribution from this is through the rational research, having originated in the North. The starting point is usually a hypothesis, and the results are not necessarily practical in nature, but something that you put in libraries, hoping that one day someone will use it. Mode 2 on the other hand is usually more practical, dealing with gaps found in Mode 1. Sometimes Mode 2 starts as a training department in a company, or a business consultancy. Its objectives include providing specific skills training for companies and other institutions – practical skills that are of immediate relevance. As Mode 2 institutions grow, they become big and flexible in terms of market reach, enabling people far apart and from different backgrounds to share knowledge. However, while Mode 2 has posed some significant competition to Mode 1, it cannot be a complete replacement thereof. Mode 1 will always have a role to play, particularly for those who aspire for a purely academic career.

Practical inventions serve the purpose of fulfilling an identified practical need in society. Examples of such are the cotton gin invented by Eli Whitney, the flexible catheter invented by Benjamin Franklin and the combine harvester invented by Hiram Moore. Even though there was no apparent urgent societal need of the aeroplane that was invented by the Wright brothers at that time, it is now unthinkable to live a life without the flexibility of the fast travel planes now provide. This has, together with the information revolution, contributed greatly to globalisation.

Knowledge creation through theories and models has also made many things possible in people's lives and in businesses in particular. It is now possible to have psychological assessments of people before you recruit them, as a case in point, to make sure they are suited to the specific jobs and levels of responsibility.

After having looked at knowledge creation in the East and West, and having lived and worked in the South, it is safe to say that there is potential for knowledge creation in all worlds. The handicaps highlighted in the South are mostly as a result of confidence destroyed through many years of colonisation, and the lack of records and documentation. Inventions are inherent in all worlds. Therefore, no particular world really stands out with regard to knowledge creation. However, we have seen also, that where two or more worlds work together, greater things happen. A good example is how Japan has benefited from Deming's contribution, and how this has improved business systems and customer focus in that country. Japan is now credited with good quality systems, yet an American statistician introduced them to this concept of quality.

Due to their pragmatic nature, Americans soon saw value in knowledge created by individuals, and quickly introduced the concept of patents. Needless to say, this is a concept that has spread throughout the world, even in the South.

Knowledge creation then, is responsible for continuously improving the quality of human life through working smarter. Ground-breaking discoveries continue to be made in the field of medicine for example, allowing doctors to cure conditions that were not curable before, and elongating people's lives.

References

Ash, R. (1974). *The Wright Brothers.* London: Wayland.

Barthelt, H., Feldman, M. P. & Kogler, D. F. (2011). *Beyond Territory: Dynamic Geographies of Knowledge Creation, Diffusion, and Innovation.* New York and London: Routledge.

Brands, H. W. (2000). *The First American: The Life and Times of Benjamin Franklin.* New York: Doubleday

Charan, R. (2007). *Know-How: The 8 Skills That Separate People Who Perform and Those Who Don't.* New York: Crown Business.

Charan, R., Drotter, S. & Noel, J. (2001). *The Leadership Pipeline: How to build a Leadership Powered Company* (2nd Ed.). San Francisco: Jossey-Bass.

Constable, G. & Somerville, B. (2003). *A Century of Innovation: Twenty Engineering Achievements That Transformed Our Live.* Washington, DC: Joseph Henry Press.

Deitch, J. W. (2001). *A Nation of Inventors.* Carlisle, MA: Discovery Enterprises Limited.

Deming, W. E. (1986). *Out of Crisis.* London: MIT Press.

Deming, W. E. (2000). *The New Economics for Industry, Government, Education* (2nd Ed.). Cambridge, MA: MIT Press.

Ellis, J. J. (2005). *His Excellency George Washington.* New York: Vintage Books.

Etzkowitz, H. & Leydesdorff, L. (2000). 'The Dynamics of Innovation: from National Systems and "Mode 2" to a Triple Helix of University-Industry-Government Relations', viewed on 5th September 2019, <www.sciencedirect.com/science/article/abs/pii/S0048733399000554?via%3Dihub>

Ewing, H. P. (2007). *The Lost World of James Smithson: Science, Revolution, and the Birth of the Smithsonian.* New York: Bloomsbury.

Fenning, K. (1929). "The Origin of the Patent and Copyright Clause of the Constitution". *Journal of the Patent Office Society*, 11, 438.

Gibbons, M., Limoges, C., Nowotny, H., Schwartzman, S., Scott, P. & M. Trow (1994). *The New Production of Knowledge: The dynamics of science and research in contemporary societies.* London: Sage.

Gitlow, H. S., & Gitlow, S. J. (1987). *The Deming Guide to Quality and Competitive Position.* New York: Prentice Hall Trade.

Gumport, P. J. (2002). *Academic Pathfinders: Knowledge Creation and Feminist Scholarship.* Hartford: Greenwood Press.

Hamby, A. L. (2010). *An Outline of US History.* New York: U.S. Department of State's Bureau of International Information Programs.

Huff, A. S. (1999). *Changes in Organisational Knowledge Production.* Denver: University of Colorado and Cranfield School of Management.

Jencks, C. & Riesman, D. (1968). *The Academic Revolution.* New York: Doubleday.

Lakwete, A. (2004). *Inventing the Cotton Gin: Machine and Myth in Antebellum America.* Baltimore, MD: Johns Hopkins University Press.

Lessem, R. & Schieffer, A. (2009). *Transformation Management: Towards the Integral Enterprise.* Farnham, England: Gower.

Martin, B. R. & Etzkowitz, H. (2000). *The Origin and Evolution of the University Species.* New York: New York University.

Navaretti, G. B., Dasgupta, P., Mäler, K.-G. & Siniscalco, D. (1998). *Creation and Transfer of Knowledge: Institutions and Incentives.* Berlin: Springer.

Nowotny, H., Scott, P. & Gibbons, M. (2001). *Rethinking Science: Knowledge and the Public in an Age of Uncertainty.* Cambridge: Polity Press.

Nowotny, H., Scott, P. & Gibbons, M. (2003). Mode 2 Revisited: The New Production of Knowledge. *Minerva, 41,* 179–194.

O'Dell, C. & Hubert, C. (2011). *The New Edge in Knowledge: How Knowledge Management is Changing the Way We Do Business.* New Jersey: John Wiley & Sons.

Senge, P. M. (2006). *Fifth Discipline: The Art and Practice of the Learning Organisation.* London: Random House.

Woodward, B. (2010). *Obama's Wars: The Inside Story.* New York: Simon and Schuster.

Electronic Sources

https://newsmaven.io/indiancountrytoday/archive/10-native-inventions-and-innovations-that-changed-the-world-M0ZwDx1Ku0mQvn4Jn0KP4Q/. Retrieved 17 July 2017.

Part IV

Co-creation

The Mode 2 University and knowledge
Creation through innovation

7 Knowledge creation and innovation at a Zimbabwean University

The Harare Institute of Technology case story

Introduction

As early as 1999 the Presidential Commission of Inquiry into Zimbabwean Education and Training detected a disconnect between Zimbabwe's university curriculum and national development. It reported that "Stakeholders wondered why poor links existed between Industry and commerce on one hand and universities and research on the other". The same report alluded to the fact that "the local universities were inflexible, failing to respond to the local development needs of the country. The curriculum was said to be elitist in that it groomed people for office and white collar jobs. Even people with technical and engineering skills do not want to make their hands dirty" the commission reported (Nziramasanga, 1999). No one has confirmed this, but this could possibly have been the seed that germinated the idea of the Harare Institute of Technology. This also sounds like a cry for Mode 2 University, even though no one realised this.

Having a nephew starting university, I became alive to the hype about the Harare Institute of Technology (HIT) where my nephew wishes to study for a Chemical Engineering Degree. I naturally became curious about what happens there and why it had now become a preferred option for Engineering studies ahead of other local universities. What I discovered is amazing, and makes a fascinating case story of good things happening in a country where, at the time of writing this, everything appears to be falling off the wheels. The programs at HIT are structured into four faculties:

School of Business and Management Sciences

- Electronic Commerce
- Financial Engineering
- Forensic Accounting and Auditing

School of Engineering and Technology

- Chemical and Process Systems Engineering
- Electronic Engineering

- Industrial and Manufacturing Engineering
- Polymer Technology and Engineering

School of Industrial Sciences and Technology

- Biotechnology
- Food Processing Technology
- Pharmacy

School of Information Sciences

- Computer Science
- Information Technology
- Software Engineering

For the purposes of this chapter, I will focus on Pharmacy as a case story within a case story.

The history of the Harare Institute of Technology (HIT)

"The Harare Institute of Technology through its charter has the most vital mandate of creation of knowledge and enabling its transfer and application to industry and commerce for the development of the economy" (Muredzi, 2018). HIT was the brainchild of the Ministry of Higher and Tertiary Education - Zimbabwe. It was apparently opened by the Zimbabwe Government in 1988 as a National Vocational Training Centre (NVTC). With time it developed into a Technical Training College, improving its offering to Automotive, Electrical and Mechanical Engineering to apprentices and soon developing a strong name for the quality of artisans they produced. This became a strong support system to Industry as the HIT artisans were capable of operating and maintaining plant and machinery with little extra training (www.hit.ac.zw/).

In 2005 HIT was granted degree awarding status following the promulgation of the Harare Institute of Technology Act (Chapter 25:26), given the good work that was evident, as well as taking into account other considerations. From that time on, HIT has not looked back but has developed from strength to strength.

HIT quickly developed into the hub of technology development and delivery of quality technology programs at undergraduate and postgraduate level. HIT claims to be Zimbabwe's most energetic and responsive institute offering unparalleled educational opportunities for those seeking highest quality under-graduate, postgraduate and continuous professional development (and I have no reason to doubt them). It is at the forefront of growing Zimbabwe's industrial base and natural resources beneficiation. While driven by the Ministry of Higher Education, amongst its significant stakeholders are the Ministry of Health and Child Welfare and Ministry of Industry and Commerce as these ministries directly benefit from the innovations developed at HIT.

HIT sees its destiny as being the stimulant of scholarship in innovation. Their cause is to cultivate commitment towards technopreneurial leadership. Their calling is to commercialise technology through professionalism rooted in integrity. Their values include innovation, leadership, integrity, commitment and professionalism. Their motto is *Success through Innovation*.

The background to an innovative approach at HIT

As one of its initiatives in 2005 the Ministry of Higher and Tertiary Education in Zimbabwe decided to upgrade Science and Technology to complement what was happening in tertiary education pertaining to Science, Technology and Engineering. HIT was therefore founded in its present form to promote technology development, incubation, commercialisation and transfer. The mandate for standard universities is to produce graduates. The approach adopted by HIT can be said to be a concept of "study while you produce" and prepares students by imparting skills of design, innovation and ability to work with minimum supervision whilst emerging as technopreneurs (Muredzi, 2018). To this end HIT has included mandatory technopreneurship courses in all its degree programs. HIT sees the production of graduates as a means to an end. To HIT, graduates are tools to enable greater industrialisation. At HIT graduates are not trained to look for jobs but to create jobs (this answered the question I always had as to why, in my many years of recruiting employees in the organisations I worked for, I never came across any candidates from HIT). They are expected to set up their own enterprises and to become employers. HIT then, views itself as a Technopreneurship and Innovation university. (HIT was the first to coin the idea of technopreneurship, focusing on technological prowess in entrepreneurship.) The main idea was to turn out people who could master technology and develop it to enable them to develop into entrepreneurs. According to Muredzi (2018) this has been more than achieved. At the time of writing this book HIT had filed for four patents with the African Regional Intellectual Property Organisation (ARIPO) and at least forty copyrights for Information Technology related applications had been registered. Hi-tech and entrepreneurial skills will drive the Zimbabwe economy back to prosperity, postulates Muredzi. "A technopreneur distinguishes logic from tradition, tradition from prejudice, prejudice from common sense and common sense from nonsense while integrating a variety of ideas from diverse groups and disciplines", he adds.

The Zimbabwean Ministry of Education introduced the Science Technology Engineering and Mathematics initiative (STEM) in High Schools in 2015 in order to promote industrialisation (Chitate, 2016). The government paid school fees for the students doing Science subjects as well as Mathematics at A Level. There was even a slogan "*If you STEMITIZE you INDUSTRIALIZE*". Linking the dots, the Zimbabwe Government could have initiated the STEM program to support HIT, among other intentions.

Curriculum structure at HIT

Like all universities in Zimbabwe, HIT's curriculum is regulated by the Zimbabwe Council for Higher Education (ZIMCHE).

In most universities the research project is done in the final year. At HIT, research and innovation is spread out through the program.

In the first year, students are introduced to HIT 200. This is a team project where a group of students is required to work together in research and innovation and bring out something tangible and workable. They are required to produce a prototype. This is designed to consolidate research and innovation skills at early stages. Competencies to do with creativity and innovation are infused early in the learning process. Success then, is measured by level of creativity and innovation.

In the third year of study at HIT students go through HIT 300, which is an individual and higher-level design and innovation project. Students are again required to produce a prototype or system. Students cannot leave the university at the end of the semester until they have successfully produced an acceptable innovation. At this stage students are really pushed to their limits with regard to creativity and innovation.

In the third year, students also undergo industrial attachment or internship for 30 weeks.

All this then culminates into HIT 400 in the final year, when the students are required to carry out a Capstone Design Project. Each student develops a technology, product or process in the form of a prototype. They also do a write up of their work. The culmination of all this is a graduate who is a technopreneur. HIT inculcates among its graduates, the philosophy of technopreneurship and develops values responsible for a mind-set shift from the traditional expectation of employment by government, commerce, and industry. The focus is to turn out graduates that have values that enable a mind-set shift to start high-tech enterprises, and in the process make an impact on the national economy by creating jobs and growing national wealth. The structure of this curriculum resonates with Kolb's experiential learning (Kolb, 1984) as the students are accorded the opportunity to experience an intense innovation process three times during their learning program.

Assessment/examination

Students are exposed to continuous assessment from first year to fourth year. Further specific assessment is carried out by the Examination Panel on the work done by students at all stages of their research to innovation journey (i.e. HIT 200, HIT 300 and HIT 400). This is a highly skilled and experienced team of examiners. The student does a *viva voce* where he articulates his innovation orally and also produces a written report and the prototype or system. Marks are allocated for:

- Continuous assessment
- The oral presentation
- The prototype or system
- The written report

HIT itself is amazed at the high-quality innovations that come out at the HIT 400 stage.

HIT's key units

HIT has some key units as outlined below.

The Technology Centre

The Technology Centre coordinates all laboratories, workshops and research facilities. Its mandate is to facilitate transformation and development of prototypes emanating from all practical project courses including the Capstone Design Project. It also translates all developed innovations into tangibles, produces what has been developed and enables commercialisation. It is manned by trained technicians and research academics, with the object of harmonising and promoting interdisciplinary research and development work from all teaching departments in the various faculties.

The centre also has a "Printed Circuit Board" manufacturing plant and a state of the art "Tool and Die" workshop.

Technology Transfer and Licensing Centre (TTLC)

This centre commercialises all technological outputs. In this process they address issues of the innovations ranging from economies of scale to factory design, from blueprint to manufacturing incubation, housing created enterprises and helping them to grow into fully fledged entities before they go into industry. When these good innovations are evident, the TTLC may where necessary and appropriate invite industry to buy the idea or acquire equity in the resultant businesses. Mamukwa, in her Calabash of Knowledge Creation, (Mamukwa, Lessem & Schieffer, 2014), points to the importance of "internationalisation" of new innovations in the process of making them explicit to a wider range of people, and HIT have actually institutionally structured this process.

I then asked why industry is not booming in Zimbabwe when such wonderful work is happening at HIT, and the answer was:

- Rome was not built in a day – the boom would come with time.
- Some good innovations required economies of scale to get the required results, which needed appropriate investment which may not be readily available.

Some of the successful innovations were listed as follows:

- To address a gap in electricity production, HIT now manufactures its own transformers. This and other initiatives have the impact of import substitution.
- For the Zimbabwe United Passenger Company (ZUPCO) HIT developed the tap and go cards to enable passengers to pre-pay their bus-fares.
- HIT developed a system for Rural District Councils to enable them to upgrade their management software.
- HIT has done a lot with regard to value addition to soya beans, developing soya milk and soya milk derivatives such as soya lacto (sour milk), soya yoghurt, and soya cheese (tofu) to mention a few things.
- Through the Pharmacy Department HIT has contributed immensely to the health sector through medical innovations and developments.

Technology Education Centre

This centre deals with Technological Pedagogy. Pedagogy deals with the essence of and approach to teaching. In broad terms, Pedagogy applies to the theory and practice of education and how this impacts the learner, and how knowledge and skills are imparted in an educational context. The relevance of Pedagogy in the HIT situation is how to find appropriate teaching methods and approached to achieve the innovation that is required. According to Shulman (1986) theories of pedagogy increasingly identify the student as an agent, and the teacher as a facilitator. Western pedagogies define the teacher as the knowledge holder and student as the recipient of knowledge. According to Mamukwa, (Mamukwa, Lessem & Schieffer, 2014) the teacher then, is the holder of tacit knowledge while the student benefits from it when it becomes explicit through a process of socialisation. HIT then, has to pay particular attention to its pedagogical approach to enable the high level of innovation expected.

To put things into perspective and give a feel of what actually happens in the different faculties, I will share the information acquired when I interviewed specifically Professor Gundidza from the Department of Pharmacy. This is a case story within a case story.

Faculty of Pharmacy

I held lengthy discussions with Professor Mazuru Gundidza, who at that time was the Chairman of the Faculty of Pharmacy. Entering his office, I was greeted by a situation where he was talking to a young, qualified pharmacist who had gone to HIT to learn about alternative medicine or African medicine. He expressed in very strong terms how she had not applied herself to the task that she had been given. She had apparently been given a task to identify indigenous fruits and research their medicinal qualities. I had to chuckle to myself as the poor young lady had included avocado, which is clearly not an indigenous Zimbabwean fruit. She was told that she had not even started the research. He added that in the area of his birth there were at least twenty-eight indigenous fruits. I was captivated. She was directed to the Botanic Gardens and other such places and she was given a myriad of instructions before she was released, thirty minutes after my entrance into the office. He looked tough and unimpressed with what she had done thus far. I thought I had been forgotten. He then turned to me and conversationally explained that he wants the young lady to realise that this was serious business, and to know where to go and who to ask. That was my introduction to HIT (this was my first interview with anyone at HIT).

Mandate of the Department of Pharmacy

The mandate of the Department of Pharmacy is to carry out research and development on indigenous or what HIT calls alternative medicines. It is driven by Ministries of Education, Health and Industry and Commerce as follows:

- Ministry of Education has an interest in any new knowledge developed with a particular interest on how such knowledge is shared. For example, when the faculty develops any new knowledge in the area of medicine and pharmaceuticals, this ministry is keen to see such transferred to other appropriate people or groupings such as doctors and pharmacists (doctors because they would then be educated to prescribe such indigenous medicines where appropriate, and pharmacists because they would be responsible for stocking and dispensing such medicines) through training them of such groupings of people. Educationally, such innovations would also impact curricula in the future.
- Ministry of health is keen to have at their disposal so that medical interventions are to a greater extend local and affordable. This would make health service delivery less expensive and more sustainable.
- Industry comes in with regard to commercialising any resultant medical or pharmaceutical innovations.

Methodology

HIT aims to develop a cadre in the health sector that is comfortable with alternative or natural medicine to cross-cut allopathic medicine, for the benefit of the patient. The faculty is continually developing and improving an African Indigenous Knowledge System. It has a database of herbs, fruits, vegetables and even trees with medicinal qualities, and this is increased and improved upon daily as new discoveries are made. Such information is continuously shared, particularly with the pharmaceutical industry. The faculty is also open to training health workers, including pharmacists and even doctors. The commercialisation of innovations in this area provides alternatives for the health professions to work with.

This African School of Natural Medicine is regulated by a number of councils:

- Natural Therapist Council
- Pharmaceutical Council of Zimbabwe
- Health Professions Authority

HIT does not copy and paste solutions but carries out its own research through its students. The structure of research to innovation is as outlined in clause 6.5, through student research at HIT 200, HIT 300 and HIT 400 levels, and this is subjected to assessment as outlined in clause 6.6.

Cross-cutting subjects for this faculty include anatomy, physiology and immunology. Artificial intelligence is also an area of research in pharmacy as well as other faculties. This ranges from artificial limbs and safety devices in vehicles, to name just a couple.

The faculty acknowledges man's ecological relationship with nature and the universe, and acknowledges therapies resulting from such relationships, such as light therapy, sound therapy, colour therapy, water therapy and oxygen therapy, to name only a few. Apparently even the earth worm is used to treat prostate cancer.

Notable innovations include cures for cancer, diabetes, high blood pressure, wounds and itching. The faculty has also developed anti-snake venom.

The faculty has three specialisation strands running at Parirenyatwa Hospital, namely the Radiography unit, Dosimetry (measurement of radiation) and Ultra Sound (used for therapeutic purposes) where HIT's contribution to health is evident.

Commercialisation of innovations

Commercialisation of notable innovations is carried out through the Technology Transfer and Licensing Office (TLLC), whose main role is to commercialise all technological outputs. Apart from handling any licensing and patent issues, TLLC also looks into practical commercialisation processes such as addressing issues of scale as well as factory design to ensure that the attendant factories have the capacity to produce at the right level. TLLC is responsible of the commercialisation process from blue print to incubation where created enterprises are nursed and helped to grow into fully fledged businesses, to disposal to industries through outright purchases or acquisition of equity.

HIT/Schweppes partnership: Another case story within a case story

I had just finished writing this book and sent it off to the Series Editor when I met Demos Mbauya for the first time at a workshop I was attending. Demos was General Manager at Schweppes at the time of writing this book. I jokingly said I hoped I would be able to stay awake as I had spent most of the previous night finalising my book draft. Demos asked what the book was about and for some reason I focused on the HIT part of the book. He excitedly explained that Schweppes had worked closely with HIT. Here is the story.

Schweppes is a beverage manufacturing company in Zimbabwe, which has strong links with Coca-Cola.

Demos went to HIT for the first time looking for moulds for manufacturing plastic bottles, only to find that HIT manufactures bottles. Schweppes subsequently purchased such bottle moulds from HIT, resulting in the first case of import substitution for Schweppes.

He then went further to explain the nature of the Schweppes partnership with HIT between 2010 and 2014. Schweppes needed training for their operators to ensure requisite skill levels and enlisted HIT's assistance with this. For Schweppes, this turned out to be an opportunity for skills improvement for its people. HIT came up with very practical programs, with assistance from the Dean of Food Sciences, Professor Ntini Moyo. HIT and Schweppes jointly designed a Beverages Manufacturing Course. A sub-committee was set up comprising representatives from Human Resources and Quality Assurance from Schweppes and representatives from the Department of Food Science. The curriculum that was developed by this sub-committee covered both theory and practice. This presented an opportunity for Schweppes managers and operators to receive value adding training, and for HIT lecturers to understand the Schweppes business. Schweppes Operators were effectively trained and tested. The curriculum and testing structure was such that the operators would be given three opportunities to pass the test.

The impact of this was raising competences and understanding the theory of beverage manufacturing. Both parties saw value addition in this partnership. There may be opportunities for HIT to develop this training to Diploma standard in the future if there are, enough numbers to make a viable proposition. Be that as it may, the training that happened with the Schweppes employees had the effect of improving employee motivation and had tremendous value addition to Schweppes as a business.

HIT and Schweppes developed this relationship further by signing a Memorandum of Understanding (MOU) annually to facilitate HIT students going to Schweppes on attachment. The students would identify problems and resolve them. HIT would be involved in coaching their students in the resolution of any work-based challenges at Schweppes. This really worked for Schweppes as there were real work-based challenges which were actually addressed.

Schweppes decided to upscale this collaboration by requesting HIT to be involved in addressing Schweppes's challenges in specific areas.

Two Schweppes business units were therefore supported by HIT in the form of capacity building and problem solving, particularly with product quality issues. It was resolved that Schweppes would be given HIT students on attachment every year. Some of these students would be accommodated by Schweppes as Graduate Learners post-graduation from HIT. While such students may not have been able to use their innovations because of Schweppes's relationship with Coca-Cola, they were very good at trouble shooting as they came from a very practical background of training. More importantly, it was an excellent confidence building opportunity for the students.

Demos saw HIT as the perfect centre for import substitution. For HIT no doubt Schweppes is a laboratory – a win-win situation. For Zimbabwe both HIT and Schweppes provide the live laboratory environment that results in real live solutions being developed, with the potential of such being rolled out to other organisations.

Lessons drawn from HIT

What seems to have made the HIT dream become reality is that it was the brain-child of government through the Ministry of Higher and Tertiary Education. To that extend, it enjoys full government support financially, materially and politic-ally. All HIT needs to do is to focus on producing the desired results.

HIT has managed to put together a strong team of passionate individuals who live and breathe innovation. Some of them have passed through Industry and Commerce, so they understand the issues from the institute's perspective as well as from the industry one. This is perhaps the biggest lesson. For an idea such as from HIT to be developed into the formidable entity that it is takes passion and commitment. At HIT such passion emanates from the top at Vice Chancellor level and permeates through the structures right down to the students.

HIT's background of starting as a Vocational Training Centre is a great strength. HIT's impetus is to produce practical innovations that can be used. They pride themselves in how many patents they have registered. This is another lesson – the measurability of the achievements. The work done by HIT goes far beyond academe. Certainly, the Pharmacy Department as an example, has set its sights on alleviating drug shortages in Zimbabwe by producing, through their research to innovation strategies, enabling increased use of alternative medicines in the health sector.

HIT has live laboratories in companies that take their students for industrial attachment, such as Schweppes. There is scope for more such laboratories being developed.

Conclusion

The Harare Institute of Technology story is certainly a very interesting and amazing one. Starting from humble beginnings as a Vocational Training Centre, HIT is poised for greater things. What would have been interesting is to follow up the HIT graduates to find out what has happened to them since comple-tion of their studies and really finding a way of measuring the success rate of these graduates as entrepreneurs and employers, but that is work for another day. Schweppes has made an amazing contribution to HIT by taking on their graduates, even post-graduation. HIT has equally contributed to the Schweppes business processes through training its operators and working with the HIT students to resolve the Schweppes work-based challenges.

Schweppes sees HIT having the potential to become a centre for import substitution. This would certainly be something worth pursuing, given the foreign currency challenges in Zimbabwe for purchase of plant and equipment, among other things.

As I move on to the next chapter, I cannot help but think that there would also be opportunities for HIT/Da Vinci collaboration.

References

Chitate, H. (2016). *Science, Technology, Engineering and Mathematics (STEM): A Case Study of Zimbabwe's Educational Approach to Industrialisation.* Harare: University of Zimbabwe.

"Definition of PEDAGOGY". Retrieved 1 July 2019, *www.merriam-webster.com.*

Harare Institute of Technology Act (Chapter 25:26) (2005). Harare Institute of Technology Website www.hit.ac.zw/. Retrieved 28th June 2019.

Kolb, D. A. (1984). *Experiential Learning.* Englewood Cliffs, NJ: Prentice Hall.

Lessem, R. & Schieffer, A. (2010). *Integral Research and Innovation: Transforming Enterprise and Society.* Farnham, England: Gower.

Mamukwa, E. S., Lessem, R. & Schieffer, A. (2014). *Integral Green Zimbabwe: An African Phoenix Rising.* Farnham, England: Gower.

Manasa, M., Madondo, M., Museka, G. & Phiri, M. (2014). *The Presidential Commission of Inquiry into Education and Training (Nziramasanga Commission): Implementation Successes, Challenges and Opportunities.* Harare: The Human Resources Research Centre (HRRC) of the University of Zimbabwe.

Muredzi, P. (2018). *10th Anniversary, Harare Institute of Technology,* ZIMIP Magazine, viewed 10th November 2019, <https://zimbabweipdevelopmenttrust.files. wordpress.com/2019/08/zimip-voice-1st-edition-2018.pdf>.

Nziramasanga, C.T. (1999). 'Report of the Presidential Commission of Inquiry into Education and Training', Harare, Unpublished.

Shulman, L. S. (1986). *Paradigms and Research Programme for the Study of Teaching.* In Wittrock M. C. 3rd ed. New York: Macmillan.

8   The Mode 2 University

The Da Vinci Institute case story

Introduction

Having discussed the Harare Institute of Technology approach of technopreneurship and their "greenfield" approach to innovation, so to speak, where they take a fresh undergraduate student and turn him into an innovator and entrepreneur, I now move on to the Da Vinci Institute, which also focuses on innovation, but with a different emphasis. Da Vinci takes seasoned leaders, executives and managers and helps them to become innovative in the way they address the challenges they face in their workplaces or communities.

Having been exposed to a variety of learning systems and philosophies in my life, I became fascinated by the Da Vinci Institute when I was introduced to this prestigious institution of higher learning by Chidhara Muchineripi, and made a decision to make this my home for the purpose of reading for my PhD. This Institute was ideal for me because it caters for what it terms the "non-traditional student", essentially mature, working students whose circumstances limit them from full time study. In this chapter I will share what I understand to be the philosophy of this institution. In this chapter then, I will share my experiences as a student of Da Vinci and Trans4M in my research to innovation journey.

About the Da Vinci Institute

The Da Vinci Institute was established in 2004 as a School of Business Leadership, focusing on developing business leaders. Warwick University decided to exit the South African environment, and the Marcus family picked it up, albeit with a different impetus. The Institute was established with the support of Nelson Mandela and Dr Ben Ngubane. When Mandela took over as President, he discovered that, much as South Africa had substantial resources (South Africa had 44% of the world's diamonds, 82% of manganese reserves and 64% of platinum group metal reserves), the South African economy was "in dire straits" (Meredith, 2010). It is understandable then, that Mandela would support institutions such as the Da Vinci Institute, which had the potential to improve the corporate world and contribute to strengthening the economy.

Professor Benjamin Anderson joined the institute in 2005 as the Chief Executive Officer, and was still there at the time of writing this book, fourteen years later. This has given stability and innovative development to the institute.

Da Vinci is modelled on a Mode 2 University, transdisciplinary in nature (Nowotny, Scott & Gibbons, 2001) focusing on creating knowledge that is relevant in the world of work, with a view to improving the bottom line. Innovations from Da Vinci however are not always relevant to work situations but can be focused on the needs of all strata of communities and society, particularly when we review the work that is happening through some of its partnerships, as we shall see below. The business community is but just a section of society. To what level Da Vinci actually operates as a Mode 2 university can be the subject of debate, but the fact is that it is probably the nearest Mode 2 institution available. Whether it focuses on work situations or communities, the innovations that result from the Da Vinci tutelage are socially relevant in whatever areas of research the students embark on. Da Vinci's brand promise is to "co-create reality". This is very different from programs run by purely Mode 1 universities (with the exception of The Harare Institute of Technology) where the focus is on the thesis, and not necessarily on the sustainability of the innovation. Professor Anderson is however quick to qualify that Da Vinci, more than being a Mode 2 university, is more focused on experiential learning. I will dwell on this later in the chapter.

Da Vinci Institute offerings

Da Vinci's strategic intent is outlined in its purpose, dream, principles and brand promise. Their purpose is to cultivate business leaders; their dream is to contribute to the development of sustainable society; their principles include seeking the truth, taking responsibility, sharpening awareness, engaging the shadow, cultivating a balance, nurturing integration and embracing holism; their brand promise is to co-create reality.

Da Vinci Institute offers a well-structured spectrum of qualifications including Higher Certificate in Management of Technology and Innovation (MOTI), Diploma in Management of Technology and Innovation, Bachelor of Commerce in Business Management, Master in Technology and Innovation and Doctor of Management in Technology and Innovation.

Their tutelage is carried out through the TIPS Framework, which stands for;

Tools/Metrics to achieve differentiation

This involves the Management of Technology (MOT). We all have to manage the technology of our time be it work tools or computers. Students at Da Vinci are therefore expected to be comfortable with the relevant technologies and tools that apply to their situation. On its part, Da Vinci enhances this in its student by giving them access to the institute's electronic management system (elms) called the Modular Object-Oriented Dynamic Learning Environment

(Moodle). This is used by students for uploading their assignments and by the institute to communicate with the students.

Ideation

Ideation is important to create and see opportunities for Innovation. Innovation rarely just happens. Ideation is the process of coming up with the ideas around an innovation while the innovation itself is the execution of the ideas generated in the ideation phase. Innovations become a reality when people at least have an idea of what needs to be improved or created and why.

Kolb's experiential learning model (Kolb 1984) concretises ideation, beginning with concrete experiences, good or bad. The ideation process is strengthened when people publicise what they have learnt, particularly the mistakes made. Reflection about what has been learnt can lead to theorising and ultimately to knowledge production.

People (human interface)

This "is about the understanding of the human bridge in implementing organisational processes and how the organisational human factor is leveraged", www.davinci.ac.za/wp-content/uploads/2018/08/CompanyProfile2018. Organisations quite often pay lip service to the importance of their people as the source of competitive advantage, but they do not necessarily pay full attention to this important statement. An organisation's people is the differentiating factor. However, people are not machines. They have a wide range of skill levels and they have thoughts and feelings. Unlike machines, people's performance is influenced by how they are treated, the culture obtaining in the organisation, their own situation at home and many other people factors. Da Vinci Institute therefore fully realises the criticality of training their students on the importance of the people factor, and what they can do to improve this for enhanced productivity and results.

Systems (organisational systems)

Systems ensure that organisational activities happen like cloak work. Good systems, when implemented religiously, ensure that everyone plays their part, the right level of productivity is achieved and the expected strategic objectives are met. Systems get us the results that we want. Kaplan and Norton (2004) describe systems as internal processes, which are critical if the organisation is to achieve its desired objectives in the form of customer and financial results.

Experiential learning

> Learning is the process whereby knowledge is created through the transformation of experience.
>
> (Kolb, 1984, p. 38)

Da Vinci subscribes to David Kolb's theory of learning through experience and believes in Systems Thinking as a Promoter of Organisational Learning. I therefore wish now to focus on knowledge creation according to David Kolb, and link this to the Mode 2 University.

Kolb is an American educational theorist whose interests and publications focus on experiential learning, the individual and social change, career development, and executive and professional education. He was a product of Mode 1, having been educated at Knox College and Harvard University, respectively. He went on to become Professor in the same Mode 1 system at Weatherhead School of Management, Case Western Reserve University, Cleveland, Ohio. His work was inspired by Kurt Lewin.

Kolb is renowned for his Learning Style Inventory (LSI) which is widely used in organisations to establish the learning styles of the key players.

In the LSI, Kolb (2015) came up with four stages in the learning cycle, namely Concrete Experience (CE), Reflective Observation (RO), Abstract Conceptualisation (AE) and Active Experimentation (AE). He developed the Learning Style Inventory (LSI) which he used to evaluate the way individuals learn. In this tool he paired AE and RO as polar opposites (doing vs. watching) and CE and AC as polar opposites (feeling vs. thinking).

Kolb (1981) contends that Concrete Experience (CE) emphasizes active involvement, with learners in this category being open minded and adaptable as well as being sensitive to their own feelings and those of others. People in Reflective Observation watch and listen, may see things differently and seek to discover meanings in the learning material.

In Abstract Conceptualisation (AC) people apply thought and logic rather than feelings to learning situations (these are more academically oriented). They tend to be good at planning, developing theories and analysis. In the Active Experimentation (AE) platform, people are good at testing theories, carrying out plans as well as influencing things through activity.

Clearly, the four stages complement one another, hence it would be preferable to have members of the team coming from all four stages to create a balance. It is however critical to note that, while an individual may prefer a particular platform, the measurement is on a continuum. Therefore, there is presence of the other stages at varying levels in any one individual, hence the use of the phrase "preferred learning style". It should therefore be possible to come up with interventions that may help an individual to migrate towards another learning style.

Kolb associates the four quadrants with four forms of knowledge. Each of the forms is paired with its diagonal opposite as follows:

- Reflective Observation (RO) and Concrete Experience (CE) and calling this group of people Divergers. These thrive on idea generating circumstances such as brain-storming and are imaginative and emotional.
- A combination of Abstract Conceptualisation (AC) and Active Experimentation (AE) was termed Convergers. These excel in test situations

where there is only one answer or solution. Comparatively, Convergers are unemotional and procedural. They prefer to work with objects rather than people. These people quite often choose to specialize in exact fields such as science and engineering.

- Assimilators are described as combining Reflective Observation (RO) and Active Experimentation (AE). The people in this group are good at creating theoretical models and tend to be more interested in abstract concepts rather than in application or in people, specializing in basic sciences and mathematics.
- Accommodators are a combination of Active Experimentation (AE) and Concrete Experience (CE). This group is good at doing things, carrying out plans and performing experiments. They are risk takers and are more easily adaptable to change. Not being very analytic themselves, they rely on other people for information.

According to Kolb (1984), a combination of all four types of learners is important as each has a role to play in problem solving, hence the importance of a balance of the learning styles in an organisation's team. (See Figure 8.1.)

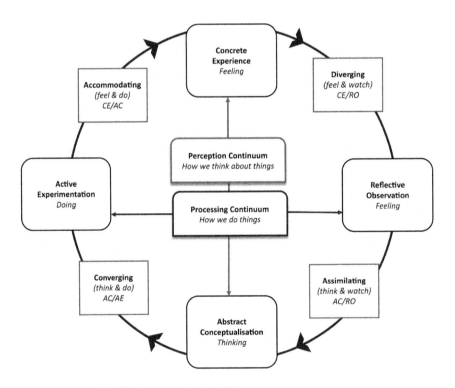

Figure 8.1 David Kolb's Learning Styles, 1984.

Source: Adaptation and design: Elizabeth Mamukwa (2019).

With regard to knowledge creation and innovation, the different learning styles will determine areas of interest and focus, as well as the type of innovations pursued.

Honey and Mumford (1982) defined this further by coming up with a Typology of Learners aligned to the four stages by defining the learning to the type of people who would use the stages as follows:

Concrete experience	Activist preferring to do and experience.
Reflective observation	Reflector.
Abstract conceptualisation	Theorist who wants to understand underlying reasons, concepts and relationships.
Active experimentation	Pragmatist who likes to have a go and try things to see if they work.

This information is important for self-awareness of the learner as well as for the teacher so that appropriate learning styles can be effectively employed. For Da Vinci Institute, it helps to align expectations according to learning styles, and it is also an indicator that people with different learning styles can innovate. What will probably differ is the way such innovation is arrived at. By implication then, Kolb implies that innovation goes beyond academe. Even those with limited academic inclination can innovate. In fact, Da Vinci Institute particularly dwells on this in the research trajectories that they encourage students to follow.

Da Vinci insist on Kolb's framework on their students, confirmed by a statement on their website:

> *There are, amongst other, four perspectives of reality that need to be considered when conducting research at Da Vinci. These are defined as concrete experiences, reflective observations, abstract conceptualisation and active experimentation.*

The subject of knowledge

In clause 2.2.3, a philosophical definition of knowledge was given as epistemology, which is the study of knowledge. In simple terms, knowledge is understanding. When we say that someone has a knowledge of marketing we mean that she understands what it is and how to implement marketing should she be required to. However, sometimes we think we have knowledge about a matter, only to find that we do not. That is why in research we make an effort to read widely and do a literature search about the subject of research so that we tap into the body of knowledge. When we do this, quite often we find that what we thought we knew was not quite correct. Knowledge therefore needs to be verified so that we in the end obtain a more universal understanding of a subject or topic.

What is an innovation?

An innovation then, is a new creation. It can take any form. At Da Vinci the innovations vary according to the work-based challenges the students decide to embark on. Such innovations range from technological, to systemic and even social innovations, to mention only three examples. Da Vinci focuses more on innovations relevant to corporate situations (Work-Based Challenge). Their Trans4M partners however tend to be more embracing of social or community-based innovations over and above the work-based innovations.

Why Mode 2 may be limited

Talking to Professor Anderson, he deduces that people do not want to confront their inner feelings. As a people we have become numb in terms of the world of experience, this is why experiential learning has the effect of stimulating that emotion that is lying dormant within us. For that reason, DA Vinci focuses more on experiential learning rather than Mode 2. Society seems to have unlearned how to develop knowledge. Experiential learning is the catalyst that stimulates the sleeping giant in people. For Da Vinci then, the concept of Mode 2 (socially distributed knowledge: transdisciplinary research carried out in a variety of institutions: thriving in geographical distances: emphasis on knowledge production) appears a bit far off. However, is Da Vinci really that far away from Mode 2? Perhaps Da Vinci is closer to Mode 2 than it realises. Some of Da Vinci's students are scattered away from South Africa, through its partnerships. Da Vinci has students in Zimbabwe through its partnership with Business Training and Development (BTD). Da Vinci's alliance with Trans4M has also resulted in students in Zimbabwe, South Africa, Nigeria, United Kingdom, Jordan and Pakistan, to name a few examples. Apart from physical distance, such Da Vinci students are unlimited with regard to the scope of their research, following the call of society with regard to the subject of research. Some of the situations that have influenced research and innovation include the need to empower communities through community-based tourism, keeping young people off the streets, the need to promote an African type of entrepreneurship (Afrintuneurship) the need to heal the land (Mamukwa, Lessem and Schieffer, 2014) and the need to feed the people (Lessem, Muchineripi and Kada, 2012). This type of research has broadened the Da Vinci offering and made the institution, through its partnerships, more relevant to communities beyond the corporate world.

Da Vinci was started as a Mode 2 dream:

> Da Vinci is a Mode 2 educational institution that is characterised by trans -disciplinary engagements in an effort to formalise an integrative process of knowledge creation, application and dissemination. It transgresses beyond existing methods of

research and acknowledges the need for joint solution finding mechanisms around a particular application, also called a "work-based challenge" (WBC).

www.davinci.ac.za/wp-content/uploads/2018/08/
CompanyProfile2018

The above statement is rendered valid by the alliances mentioned above. In particular, the partnership with Trans4M has resulted in some of the Da Vinci students pursuing the Integral Research trajectory (Lessem & Schieffer, 2010).

Lessem and Schieffer, associates of Da Vinci, developed the Integral Worlds Model. The most significant part of the Four Worlds is the southern relational world, for the simple reason that it grounds one (if we follow the GENE trajectory). Once **G**rounded you are reminded of who you are, and you can face the world with confidence and achieve much. You will become more comfortable to **E**merge in the eastern world of spirituality, deal with the **N**orthern part of reason and embrace the **E**ffectiveness of the pragmatic west. The issue here is that Da Vinci and its associates will break down the barriers to creativity and innovation to enable students to come out of their shells, confront their demons and scale new heights.

In a way this draws a parallel with the TIPS introductory module (Self, Other and Social Context) in which the student is encouraged to reframe themselves in the quest to bring developmental change to themselves as well as their situation. Such developmental change is enhanced where the student understands the strategic impetus of the organisation that he works for and seeks to impact. Such strategic understanding also enhances sound decision making, buttressed by Management of Technology, Management of Information and Management of People as strategy implementation tools. It also promotes the creation of new knowledge and innovation as it empowers the students by strengthening their basic understanding of their own work (or social) situation as well as opening their eyes to possibilities for knowledge creation and innovation.

Student support

As a former student I found the Da Vinci's student support amazing. They bend over backwards for students and really go out of their way to accommodate student needs. The Institute is focused on developing business leadership competence among students. These are some of the initiatives for student support:

- Da Vinci supports students through Program Coordinators and Conveners to ensure constant contact.
- The institute utilises the services of Student Support Specialists to run student support sessions in an effort to stay close to their students and address any problem areas as they arise.
- As highlighted earlier, students are given access to the institute's learning management system.

- The institute carries out the assessment of study and work habits of the students through the Shadowmatch profiling to assess the required areas of development to ensure success in the student's academic endeavours.

How innovations are shared with society

A number of actions have been put in place to acknowledge good performance by students, as outlined below.

Notable awards are on offer to outstanding students, such as The Da Vinci Laureate: Social Architectuaris for a student who has made an outstanding contribution in terms of redefining a social system; The Benjamin Anderson Award for the best Bachelor of Commerce student in terms of planning and executing a work-based challenge; The Da Vinci Community Services Award to recognise students who demonstrate community involvement in their research; The Mandala Award for recognising a student who integrates different parts into a synthesized archetype of subjective truth; The Da Vinci PhD Excellence Award to acknowledge academic excellence; The Da Vinci President's award to recognise students who demonstrate excellence in applied research and contribute to an alternative understanding of what constitutes the Da Vinci Institute's offerings related to Managerial Leadership in Technology, Innovation, People and Systems.

With support from partners such as the Department of Science and Technology, Eskom, PwC and IDC, Da Vinci hosts the tt100 Business Awards Program. This is designed to develop a local culture of technological innovation and excellence. The write up on the website says,

> *tt100 has evolved into one of the foremost business award programs that laud South African companies for their prowess in the Management of Technology, Innovation, People, Systems and Sustainability, regardless of their industry. The program is an effective vehicle for achieving growth and innovation advancement in our country …*

Some Da Vinci Institute learning outcomes

There are many outcomes of the learnerships at Da Vinci. I will focus only on those that familiar with.

The first one I wish to dwell on is the Chinyika Socioeconomic innovation (Lessem, Muchineripi & Kada (2012). Through the Da Vinci PhD program Muchineripi and Kada re-engineered reality to alleviate starvation in Chinyika by re-visiting traditional agricultural practices and crops by combining traditional and modern practices to avert hunger and starvation to thousands. This innovation has stood the test of time and was going strong at the time of writing this book.

Dr Father Anselm Adodo, during his PhD journey, transformed Ewu Village in the Edo state in Nigeria by developing a community enterprise in the form of Paxherbal (Adodo, 2017) (although this may have started before the commencement of the PhD studies, the Da Vinci PhD program gave this momentum and direction). Apart from the manufacturing of the herbal medicines, there was community transformation through job creation and effective utilisation of land.

Chinyuku developed and implemented an industrial ecology for paint manufacturers in Zimbabwe; Mamukwa developed the Calabash of Knowledge Creation to marry indigenous rhythms and exogenous workplaces as well as promote the sharing of old knowledge and use such to develop new knowledge; Mandevani developed community-based tourism (Mamukwa, Lessem & Schieffer, 2014); Matupire developed the Integral Ubuntu Leadership Model which he is now using to develop leadership training modules for business leaders; (Matupire, 2017); Nyambayo developed the Integral Marketing Model (Nyambayo, 2017).

Another Zimbabwean result is the setting up of Pundutso Centre for Integral Development which has not stopped evolving since its conception in 2014. More will be shared later in the book about Pundutso.

These are only a handful of innovations resulting from the Da Vinci PhD program, as I have limited myself to the Zimbabwean chapter. There is a lot more.

Conclusion

Da Vinci Institute offers amazing programs that promote the effective resolution of challenges at the workplace. Students are pushed to the limit to come up with innovations to address work-based challenges. Meaningful student support is rendered to ensure that such students develop into effective innovators. An array of awards has been put in place to recognise achievers. Commercialisation of the resultant innovations is limited as the focus is on creatively addressing work-based challenges. However, some of the innovations naturally become commercialised as a result of their nature, Paxherbals being one such example.

Da Vinci has focused on the niche of mature, working students. While focus for Da Vinci has been students in the corporate world, Da Vinci's partners (particularly Trans4M) have widened the net to incorporate other aspects of innovation to include social innovation to improve the quality of life of communities.

References

Adodo, A. (2017). *Integral Community Enterprise in Africa: Communitalism as an Alternative to Capitalism.* New York: Gower.

Honey, P. & Mumford, A. (1982). *The Manual of Learning Styles.* Maidenhead: Peter Honey.

Kaplan, R. S. & Norton, D. P. (2004). *Strategy Maps: Converting Intangible Assets into Tangible Outcomes.* Boston: Harvard Business School Publishers.

Kolb, D. A. (1984). *Experiential Learning.* Englewood Cliffs, NJ: Prentice Hall.

Kolb, D. A. (2015). *Experiential Learning: Experience as the Source of Learning and Development.* New York: Pearson Education.

Lessem, R. & Schieffer, A. (2010). *Integral Research and Innovation: Transforming Enterprise and Society.* Farnham, England: Gower.

Lessem, R., Muchineripi, P. C. & Kada, S. (2012). *Integral Community: Political Economy to Social Commons.* Farnham, England: Gower.

Lewin, K. (1942). *Field Theory and Learning* in Cartwright, D., ed. (1951) *Field Theory in Social Sciences: Selected Theoretical Papers.* London: Social Science Paperbacks.

Mamukwa, E. S., Lessem, R. & Schieffer, A. (2014). *Integral Green Zimbabwe: An African Phoenix Rising.* Farnham, England: Gower.

Matupire, P. M. (2017). *Integral Ubuntu Leadership.* New York: Routledge

Meredith, M. (2010). *Mandela, a Biography.* London: Simon and Schuster.

Nowotny, H., Scott, P. & Gibbons, M. (2001). *Rethinking Science: Knowledge and the Public in an Age of Uncertainty.* Cambridge: Polity Press.

Nyambayo, A. (2017). *Integral Marketing* Durban: Mepho Publishers.

Part V

Co-creation

Research methodology

9 My research to innovation journey
Research methodology

Introduction

This chapter will provide a practical demonstration of the Da Vinci (and Trans4M) research to innovation methodology. This is one of many different examples of PhD students who walked a similar journey.

In 2014 I completed my PhD degree, where I travelled my own research to innovation journey. In this chapter I will share the research methodology I used in my PhD, which research resulted in the creation of The Calabash of Knowledge Creation *(Denhe re Ruzivo)*. In 2013 I undertook the research in fulfilment of my PhD degree. The burning issue driving this research was the loss of critical skills which resulted in a near paralysis of a large manufacturing plant, Turnall Holdings.

Conventionally based, in "Mode 1", academic research, which proliferates, most especially in developing societies, demands that a hypothesis be tested. In doing this, sampling becomes a very critical aspect in order to make the results of this research authentic (Moser & Kalton, 1979). Information is collected by desk research, interviews and questionnaires, to name just a few methods. The researcher is external to the process – he is the specialist looking at the problem from outside. The results are tested by statistical methods (Huysamen, 1984). Integral research, on the other hand, (Lessem & Schieffer, 2010) is focused on social innovation rather than merely analytically based research. In embarking on an integral research and innovation project I was asserting the need for a problem-solving approach which distinguishes this methodology from the academically oriented research methodologies. The focus is not on a hypothesis and statistical calculations, but on real visible contributions to improving enterprise and society in a way that is permanent. The researcher becomes part of the community, and not a specialist looking from a distance.

The issue of Mode 1 and Mode 2 universities was adequately addressed in Chapter 5. Suffice to say that Mode 2 knowledge production is the philosophical basis upon which this research was anchored. In this research the economic and social applications to be addressed concerned the creation and sharing of knowledge at Turnall Holdings, a manufacturing entity, and the systems that were aligned to this so that Turnall would not experience serious losses in productivity at the loss of specific employees for any reason. The specific purpose of the research was to come up with an innovation that enables this. This was achieved through a transdisciplinary research team of heterogeneous origin. The ultimate result of the innovation that was developed of necessity resulted in operational efficiency in all circumstances, leading to satisfaction of a wide range of stakeholders, and resulted in commercial success for Turnall Holdings and the other participating companies. For this research to come up with sustainable solutions, it became important to go back to the indigenous rhythms as a starting point in order to tap into the wealth of indigenous knowledge, emotion and energy in the process of developing and creating knowledge. The evolutionary aspect of the innovation product therefore moved the Turnall team towards the desired destiny, which is the social innovation.

The Four Worlds Model

As a prelude to the research journey, I wish to dwell a little on the Four Worlds Model (Lessem & Schieffer, 2010) as it will help to clarify why a model developed in the East or West may not be entirely effective in a Southern Relational environment.

The Four Worlds Model is the philosophical background to the research methodology. The proponents of the Four Worlds Model (Lessem & Schieffer, 2010), divide the world of research into four categories, namely, the South, East, North and West. In their proposition, the South is imbedded in relational humanism, the East in holistic renewal, the North in rational reason and the West in pragmatic realisation. While premised on the physical worlds, the Four Worlds Model does not necessarily refer to the physical world but to an intellectual approach to resolving societal issues. The integration brought about by this Four Worlds Model is what enables us to release the GENE-ius of transformation. Integral research is therefore about bringing transformation and social innovation to society in the process of finding solutions to societal problems.

The Four Worlds Model is the vehicle that brought integrity to this research. The four possible paths to follow in integral research are discussed below.

I will introduce another concept – the GENE. The stands for Grounding, Emerging, Navigating and Effecting (Lessem & Schieffer, 2010). Grounding is aligned to the Southern Relational World, Emerging is aligned to the East, Navigation is in the Northern World of Reason and Effecting is aligned to the Pragmatic West. This research then was started by grounding, when I sought to seek a deeper understanding of myself, my community as well as the society that I grew up in. It is by understanding one's background and identity that one can make greater sense of the world. Indigenous rhythms clearly played a prominent role in my life and as such helped to define the person I am today. This

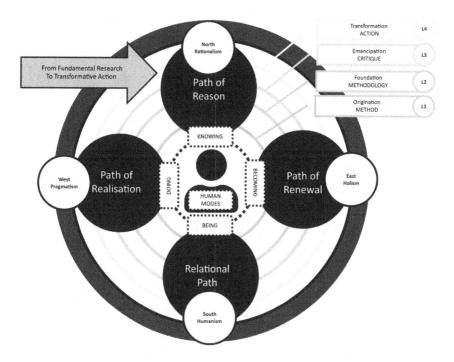

Figure 9.1 The Four Worlds Model.
Source: Lessem and Schieffer (2010).

was followed by dwelling on the burning issue in the manufacturing entity and the Zimbabwe Manufacturing Sector in general. The absence of indigenous rhythms in the workplace was a real issue, and such absence had the effect of thwarting creativity as workers were operating in a "strange" environment.

Research methodology

There is often confusion between "research methods" and "research methodology". While "research methods" are the techniques used, research "methodology" is the philosophy followed in the research process. However, research method is a part of the methodology as the methods used are informed by the methodology, and vice versa. While the methodology is informed by the problem context, it in turn informs the methods to be used at each stage of the research and innovation process.

The Four Worlds Model outlines the life forces, or indeed ontological realms underlying integral research. As an African steeped in the African culture, my natural research style turned out to be the Southern relational.

In the same rhythm of research, Lessem and Schieffer also highlight OFET which, in integral research, stands for the four dynamic and interconnected rhythms of Origination, Foundation, Emancipation and Transformation. The Four Worlds, the GENE and OFET are all superimposed and support one another in this research trajectory.

Purpose of research

It is pertinent to highlight at this juncture that the research was carried out in order to empower and emancipate specifically Turnall, a Zimbabwean manufacturing company that was marginalised by skilled employees who held it to ransom, particularly during the hyper-inflationary period. Employees would leave without notice, and sometimes tender their resignations by email as soon as they secured other jobs outside the country, never giving consideration to how the company would manage with the huge skills gaps, without any time to craft plan B. The objectives of the research do not include finding out why the employees left. We know why they left and appreciate the difficult circumstances that led to the skills exodus, but this does not take away the serious challenges created by the said exodus. The objective of the research was to come up with a sustainable solution, indeed a social innovation, to the problem that was caused by the departure of the employees and the skills that resided in them. By extension, this emancipation will also benefit other manufacturing companies and businesses in general in Zimbabwe and globally. The research will also contribute to the body of knowledge.

As highlighted in an earlier chapter, the problems that came to the fore in most Zimbabwean companies were a typical example of a culmination of societal problems, ranging from the time when indigenous Zimbabweans were forcibly evicted from their land by the colonisers, which resulted in a changed way of life. They were forced to look for work on farms and in the city instead of tilling the land and hunting, which was their normal way of life. With this came a different way of learning that was imposed by the same colonisers. The indigenous Zimbabwean here came face to face with an exogenous way of learning and doing things in general, because this was the way of the colonial master. However, they learnt to separate the things that the colonial masters expected them to do (and indeed they did these things) and their own way of doing things. Hence, when a Zimbabwean is at work, he is a different person doing things in an expected exogenous way. As soon as he leaves work, he becomes his own indigenous self, doing things the African way. This has had a bearing on how people learn and create knowledge. This even spills into issues of spirituality. While the average Zimbabwean proclaims his Christianity, it is not surprising to see him performing his traditional spiritual rituals when the need arises.

The long and short of it is that the average Zimbabwean divides himself into two, urban and rural, exogenous and indigenous, and has generally not been enabled to fuse them together, into a unique synthesis. In this thesis, the diversity of the indigenous and exogenous approaches to knowledge creation and societal learning will be embraced to come up with a fusion that is relevant in a local and global context. Such fusion can only happen, in my view, when indigenous rhythms are given space as a starting point, to leverage creativity and innovation.

Therefore, in the process of solving the highlighted problem, it was expected that a new knowledge creation paradigm would emerge, based on our own indigenous rhythms, tempered with exogenous ones, leading to a fusion of rhythms, lending the solutions to a global context.

Southern Relational Path

In this research trajectory, the focus is on "being" – who are we? Knowledge creation has to rely on who we are. In this instance, the people that we are is very much coloured by our indigenous rhythms, which is an aspect that was given prominence in this research. Indigenous rhythms are by nature relational as rhythm is an end result of a coordinated relationship between two or more instruments.

This specific research has, among other things, sought to provide answers to the following questions:

a. How do we facilitate genuine employee involvement in order to increase their creativity?
b. How do we leverage the indigenous rhythms of employees to increase this creativity?
c. How do we learn skills from one another and from other sources, and how can this facilitate and promote knowledge creation?
d. How can we share such knowledge with one another?
e. How can we turn individual knowledge into organisational intellectual property that is able to endure the departure of individuals for any reason?

These questions were, in this research, answered through following the OFET trajectory of the relational path which involved working with co-researchers and sharing experiences and knowledge. This experience and knowledge in the first place included and involved our indigenous rhythms.

Description in this trajectory is used to reveal the origins, nature and scope of human experience. The major departure from conventional, empirically based scientific research is that, in this method, experiences are uncovered through careful and comprehensive descriptions, as opposed to measurement used in the empirical approach to research. An experiential approach is therefore adopted in this Originative phase of this relational trajectory.

A phenomenological approach to research was taken, as the very Foundation of this path, in that the researcher made herself part of the community being researched by immersing herself into that community. Thirdly, as we proceeded from relational Foundation to Emancipation, Feminism was relevant for knowledge promotion and liberation. It involved uncovering indigenous knowledge (and rhythm) which was used to promote knowledge and wisdom for the purposes of personal liberation and not oppression, and it also represented natural diversity as already highlighted in Chapter 3. Feminism is what enabled me to look at both indigenous and exogenous knowledge objectively and come up with a fusion that is relevant in a local and global perspective.

Participatory Action Research (PAR), finally with a view to Transformation (as pointed out later in this chapter, I in fact used Cooperative Inquiry rather than PAR as my action research orientation), is then used as the mode of alleviating the communal or societal challenge, in this case, knowledge creation and societal learning. This is collective research which is carried out through dialogue, collective memory, and where culture is valued. It involves the full active participation of the community (Lessem & Schieffer, 2010). In PAR, collective problem solving is used as a way of promoting self-reliance. The navigation strategy is to begin where people are, to encourage them to carry out an analysis of their situation and come up with actions to improve the existing situation. It is also critical to encourage regular self-reviews to monitor progress. I imagine this is exactly what happened with the Chinyika project where the starting point was "the people are starving" (Lessem, Muchineripi & Kada, 2012). For my particular research, the starting point was "we are losing knowledge". This therefore raised a number of questions on why we are losing knowledge, how we have kept knowledge in the past and how we can reduce such loss of knowledge and indeed create new knowledge.

This is the path that I predominately used in this research project.

Outline of envisaged path

The research methodology, overall then, was based on the Southern Relational Path which involved the Description of the situation, Phenomenology, Feminism and Participatory Action Research. However, aspects of other methodologies, such as Eastern Path of Renewal, Northern Path of Reason and the Western Path of Realisation, featured intermittently where necessary in order to give balance and a measure of completeness arising from the Four Worlds Model that necessarily had to be integrated. In fact, as highlighted above, I used Co-operative Inquiry in this research. Details of the Southern Relational Path are outlined below, aligned to the GENE concept.

Grounding: origination: descriptive

Description is used for grounding, where researcher puts herself into context of the problem or opportunity and the necessary innovation. This is the origination behind the innovation and is based on the premise that for one to be able to contribute meaningfully, they need to understand their origin and what they can learn from it. They need to take into account their indigenous rhythms. In addition, the way one contributes is related to their background.

For the Chinyika community for example, the solution to hunger and poverty could only be unravelled when they went back to their roots and revisited their history (Lessem, Muchineripi and Kadaa, 2012).

Emerging: foundation: phenomenology

Phenomenology is a humanistic approach to research, where the researcher immerses himself/herself into the community (and the problem) to be researched. In other words, the researcher becomes part of the subject of research. He/she carries out research with, and not on the community. In this research orientation, the objective is to understand the phenomena from within, before any explanations can be imposed. Emerging occurs when there is a blending between the local and global, when we begin to look beyond our own environment.

The tenets of phenomenology include the immersion of oneself into the world of the study, concentration on illuminating your inner self as an important aspect of the life world, and the location of every unique cultural history. In this research I was therefore phenomenologically involved in the research process at Turnall.

Navigation: emancipation: feminism

In Navigation the researcher aims at coming up with theories, concepts and frameworks which are globally constituted and recognised, such as "*kaizen*" in Japan and "*ubuntu*" in Africa. In my Southern Relational Path these theories and concepts were arrived at after the process which involves starting where the people are, encouraging self-analysis, mobilising and organising people and facilitating actions for change. The building of loving relationships would normally occur in the relational path. In this instance, these loving relationships are expressed through the indigenous rhythms, which define the give and take of human interaction.

Effect: transformation: PAR/CI

The Effect is the implementation. This is when I would actually apply Participatory Action Research (PAR), within my company, whereby the social innovation would become a reality. PAR is the normal trajectory for the relational path where the expected effect is community building and healing. However, as mentioned earlier, Cooperative Inquiry (CI) was in fact applied, which brings transformation, and in its own way brings social innovation albeit in a more holistic way. On the whole then, I applied a hybrid trajectory to the innovation, ranging, on a continuum, between PAR and CI.

I saw the Southern Relational Path being the prominent path for me to use in this research, particularly as I carried out the research within Turnall Holdings.

OFET

OFET, more specifically then, stands for the **O**rigination behind the innovation (Grounding), the **F**oundation of innovation (Phenomenology), **E**mancipation towards innovation, and the **T**ransformation for innovation. OFET works hand in hand with the GENE.

Eastern Path of Renewal

In the Eastern Path of Renewal, narrative methods and storytelling are used to uncover the existing story. Hermeneutics is the Renewal approach to research. Unlike phenomenology where you immerse yourself in the community under research, hermeneutics prescribes that you identify and empathise with the subject of research, and you seek a deeper meaning in what may seem apparent. You give the other a voice. Part of your methodology is to develop the ability to understand things from another person's perspective. This helps to develop dialogue and to fuse horizons. In navigation, the researcher pursues ultimate meaning in the situation under research.

Hermeneutics leads to critical theory, whose tenets include uncovering power relations and focusing on promoting liberation.

In this overall renewal trajectory, co-operative enquiry is ultimately and transformatively used to uncover shared potential. This method is used among peers who view themselves as equals. The strategy is to agree on actions to be taken then democratically come up with consensus on the outcomes. The effect in this trajectory is conscious evolution.

While my chosen path was the Southern Relational one, in the course of the research I found myself borrowing from the Eastern Path of Renewal, especially for the purpose of sharing specific strategies with peers in other organisations as well as in my organisation then getting consensus on the outcomes of the said strategies. This was done through Co-operative Inquiry, which, according to Lessem and Schieffer (2010), is a participative form of inquiry as well as being a knowledge-oriented process which is experiential. I also benefitted from the works of writers from this background such as Nonaka and Takeuchi (1995), and Jaworski (2011), to name a couple.

Northern Path of Reason

In this trajectory, research is based on scientifically proving a given hypothesis. In Critical Rationalism, emphasis is placed on searching for the truth. The way to the truth is through some ordered data which is organised to give answers to address the hypothesis. In this research path, the researcher is the "expert" who searches for answers by studying others who become the objects of research. Tenets of Critical Rationalism include the desire to falsify rather than verify. This often results in multiple truths emerging at different times and in different circumstances.

Research leads to Socio-Technical design, which adopts a problem-solving approach. The research should result in action towards improving society. However, there does not necessarily have to be consensus. The effect of this trajectory is knowledge creation.

In the process of carrying out my research, while I did not specifically utilise the Northern Path of Reason, I remained open to its suggestions in order to benefit from the diversity. However, it is in the Northern Path of Reason that my model was crystallised.

Western Path of Realisation

This trajectory is grounded in survey and experimentation. Researchers here have the capacity to ask good questions, to listen and be adaptable. They have to be able to see opportunities that arise. The survey methods incorporate experimentation which leads to empiricism. The tenets of empiricism include searching for the truth, seeking the positive facts and separating facts from values.

The research philosophy emerges in the measurement of people as well as things. In the navigation arena this trajectory focuses on uncovering reality, through critical realism, focused on "real" generative forces. Action Research is the transformative method ultimately used in this trajectory. This incorporates undertaking social research for social change, placing emphasis on the "how" rather than the "what" and incorporating action learning. The ultimate role of action research is to empower people.

Again, my involvement with this trajectory was to be informed by it but not to focus on it. It is however in the pragmatic West that the implementation of my innovation resides. I also benefitted from works by writers from the western perspective such as Kolb (1984), Kotter (1996, 2006), Charan, et al. (2001) and Senge, et al. (2005) – again, to mention a few.

Why the chosen path (Southern Relational)

There are a number of reasons why I chose to use the Southern Relational Path in this research. According to Lessem and Schieffer (2010), however, while integral research can be based on a specific life world, "… it accommodates all four worlds … spanning individual (pragmatic) and institutional (rational, interpersonal), (holistic) and societal (humanistic)". Although I focused on a particular path in this research then, I could not be completely closed off from the other paths. This is what made the research fully integrated. The reasons for focusing on the Southern Relational Path are highlighted below.

Personal inclination

I have a passionate inclination towards resolving the knowledge gap issues, having worked in corporate organisations for thirty years. My background, having been born and raised in the traditional Shona set up, inclines me towards a relational approach. The Shona society is essentially a humanistic one. I had no problem with immersing myself in the community of my organisation because I was already part of this community and had over the years contributed significantly towards what the company had become. I also believe in the emancipation of all and would love to see organisations emancipated from the problem of skills loss and the resultant knowledge gap, to come up with a sustainable solution to this.

Cultural perspective

Coming from a typical African background, my culture, and that of the company I seek to liberate is set in relational tradition. The Shona culture in particular is very relational. Everything that happens in the village has a bearing on other members of the community, and the community as a whole is interested and curious about what is happening to everyone else. This is the way I was raised. It therefore is a natural progression that my chosen research path is Southern Relational, which falls into line with my cultural background.

Objectives of the research

My desire to heal my organisation as a community and Zimbabwe as a society of the ills of the dearth of new knowledge made it apparent that I use this research path. The desire to bring about social change further endorsed the relevance of the chosen trajectory. Further to this, it is my belief that the solutions to organisational problems lie within the organisations themselves, in as much as I believe that the solutions to Zimbabwe's problems lie within Zimbabwe.

Secondary path: Eastern Path of Renewal

As a secondary research path, the significant contribution that the Eastern Path of Renewal made to this study was to promote fusion. This fusion is between different organisations in Zimbabwe as well as in a more global perspective. The path promoted the act of giving "the other" a voice. This happened through co-operative inquiry (CI) specifically, where a CI group of eleven people was identified to carry out this research. These employees were given "a voice" to air their views in the course of the research and share their observations. Additionally, I started a "community of practice" through where I also shared information with colleagues on the PhD program while working through the research. This community of practice was also given "a voice".

Design of research and innovation

The research design involved the four aspects of the Southern (humanist) relational path involving the four levels of integral research consisting of method (Description), methodology (Phenomenology), critique (Feminism) and action

(Co-operative Inquiry). The Descriptive method translated to origination or grounding, the methodology of Phenomenology coincided with foundation or emergence, Feminism which relates to emancipation or navigation, and Action (CI) which related to transformation or effect. Details of the above levels of the research innovation trajectory are given below.

Method/descriptive

Method is the technique used for doing each phase of the research. The method that was employed, which is embodied in the context, is the "Descriptive" one, which was used to start the research journey. This method was used to characterise the origins of the problem, to describe self as participant during the problem-solving process and as co-researcher in solving same. It was also useful in engaging self as a participant and for illuminating the observations made as the research uncovers experiences.

This method was also used to describe the context in which our people lived in harmony with nature, living sustainably amongst themselves by embodying the spirit of ubuntu/unhu/humanism (Uri munhu here? / Are you human?). This philosophy provided the grounds for learning about the cultural, survival and entertainment /leisure knowledge of the people and how this knowledge was to be passed from mother and father to daughter and son, from aunt and uncle to niece and nephew in a rich cultural context that provided a free and conducive learning environment. I also wanted to understand to what extent the cultural indabas *(dare)* and other learning platforms were constructed to provide an environment for creative learning and knowledge dissemination that enabled our ancestors to survive what the colonialists describe as harsh, tropical conditions. The research endeavored to understand the historical context in which knowledge was created and shared among the ancient and to see how this may also be applied today in order to enhance knowledge creation and dissemination in a local/global context.

Methodology-phenomenology/hermeneutics

In phenomenology the researcher immerses himself/herself in the life world of the lived experiences. He/she concentrates on illuminating the inner self, and also treats every unique cultural history as part of the larger story. In hermeneutics the researcher reconstructs self and society by moving from being a mere spectator to an active agent (Lessem & Schieffer, 2009). I therefore evolved from being interpretive to being transformative. I also needed to reconnect with my source by going back to the roots, for this is where meaning is found. It is through fully understanding self that one can make sense of the world as well as make a meaningful contribution to same.

Here I sought to understand, through experience, how the indigenous Zimbabwean people have been able to create, share and preserve life sustaining knowledge about our culture, indigenous agriculture and other methods of

food production, processing and storage, knowledge about leisure and entertainment and other forms of cultural knowledge such as marriage, child rearing,
rainmaking, healing and counselling, which gives us an identity and binds us
together as Zimbabwean people and Africans. The critical aspect was to link this
to the problem at hand and use this background knowledge as a springboard for
coming up with solutions to current problems.

The researcher becomes part of the structures that form platforms for innovation and becomes a catalyst thereof. To what extent do we learn from this, as
we seek to improve our knowledge creation, sharing, dissemination and pres-
ervation in the post-modern economy as a basis for improving our organisational competitiveness in the local and global context? To what extent do we
pay attention to our own indigenous rhythms, for only when we do that will
we have the capacity to recognise the rhythms in other cultures? How do we
fuse horizons (urban and traditional, indigenous and exogenous) in an effort to
come up with a high-breed that fosters better and more effective knowledge
creation in organisations, in coming up with social innovations that improve
society? How do we work with others to develop and create knowledge using
the cultural and spiritual history in order to create a more modern innovation
that benefits both the traditional and the urban life worlds that are sustainable
in terms of local/global competitiveness?

On the other hand, hermeneutics (Eastern Path of Renewal) were employed
in this research. In this regard I was seeking to display empathy with co-
researchers in other organisations as well as my own, seeking to understand
their problems, including the historical aspects of such problems. I sought a
deeper meaning within any outward appearances. Above all, I sought to understand things from the other party's perspective. Hermeneutics seeks to bring
about a fusion of horizons – unity in diversity. In the process of linking with
co-researchers in other organisations and my own organisation in this research,
I hope I have achieved this fusion.

Critique/feminism/critical theory (emancipation)

Feminism is the critical tool of this methodology. It demands that the research
brings about positive social change, the knowledge gained being used as a tool
for liberation and not oppression. Feminism therefore represents human and
natural diversity and will therefore be used to critique the relational path. It is
important to remember however that the hybrid trajectory used in this research
all the more demanded an equally hybrid critique approach. The likely critique method therefore ranged, on a continuum, between feminism and critical
theory, leading to co-operative inquiry.

I sought to understand and appreciate the pre-colonial traditional tenets
that characterised the way men, women and children were empowered in our
traditional set up, and how traditional roles were clarified and respected in line
with the different roles that were expected of them, and how we can learn from
this in order to come up with a blue-print of unity in diversity with regard to

empowerment. For example, there were channels to be followed when dealing with disputes in the home, in an open and democratic manner. This can only enrich the way we deal with empowerment issues in modern day organisations, ensuring that the marginalised are given a voice.

Knowledge empowers people and communities, particularly when that knowledge brings social change to communities. An example is the Chinyika community whose "new" knowledge of finger millet has liberated them from hunger and poverty. The community has therefore gained respect in society because they have become self-sufficient and economically independent. The research therefore sought to uncover possibilities of social innovations in knowledge creation in order to liberate Zimbabwean companies.

On the part of the subordinate Eastern Path of Renewal, critical theory was oriented towards changing society as a whole in the field of knowledge creation and societal learning. This self-reflection that happened reduced the chance of the concerned organisations being affected in the same way by skills flight in the future. If this happens, the organisations would have liberated themselves from domination by skilled employees. The balance of power would have been restored.

This hybrid approach has resulted in emancipation, both for the organisation in question and for the other organisations participating in the research, and by extension, to many other organisations beyond this circle.

Participatory action research/cooperative inquiry

Daniel Selener, as quoted in Reason and Bradbury (2006), says, "Participatory research is a process through which members of an oppressed group or community identify a problem, collect and analyse information, and act upon the problem in order to find solutions and to promote social and political transformation". This really sums up my following discussion on PAR. The subject of "methodology" is therefore the roadmap to follow in achieving this. The choice of PAR is ideal in that, it is recognised as an "appropriate epistemology for the vision of more than just and equitable social transformation" (Brown & Tandon, 2008).

PAR is about community involvement, participation and transformation, usually targeted at the poor, the exploited, the oppressed and the marginalised. It creates an awareness of what resources are available in the community. McIntyre (2008) contends that the following tenets inform the majority of PAR projects:

- A collective interest to investigate an issue or problem,
- A desire to engage self as well as collective reflection to gain clarity about an issue,
- A joint decision to engage in individual and/or collective action that brings a solution to the problem to the satisfaction of those involved, and,
- Building alliances between researchers and participants in the planning, implementation and dissemination of the research process.

For Chinyika for example, these four tenets are very appropriate and relevant. Although there was a catalyst in the form of Dr Chidhara Muchineripi, the collective commitment was there, as was the desire to seek clarity in the situation, leading to a joint decision to embark on a sorghum growing project, and the alliances between researcher and participants are obviously very strong. It is no surprise therefore that the project is enjoying such a high level of success. For my project research, it was important to learn from Chinyika and seek to get buy-in from my co-researchers and participants.

The issue of resources is of some significance in PAR, depending on the nature of the project. Although it is a very poor community, the resources available at Chinyika included land, finger millet seed from the few that had been growing it, and indigenous skill and knowledge. A bonus resource is a borehole that has enabled twenty-six families to embark on a very successful market garden to supplement the finger millet project. The resources need not be a lot of money or expensive equipment but can be the everyday things that people take for granted and under-estimate.

The next action is to mobilise the community for self-reliance, with the ultimate goal of transforming the community.

My organisation, like many organisations in Zimbabwe, went through a period of exploitation and marginalisation from skilled workers who had a very wide variety of employment opportunities to choose from, regionally and internationally, with permanent workers leaving without serving the stipulated notice period, because they were in a position of power at that particular time. The research seeks to transform organisations by balancing power in the organisation so that the companies are not left vulnerable. This will be achieved through an innovative way of knowledge creation, development and management.

Participatory Action Research will enable organisations to identify the resources that they possess, such as the knowledge that resides in the experienced employee, which can be harnessed using social innovation. The research will involve the object of research and other organisations to mobilise people for self-reliant development in the field of knowledge creation. The ultimate goal of the research was to transform the way companies create, harness and manage knowledge.

Participatory Action Research, therefore, is intended to directly contribute to community organisation and action. The research process is considered to be just as important as the results. This is because regardless of what the results come out like, the participating community has been changed and will have been introduced to the philosophy of taking control of their situation.

However, in this research, co-operative inquiry was employed.

CI is more integral as it has aspects of the other three epistemologies, i.e. "humanism, rationalism and empiricism" (Lessem and Schieffer, 2010). It is however more steeped in the Eastern Path of Renewal and is aligned with narrative methods (where PAR is aligned with description), hermeneutics and critical theory, leading to a process of "becoming".

CI involves research involving other people who are equal co-researchers. The research becomes political in that the participants have the right to participate and to identify their own aspirations and preferences in the research process. These participants are empowered during the research. The research process avoids disempowering the co-researchers so that they are not misrepresented by the originator of the research. In my particular case, while I had my own objectives of the research, the objectives of the co-researchers were to be taken cognizance of so that they were not disempowered. Together therefore, we mapped out the objectives of the research from the angles of all co-researchers.

Heron (1994) highlights multiple ways of knowing, which range from practical knowledge, conceptual knowledge, imaginal knowledge and knowing, experiential knowledge and knowing, conceptual knowledge and finally practical knowing which will lead to the research innovation. He contends that validity of the outcomes of co-operative inquiry lies in these four modes of knowing. This is a process that researchers have to go through, leading them to social innovation.

CI, as any form of Action Research therefore involves research with and not on people, where experiences are shared. The co-researchers go through personal transformation for participating in the research. In the process of coming up with a social innovation, the participants to the research are also transformed.

For the research that I carried out together with my co-researchers, these four modes were therefore paid particular attention to in order for us to claim validity of the outcomes of the research.

Specification of research method

As highlighted above, the methodology used was the relational path. The research method was therefore mostly the "descriptive" method which research method was applied to all aspects of the research process.

The Eastern Path of Renewal also came in handy, particularly when I borrowed from Eastern writers such as Takeuchi and Nonaka, and when I used Co-operative Inquiry for my research.

In Co-operative Inquiry, a selection of six to eight co-researchers from a cross section of specialist areas such as financial, educational and health institutions was to be selected to participate in this research. I benefitted from using the Confederation of Zimbabwe Industries (CZI) as part of my research. This was facilitated by my co-researcher, Joshua Chinyuku, who, at the time of carrying out this research, was the President of the Mashonaland Chamber of CZI.

Research to find out whether (and how much) knowledge management has affected companies, and to see how interventions of knowledge creation, turning the companies into learning organisations, improved the local and global competitiveness in the organisations.

I drew on Wenger's communities of practice (1998), Senge's Learning Organizations (2005) and Charan, Drotter and Noel (2001) on the Leadership Pipeline (for talent development and retention) in the process of executing this research, among other works.

Conclusion

Lessem and Schieffer (2010) contend that in co-operative inquiry "... human persons are linked in a generative web of communication with other humans and the rest of creation". This resonates with the approach that I took in the context of co-operative inquiry in this research, where I indeed created a web of communication through my team of co-researchers and the community of practice that I developed. Lessem and Schieffer (2010) go further to say, "Human persons do not stand separate from the cosmos; we evolved with it and are an expression of its intelligent and creative force". This brings me back to the issue of rhythm, as part of the cosmos. I am reminded of a holiday I took to Mauritius and stayed at a hotel overlooking the beach front. The waves created a certain rhythm which was apparent to the eye and the ear. I have no doubt that the indigenous Mauritians have developed a communication with and an understanding of this rhythm. They have to, for their own survival. They have to understand when it is safe to take the children for a swim at the beach and when it is safer to stay as far away from the beach as possible because a storm is brewing. By extension, there is need for owners and managers of companies in Zimbabwe (and indeed elsewhere), to develop an understanding of, and communication with the indigenous rhythm, for such understanding makes us one with the cosmos. It is my assertion that, even in problem solving, we are more likely to come up with more sustainable solutions if we listen to the rhythms and allow ourselves to be informed by them. In the research on knowledge creation and societal learning therefore, I will make an attempt to listen to and make sense of the indigenous rhythms.

The Research Methodology outlined in this chapter is the process that was to bring a solution to the burning issue of my research, and this solution should bring transformation to the organisation, the manufacturing industry, the business community and also in a global context. Integral research can bring this transformation, not academic or scientific research. Integral research, is not just for the sake of knowing, but for transforming individuals, communities and society.

The Four Worlds Model becomes extremely relevant because of the integration it brings to the research, from a local/global perspective. The hybrid research trajectory of the Southern Relational Path with a contribution from the Eastern Path of Renewal helped the research teams to come up with an innovation that is more meaningful and relevant to a wider audience, as the transformation will not be as a result of work done at the organisation only.

Finally, the research has impacted the individual members of the research teams in a way that is permanent, even from the thinking process and from a problem-solving perspective. Most of all, I was the most changed person of all, having gone through the whole research philosophy and having experienced the entire research process.

References

Bates, S. M. (2012). *The Social Innovation Imperative: Create Winning Products, Services and Programs that Solve Society's Most Pressing Challenges.* New York: McGraw-Hill.

Brown, L. D. & Tandon, R. (2008). Ideology and Political Economy in Inquiry: Action Research and Participatory Research, *Journal of Applied Behavioral Science,* 19 (3), 277–294, viewed 7 December 2019, <https://www.researchgate.net/publication/250959282_Ideology_and_Political_Economy_in_Inquiry_Action_Research_and_Participatory_Research>.

Charan, R., Drotter, S. & Noel, J (2001). *The Leadership Pipeline: How to build a Leadership Powered Company* (2nd Ed.). San Francisco: Jossey-Bass.

Coghlan, D. & Brannick, T. (2010). 3rd Edition. *Doing Action Research in Your Own Organisation.* London: Sage.

Gibbons, M., Limoges, C., Nowotny, H., Schwartzman, S., Scott, P. & Trow, M. (1994). *The New Production of Knowledge: The Dynamics of Science and Research in Contemporary Societies.* London: Sage.

Heron, J. (1994). *Co-operative Inquiry.* London: Sage.

Hoppers, C. (2002). *Indigenous Knowledge and the Integration of Knowledge Systems.* Capetown: New Africa Books.

Huysamen, G. K. (1984). *Introductory Statistics and Research Design for Behavioural Sciences, Volume ll.* Capetown: Huysamen.

Jaworski, J. (2011). *Source: The Inner Part of Knowledge Creation.* Los Angeles: Berret-Koehler Publishers.

Kindon, S., Pain, R. & Kesby, M. (2007). *Participatory Action Research Approaches and Methods: Connecting People, Participation and Place.* London: Routledge.

Kolb, D. A. (1984). *Experiential Learning.* Englewood Cliffs, NJ: Prentice Hall.

Kotter, J. (1996). *Leading Change.* Boston: Harvard Business School Press.

Kotter, J. (2006). *Our Iceberg is Melting: Changing and Succeeding under any conditions.* New York: St Martin's.

Lee, J. Cronbach and Associates (1980). *Toward Reform of Product Evaluation.* San Francisco: Jossey-Bass

Lessem, R. & Schieffer, A. (2009). *Transformation Management: Towards the Integral Enterprise.* Farnham, England: Gower.

Lessem, R. & Schieffer, A. (2010). *Integral Research and Innovation: Transforming Enterprise and Society.* Farnham, England: Gower.

Mamukwa, E. S., Lessem, R. & Schieffer, A. (2014). *Integral Green Zimbabwe: An African Phoenix Rising.* Farnham, England: Gower.

McIntyre, A. (2008). *Participatory Action Research.* London: Sage.

Moser, C. A. & Kalton, G. (2nd Ed.). (1979). *Survey Methods in Social Investigation.* London: Heinemann.

Nonaka, I. & Takeuchi, H. (1995). *The Knowledge Creating Company: How Japanese Companies Create the Dynamics of Innovation.* Oxford: New York.

Nowotny, H., Scott, P. & Gibbons, M. (2001). *Rethinking Science: Knowledge and the Public in an age of Uncertainty.* Cambridge: Polity Press.

Nowotny, H., Scott, P. & Gibbons, M. (2003). *Mode 2 Revisited: The New Production of Knowledge.* Minerva 41, 179–194.

Reason, P. & Bradbury, H. (2006). *The Sage Handbook of Action Research: Participative Inquiry and Practice* (2nd Ed.). London: Sage.

Senge, P. M., Scharmer, C. O., Jaworski, J., & Flowers, B. C. (2005). *Presence: An Exploration of Profound Change in People, Organisations and Society.* New York: Doubleday/ Currency.

Thomas, G. (2009). *How to do Your Research Project: A Guide for Students in Education and Social Sciences.* London: Sage.

Wenger, E. (1998). *Communities of Practice: Learning, Meaning and Identity.* New York: Cambridge University Press.

Williams, B. & Figueiredo, J. (2009). *Phase Change in Engineering Knowledge Production – From an Academic to an Entrepreneurial Context.* (Proceedings of the Research in Engineering Education Symposium 2009, Palm Cove, QLD), <https://www.researchgate.net/publication/257651075_Phase_change_in_engineering_knowledge_production_-_From_an_academic_to_an_entrepreneurial_context>.

10 Co-operative Inquiry

Towards new forms of knowledge creation

Introduction

Many long-standing African manufacturing companies came into being to meet the needs of the colonial settlers, with exogenous skills and machinery, but with an indigenous workforce that had to sacrifice its indigenous nature in order to fit into an exogenous realm. Obviously, this compromises the quality of what they do as well as their sense of who they are at the workplace. Indigenous workers seem to separate who they really are from who they are at work. Consequently, although many companies boast of being systems organisations, these systems are not really working as well as they should for the said organisations because the critical link, the people, find themselves in a dysfunctional situation. In the absence of true African values, and the indigenous rhythms, the African person cannot be true to himself.

A lot has been said about the "Four Worlds" perspective (Lessem & Schieffer, 2009, 2010) in this thesis. In this research, therefore, the Southern Relational path was identified as the preferred path. However, the research itself was carried out using Co-operative Inquiry, which is actually from the Eastern Path of Renewal. In this chapter I will begin to explore this research to demonstrate how, using Co-operative Inquiry I worked with co-researchers to try and unlock new knowledge and develop new concepts relevant to Turnall and other manufacturing companies in Zimbabwe and beyond. My initial task in this chapter will be to define Co-operative Inquiry, in the process of getting a full grasp of what it is, how it is implemented and the benefits that can be derived from it, and indeed demonstrating how Integral Research can play a pivotal role in the creation of new knowledge. The best and most straight forward way of doing this is simply to carry out a narrative of how the Co-operative Inquiry research with my co-researchers transpired at Turnall.

Standing on the shoulders of giants

It was pertinent for my co-researchers and I to understand Co-operative Inquiry and how it works in order for us to use it to full advantage in this research project. What better way to do so than to listen to the "giants" in this regard.

Heron (1996) postulates that Co-operative Inquiry (CI) has its roots in Kurt Lewin's work. However, the dimension brought to the table by the likes of Heron (1996) and Reason (1988, 1994) takes this to a different level and plane. CI is a form of action research aligned to the Eastern Path of Renewal (Lessem & Schieffer, 2009). It involves two or more people researching a topic through their own experience. In my CI at Turnall there were twelve co-researchers. In CI, co-researchers research with, and not on one another. No one is more superior to the other, but all are equals. People are treated as active agents, and not as passive subjects (Reason & Bradbury, 2011). Participants are therefore both co-researchers and co-subjects (Reason & Bradbury, 2008). This form of research is transformative by nature (Heron, 1996: Lessem & Schieffer, 2009).

Stages of Co-operative Inquiry

Heron (1996) came up with four recognised stages in CI. Stage 1 involves bringing a group of people with a common interest together and identifying issues to be researched. This is the first reflection stage where the researchers choose the area of focus for their research, come up with a launching statement for the topic of inquiry and an action plan for this first phase. Researchers also agree on how experiences are recorded.

In Stage 2, which is the first action stage, the researchers explore in experience and action the inquiry topic, applying an integrated range of inquiry skills. It involves applying agreed actions and observing and recording the experience. Keeping records of the experiential data remains a critical aspect of the research process.

In Stage 3 researchers fully immerse themselves in the action phase, remaining open to experience. In Stage 4, which is the second reflection phase, researchers share the data from the action phase, review and modify the inquiry topic in the process of making sense of the data, and choose a plan for the second action phase.

Four epistemologies

Heron (1996) identifies four types of knowing, namely, experiential knowing, presentational knowing, propositional knowing and practical knowing.

Experiential knowing involves knowledge created by consciously being, grounded in the sensory environment. In my CI group, experiential knowing was explored as co-researchers shared their experiences at Turnall and the challenges they saw the business facing with regard to the creation and management of knowledge.

Presentational knowing involves reflection and knowledge generated through artistry and imagery. Here poetry, song and dance, producing rhythm through playing the African drum, among other artistry, was employed.

Propositional knowing then is the formal theoretical, conceptual knowledge expressed through language. Here, co-researchers can come up with theories and models. Practical knowing involves practical application where the theories and models are implemented and validated. In a way, this is the most important part as it defines whether the theories and models are usable or not, and how valid their applicability is.

Practical experience of setting up a CI group

Purpose of research

The challenges faced by Turnall have been highlighted. The purpose of this CI research was therefore to bring transformation to Turnall in the area of knowledge creation and societal learning. The co-researchers agreed that this was an area of concern, given that many critical skills were lost (and by extension, knowledge was lost), during the hyper-inflationary era.

Structure of the Co-operative Inquiry group

The first thing I did was to approach the Managing Director of the company with the intention of getting buy-in from him, and by extension, getting access to the workers and permission and support to carry out the research. As a candidate of the PhD Program himself, in addition to being a progressive person, the Managing Director came on board. His role was that of promoter/patron/technical supervisor.

In my choice of co-researchers from the Management team, I considered the roles that these co-researchers would play when it came to the implementation of the outcomes of the research. For this reason, I chose the Works (factory) Manager, because the outcomes would have a direct bearing on his factory, hence he would be definitely interested. I proposed the role of facilitator for the Works Manager because he had good rapport with the workers and had the ability to extricate information from them in a friendly and sometimes humorous manner. I also chose one of the Human Resources (HR) Managers, specifically the Harare one, as this is where the initial research was to take place. The HR Manager would play a critical role in assisting to roll out the outcomes of the research to the other sections of the company. I proposed the role of recorder for the HR Manager. She would be responsible for keeping a record of all the meetings in a minute book. The initial area of research would be the factory, where the results of the skills and knowledge loss were most obvious. Two members of the general factory workforce were also included in this first grouping. What they brought to the table was informal worker leadership, which I felt would be useful in terms of bringing the other workers on board.

Together with these four co-researchers, we chose six other co-researchers. The group felt it was important to choose good performers in the different functional areas in the factory who had something to bring to the table, and who were serious and committed to work. The worker representatives represented the institution, and would have the added advantage of bringing first-hand information on how the workers viewed the challenges faced by the company. The CI group's representation therefore cut across all ranks, with four shop-floor employees, three supervisors, one foreman, two managers and one executive director.

My role was that of catalyst, but on the whole, I was a co-researcher working together with the other researchers on an equal footing. What I brought to the table was a more enhanced understanding of Co-operative Inquiry as a research method, in addition to other tools that might be necessary to use, such as Kolb's Learning Styles Inventory (LSI).

The CI group named itself *Denhe re Ruzivo* (the calabash of knowledge). In the African culture a calabash is used for storing and sharing beer or water, with people actually drinking from it. The concept then was to gather knowledge into this metaphorical calabash then give it to others in the company and beyond to quench their knowledge thirst.

Outside of this CI group is what I will term the *de facto* CI group consisting of the Management Committee. Any critical discoveries were shared with these people, and this way they also had the opportunity to bring their observations and inputs to the table.

There was of course my CI group of co-researchers from the PhD group, consisting of Joshua Chinyuku, who was at that time General Manager of Astra Paints, and Passmore Matupire, then Board Chairman of ART Corporation. In this group we shared observations and tried any new discoveries on the other two companies, to validate whatever would be happening at Turnall, and vice versa. We would meet on a regular basis to exchange notes and share experiences on our different CI groups. We decided to call this group *Pundutso* (positive transformation), for we believed that at the end of our varied research projects would be some positive transformational outcomes.

Stage 1

The first thing that we did as a group was to get to know one another. We shared our different totems, where we come from geographically, our family situations, how we perceived our work to be and the role it played in the overall achievement of the company's objectives and those of employees. Just talking about ourselves and what we did seemed to inject some energy and enthusiasm in all of us. What became apparent was how all the bits and pieces of work that we did contributed to the greater whole, and how important it was therefore, for every one of us to do our best in our little corner to enable the company to achieve success so that jobs are preserved. Sharing our personal information appeared to bring us closer together, and also as individuals to remind us that we were all important individuals in our own right, bringing our individuality to Turnall and becoming a force to reckon with as a workforce. We started greeting one another in our traditional way, which seemed to relax all of us and boost our egos in a positive way.

Following Heron's four stages of Co-operative Inquiry (1996), we started with Stage 1. Here as co-researchers we discussed and agreed on the focus of inquiry, in this case knowledge creation and societal learning using the Turnall case story. We agreed on how often we would meet (which was once a week) to discuss these issues, how we would record our discussions, and how important it was to share our practical experiences. The specific key objectives of the research were discussed, resulting in the following being adopted:

- To come with an innovation that has the capacity to transform knowledge creation and societal learning at Turnall,
- To identify problems/challenges faced in the factory, and focusing on finding sustainable solutions to such,
- To convert tacit knowledge gained from past/current experiences in the factory into explicit knowledge, and to keep a knowledge repository in the organisation for current and future use,
- To incorporate our indigenous practices, languages and norms and blend these with exogenous learning practices to enhance organisational learning and continual improvement, and
- To manage information and learning in a practical but sustainable way.

In the *Pundutso* CI group we met every fortnight, and apart from discussing any sticking issues in our various research areas we shared whatever was of interest and compared notes from the results of our company-based CI groups. As my colleagues were still a bit behind in their research processes, initially I shared with them what I was doing at Turnall with regard to the research process. This had the effect of motivating them to pursue their own research.

Stage 2

In the second stage in *Denhe re Ruzivo* we discussed how we would engage on agreed actions. We agreed that, as we continued the journey of our CI group, we would stumble on information that needed immediate action, and this would be immediately implemented. We also agreed that we would discuss the outcomes of this implementation to see what difference it was making.

Some of the observations made were as follows:

- "Young people are not keen to learn as they are not willing to do any additional work to what they have been assigned. Consequently, they often miss opportunities to learn new processes".
- "The elders in the workplace on the other hand take a back seat with regard to correcting and admonishing errant young people, in line with our African culture and values".

Over and above this, we agreed that we would observe and record the process and outcomes of our experiences and explore these outcomes. We would be guided by the concept of what we believed we wanted to achieve, namely, a situation where, when people leave the organisation, the said organisation would not be crippled as a consequence of lost skills and knowledge. Of importance to us was how we could marry the African (indigenous) perspective with the exogenous workplace, with a view to improving and enriching the workplace as well as the employees' work experience.

Experiential knowing

A lot of time was spent in *Denhe re Ruzivo* on co-researchers sharing their experiences at Turnall during a total of 260 years of combined service. This became the ice breaker, as people went down memory lane, reminiscing about their careers, their practical experiences, the good as well as the bad times. Co-researchers really began to warm up in this session, and we agreed to give this more time so that all members would get the opportunity to share. We tried to distil the experiences to get the lessons learnt for the past as well as for the future.

Specific problems encountered in the company

The CI group identified the following problems as be-dogging the factory:

- Low production outputs
- Poor product quality
- Old equipment
- Limitations in skills to repair key machine components, a sign that we have performed poorly over the years with regard to the passing on of tacit knowledge.

On asking why some employees did not have the skills to repair the machines after working with the said machines for a long time, some members highlighted that, on being taught these skills, not enough time was spent on according them the opportunity to practice the skill, so sometimes they internalised things that were inaccurate or incomplete. This is because supervisors were keen to move on and use people who know the skill so that they can reach their targets. They did not have time for people who were slow to learn. A significant amount of time was spent discussing this.

On digging deeper as to why there were poor production outputs and poor-quality products, the members blamed this on the issue of targets. They felt that Management pushed for certain targets, regardless of circumstances. For example, in a situation where there are machine operators whose job it was to work closely with and monitor the machine, they cited members of management in Production who would just come and ramp up the machine without bothering to consult the operators. One member said, "*Chinoziva ivhu kuti mwana wembeva anorwara*" (it's the soil that knows when the mouse is sick). What he then went to explain was that, working with the machine, he feels the heat of the machine, listens to the sound that it makes, and so on. Therefore, at any one time, he would understand the strengths and limitations of his machine. When a manager or foreman just comes from his office and ramps up the machine, this is often done without full knowledge of the state of the machine at that particular time. Therefore, quite often the machines were pushed beyond their sustainable capacity, and by the time this was realised, a lot of defective product would have been produced resulting in poor quality and high levels of waste. The facilitator (Works Manager) took this issue on board for immediate implementation. He encouraged his managers and foremen to engage the machine operators before making any changes to the production process. This was subsequently incorporated into the works procedures and would be monitored to see the outcome of this intervention.

On the issue of consulting shop-floor employees, there were others in the management team who felt that, sometimes certain approaches needed to be used in managing the said employees to avoid anarchy and disorder. Some felt that employees tended to want to complain about the way they were treated, ignored and not consulted; this was their nature. On looking at the results of the profiling of the Kolb Learning Styles Inventory, I discovered that, by some coincidence the managers with these views were pragmatist. The challenge was to show both sides that there were more merits than demerits in working together and consulting one another, and to show members of the management team that employees were not little devils that needed to be always whipped into line. They too had a meaningful contribution to make when given an opportunity. As one of the employees said, "If you treat people like machines, they will behave like machines".

On sharing this in *Pundutso,* Passmore (the leadership guru of the team) saw a leadership gap that needed to be addressed (Mamukwa, Lessem & Schieffer, 2014). He felt that when Management just walks to the machine to ramp it up without consulting the machine operator, they were alienating the workers and failing to fully appreciate that we get results through people. There were therefore limitations in the leadership effectiveness as such leaders actually tend to de-motivate employees by ignoring the chain of command. Josh saw this from a micro-ecological point of view, explaining that lack of the relational aspect at work has the effect of hindering knowledge sharing and creation. He further expressed that lack of observance of cultural norms such as *ubuntu* can hinder performance at the workplace, for if a person is not emancipated, such "oppression" retards the acquisition of knowledge.

Josh shared an experience which all three of us identified with. He said when he joined Astra as a cadet, he and his peers were told by a white manager who was in charge of their training, "Welcome to the world of work, but here you can throw your degree out through the window and start learning". The message was the degree was useless and irrelevant to the work situation, which was strange as the company had gone all out to look for chemistry graduates for this cadetship program. The approach did not foster co-operation, and can encourage silos and camps. It disturbed ecology at enterprise level and killed enthusiasm as well as creating a fear culture. As a result, at that time it took five years to train a cadet. With a friendlier, more relational approach, the same program was reduced to two years.

When Josh took over as manager from the white incumbent, he realised that the old approach would not yield the desired results. We all agreed that a relational approach to knowledge sharing and creation bears more positive results. For example, in most companies including our own, there are some older people who have done their jobs for a long time. Unless one builds a relationship with them, they will not share their knowledge. In fact, not sharing one's knowledge was perceived as a way of securing one's future, for as long as no one else could do your job, you remained critical and relevant to the company. There is therefore a need to relate properly and gain the confidence of the more experienced people before they can share their knowledge and skills with you. Such confidence has the effect of assuring them that they are important to the enterprise, even if they are not the only ones with a given skill.

Further discussions at *Denhe re Ruzivo* highlighted the fact raised earlier, that some people lacked a skill they should have because the method used to transfer that skill did not accord the learners enough practice for them to gain confidence in executing the skill. At the time of carrying out this research the company was installing a concrete tile machine, and the Italian supplier had sent some engineers to install the plant and train local employees on how to operate the machine. Members of *Denhe re Ruzivo* used this example to illustrate that people were learning fast because the Italians were demonstrating things and allowing the employees a lot of practice until they had confidence in what they were doing. They pointed out that this did not always happen in such a way when fellow employees were transferring knowledge and skills to one another.

Another indigenous lesson brought to the discussion was, "It takes a village to raise a child". The question was, how do we apply this to the workplace situation? Comments were to the effect that, while traditionally it was expected that the elders would admonish a younger person caught doing something wrong, this did not happen at the workplace. It was agreed that, such an approach would result in some kind of "peer review" system where older peers would correct younger ones where necessary, and that this might have the effect of reducing the number of formal disciplinary hearings. It was also suggested that in leadership positions and at work stations, it would be useful if older employees were paired with younger ones, both for the purposes of passing on knowledge from one generation to the other, as well as to inculcate the right attitudes and culture at the workplace. In other words, a coaching and mentoring system would be introduced to address this situation.

"We do not expose our armpits"

A visit to the CI group was carried out by Professors Lessem and Schieffer, the field supervisors (Chidhara and Kada) as well as my PhD co-researchers (Chinyuku and Matupire). I was expecting the members of the CI group to talk about all the things that they had discussed in past meetings, such as the younger workers being lazy and not willing to learn new skills, the managers being over-bearing with regard to the production process, among other things. To my surprise, they started talking about how Turnall is their home, how they were happy with Management, and how Management would assist them whenever necessary. One of the field supervisors immediately understood what was happening. In the African culture you do not air your dirty linen in public ("*Haufukure hapwa*" – you do not expose your armpits). Therefore, the armpits would not be exposed in the presence of these "strangers". This was very informative with regard to the use of outside people, such as consultants. The question that begs to be asked is, how accurate is the information given to consultants? Time will tell. However, some issues began to surface, such as that it is not African to call one another on a first name basis, particularly when it comes to elderly women. It is a sign of disrespect, they insisted.

The major lesson for me then was, for one to fully benefit from research in a co-operative inquiry setting, some level of cultural appreciation is helpful, or at least a willingness to try and understand things from a cultural perspective.

Expectations of the workforce in terms of the outcomes of the CI

In the course of the CI group, the core members of the research group would, without consultation, co-opt briefly a colleague into the CI group. Whenever this happened, I observed that it was because the members of the core group felt that such a person had something useful to contribute. I tacitly let this happen. What it showed me was that the members felt that this was their group, and they were in control of the activities of the group. They did not need permission to invite a colleague to a meeting. I saw this as something positive.

In addition to this, the fact that the CI meetings happened right inside the factory, in full view of all employees gave the whole exercise some transparency, making the entire workforce comfortable with the research. There did not appear to be any suspicions about what was happening. It was clearly understood in the factory that the CI group was carrying out research for a degree program that I was doing. They openly talked about this aspect, and declared that they would do all that was necessary to make sure that I achieve top grades in my studies. It was also appreciated that practical, transformational outcomes of this research were expected, and would be implemented to improve the way we do things in the factory and in the company as a whole. For this reason, the floodgates of information were opened. People were very eager to share information about themselves as well as past events in the company, hoping that this would help clarify issues and pave the way for positive outcomes of the research.

As this research happened at a time the company was experiencing some difficulties as a consequence of the economic dynamics in the country, it was evident that co-researchers and those outside the centre of the research were expecting some wonderful things to happen in this research, and hoping that the research would make a difference to the problems being encountered.

Bringing our African-ness into the exogenous workplace

We kept pushing the issue of how we can bring our African-ness into the workplace. It was amazing that, when we kept asking this question, the issue of spirituality was raised, and on pushing further, co-researchers came up with the point that we need to pray for the company. This came as a surprise to me. I was expecting them to come up with traditional forms of spirituality, but they came up with prayers from a Christian perspective. This further buttressed the concept of the merge of indigenous and exogenous rhythms, this time from a spiritual perspective.

Some spiritual revelations

In 2009 the chrysotile asbestos mines in Zimbabwe became incapacitated to provide fibre for the Turnall manufacturing process. This became a serious nightmare for Management. Many meetings were held on the issue of viable options for the procurement of chrysotile fibre. The company was at the same time experiencing serious cash-flow challenges, and prospective suppliers were demanding cash for their fibre. By some coincidence Management managed to convince one supplier to send fibre from Russia and Brazil without an upfront payment. This was a true life- saving situation for the company, and we were all very pleased that we had managed to negotiate this deal.

Unbeknown to Management, there was a group of workers that was meeting every evening at 5:00 pm to pray for the fibre situation. When Management reported a break-through in the fibre situation, this group of workers felt that their prayers had been answered. I only got to know about this when, in one of the *Denhe re Ruzivo* meetings we asked co-researchers what we could be doing, from an indigenous perspective, that we were not doing, and they said "pray". They believe that the solution to the company's fibre challenge was a result of their prayers. When I shared this information with my colleagues in the Management Team, they were equally surprised and touched that these employees had taken the initiative to pray for our situation, and embarrassed that we never knew about this. This pointed to the fact that we had not stayed close enough to our employees. We had not really gone out of our way to communicate with them the extent of the challenges faced by the company, nor had we given them the opportunity to communicate to us what they thought would be solutions to these problems.

The co-researchers went further to request that we start and end the *Denhe re Ruzivo* meetings with a prayer so that God can reveal His wisdoms to us.

They went further to request that we commit the new concrete tile machine that was about to be commissioned to God through prayer. On sharing this with the Management Committee, the suggestion was taken on board. There has generally been an enthusiasm from management to share the outcomes of *Denhe re Ruzivo* meetings and tap into such.

It has been said that African people are very spiritual. However, my colleagues in Management and myself had underestimated how much the Christian faith had permeated the African people in Zimbabwe, if the Turnall employees are to be used as a sample. What became apparent here was an indigenous rhythm represented by African people that has merged with an exogenous religion. The issue to note is that the workplace should take cognizance of the spirituality of the African workforce so that there is no disconnect between the workers and the leadership. Instead, Management should seek to accommodate the spirituality of the workforce, consequently accommodating one another. There should in fact be opportunities for communalism, where Management becomes part of any spiritually motivated rituals, such as participating in the ceremony to spiritually dedicate the concrete tile machine at Turnall. In this instance, Management committed to participate in this, therefore bringing harmony to the situation. While Management pursues their own solutions for challenges that may arise, such as the fibre situation at Turnall, it pays to acknowledge and encourage the solutions brought on board by the workers, such as praying for the fibre situation. This way, the impression given is that a multi-pronged approach to the problem is being pursued, and this fosters a sense of togetherness in the greater team.

I also observed that there was a tendency in the Management Committee meetings to be more open about spiritual issues, with people quoting the bible to illustrate a particular point. Management at Turnall, like in most Zimbabwean companies at the time of writing this, consists of predominately African people. What this has shown is that even the so-called senior employees are deep down just African people dying to bring out their spirituality.

At Turnall we in fact only had one white man who had been with the company for over forty years. We jokingly nicknamed him *Chipembere* (rhinoceros), implying that he was an endangered species. Chris Whyte would openly state that he is not spiritual at all.

Presentational knowing

An explanation was given on presentational knowing (Heron, 1996), followed by a discussion on how this could be executed. The co-researchers came up with many ideas, including *majakwara* (group work, where an entire village work together to kill a task), story-telling, poetry, art, music, fables about how people live and work together, and skits about knowledge creation and management at the work place. They were encouraged to come up with specific presentational knowing activities, which would be practically presented in a subsequent CI meeting.

In addition to this, the co-researchers also came up with ideas about improving the way the company recognises outstanding performance in the field of knowledge as well as in other areas. First of all, they felt that there should be a difference in the way feedback is given about outstanding performers. It was intimated that there could be a problem with supervisors who created a barrier here, because they claimed the good performance of their sub-ordinates as their own. It was therefore critical to involve the workers themselves in identifying outstanding performers. Co-researchers felt that a change in this area would motivate workers to become more productive as well as to share their knowledge and skills more with others, if this was made one of the parameters for identifying exceptional performers. I made a mental note of this as an issue to be pursued and implemented, parallel to the research.

As part of "Presentational Knowing" some members of *Denhe re Ruzivo* came up with a little play. The introduction song was "*Tsanga yangu yawa: hutetena*", which broadly means that we eat what we produce. The essence of the play was a discussion on the political situation, and what bearing it could have on Turnall as a company and the employment situation of its employees. This was an indicator of what constituted the fears of employees. The discussion, purportedly by the management team, was specifically about the then president's (Robert Mugabe) threat to pull out of the Southern African Development Community (SADC). In the discussion, they saw the consequences of this including the closure of our borders, resulting in the company's failure to bring in imported fibre. It was therefore necessary to purchase and commission a concrete tile machine, which would only need local raw materials. In the discussion it became clear that the important issue at the time was not high wages, but to keep the company open and people employed. After the play the entire *Denhe re Ruzivo* carried out an analysis of the play and its implications, and it became very clear that employees were afraid of losing their jobs due to the continued decline of the economy. They saw around them many companies that had closed, and this worried them. They saw poor performance of the machines resulting from poor fibre quality, and a management team that did not consult them as to what the possible cause of this could be. Knowledge sharing was therefore not implemented when it was most necessary, and this concerned them.

Another play was carried out about the poor quality that was experienced in production at a given time. Although the reason for this poor quality was identified as poor-quality fibre, it was acknowledged that there was also a significant element of poor knowledge of processes emanating from poor problem diagnostics. The message was, we cannot expend our knowledge to throw away product, by implication throwing away money. The essence of the message was the importance of relationships and consultation in the production process. It extended to relationships in the whole knowledge sharing arena, as well as the criticality of practice when new skills were learnt in order to ensure that the said skills were internalised.

This was shared with the relevant members of the management committee, who promised to change the ways of doing things to incorporate the highlighted shortcomings. It was agreed that where a machine breakdown or poor machine performance occurred, particularly when it was not clear what the problem could be, a *dare* (short meeting) would be held between the managers, foremen and operators to brainstorm. There was need in such situations to accentuate the relational aspect and allow everyone to participate in the problem-solving process. In other words, the rhythm between the workers and their supervisors needed to be enhanced.

In my *de facto* CI group (Management Committee) there was a presentational knowing situation in one of the meetings. The Managing Director bemoaned poor levels of profitability, emanating from low production levels resulting from disruptions caused by machine breakdowns and poor planning. This is how he dramatised this situation:

> Imagine you are in an aeroplane travelling to Europe. While in mid-air, someone shouts that the plane has had a breakdown. Then the pilot turns to the Procurement Manager and asks whether he remembered to order the spares required to fix the plane. The Procurement Manager says he asked the Finance Manager to pay for the spares, but he had other priorities.
>
> The engineer then comes up with a daily schedule of breakdowns and time lost by the plane through breakdowns.

Everyone was smiling sheepishly, because they realised that the approach used to manage machines at Turnall would not work for an aeroplane, as lives would be lost if people were so casual about looking after the aeroplane.

His very strong message was that we seem to have given control over to the machine, instead of us being the ones in control. He emphasised that we were entrenching incompetence in the team in the way we were managing. The question then remains, what is it that we can do to change this? The presentational approach he used left the team in a very clear mind as to what needed to happen.

On looking closely at this, there was alignment between what the Managing Director was saying, and the sentiments of *Denhe re Ruzivo,* whose sentiments were that we could be in better control if we worked together more closely to deal with machines and other challenges.

In *Pundutso* we shared stories about our experiences in the work situation. Josh shared his story about the cadetship program. Passmore shared a story about a manager in his stable who had to be relieved of his duties because of a dishonest act. The issue was that the manager had failed to live up to one of the company's values, *integrity*. The reasons for relieving him of his duties was that he was setting the wrong example to those he led, bringing in the old adage of "do as I say, not as I do". The message was that if a leadership team comes up with values, they should hold themselves accountable to such.

I shared a story of how I had to befriend a white man perceived by other workers to be very racist when I worked for Anglo American, because I needed to learn the systems from him. As a result of the relationship I took the trouble to establish, he shared all the necessary information with me. In addition, I discovered that deep down he was just another insecure human being seeking to remain relevant to the organisation. The friendship lasted way beyond me learning the job, and we continued to support each other through any difficult times that we went through.

The power of enhanced communication

The work carried out in the CI group so far has highlighted the importance of communication. When the CI group started explaining things from their perspective, such as the fibre challenge in 2009, it became apparent to Management that there was a communication gap. This was made worse when the group asked when the concrete tile machine that was being installed would be commissioned. Somehow in the hustle and bustle of installing the concrete tile machine, Management had omitted to pay attention to the soft issues of how to bring the rest of the workers on board in this new project that was viewed to have a life changing potential for the business and its people. The CI group requested that the ordinary worker be involved in the commissioning, and further requested that a man (or woman) of the cloth be invited to pray before the machine started effective production. The CI group also highlighted the importance of communicating a date for the official launch of the concrete tile machine, even if the date would be changed for whatever reason. The CI group were beginning to communicate very clearly Management's communication gaps, and gently suggesting ways to bridge these gaps. The clear message was that the workers are part of the deal, and to please not leave them behind.

What was heart-warming was that these suggestions were not being made as criticisms, but merely as areas that needed improving. The CI group in a way became the mouthpiece of the workers, and Management's conscience. It was most interesting to note that Management began to listen to this voice and to take action on the issues raised. For example, the Managing Director felt that it was necessary for him to address all employees, in manageable groups, in order to give an update on the state of the company, and to also give an opportunity to all employees to share their views on the things that the company needed to do to deal with the challenges that were obtaining in the business. He felt that this move was necessary as a message that we are one family that needed to face our challenges together, and also to send the message that the opinions of all employees were valued by Management. Most important of all, he genuinely wanted to know what the employees were thinking and feeling about the business that was sustaining all our livelihoods.

The challenge addressed to the CI group was:

> *How do we involve other employees to share useful ideas about incorporating useful traditional practices into improving the way we do things in the business?*

The message was that, in as much as Management had a role to play, the workers also needed to mobilise one another so that ideas are shared. The communication gap needed to be bridged even between worker and worker so that what the CI group eventually came up with was representative of the entire body of the business. Therefore, the homework of all members of the CI group was to engage their various constituencies, so to speak, sharing ideas and gleaning from others what wisdoms can be useful in moving the business forward by doing things differently in the area of knowledge creation.

Some indigenous wisdoms

This report would not be complete if I did not share some of the "indigenous wisdoms" that came up during the *dare* (meetings) of the *Denhe re Ruzivo* CI group, for these wisdoms may have a bearing on how we need to do things in the future.

The richness of the Shona language became apparent in these meetings. On asking why some employees were more self-motivated than others, someone said, "*Simba regavi rinobva kuma svuuriro*" (the strength of the rope depends on the bark from which the rope originated). This has implications on digging into the home background of people on recruitment, for this background is likely to have a bearing on the kind of worker that a person becomes.

On the issue of working hard to get the correct results, someone said, "*Simba mukaka, rinosinira*" (energy, like milk, is regenerated on a continuous basis). This has a bearing on motivating employees to rise to the occasion when the situation demands real muscle hard work. There are situations when a machine breakdown results in people working round the clock to solve a particular problem, and such motivation becomes necessary.

On planning and carrying out certain tasks that do not bear immediate visible results, someone came up with the expression, "*Chisi hachiere musi wacharimwa*", which basically means the same as "Take two aspirin and wait".

The CI group also encouraged candor in communication with one another. Here someone put it this way, "*Huroyi, ukahunyara, kana hwaambuya hunouraya*". The literal translation of this is that, if you see your mother-in-law poisoning your food, do not eat the poisoned food out of politeness, for it will kill you. This means that, unless we are frank and candid with one another, we will put up with practices that are harmful to the business that we are trying to build.

Perhaps the most fascinating of these expressions for me was, "*Zizi harina nyanga, makushe*". Literally this means that an owl does not have any horns, but just horn looking feathers. The interpretation is that we must not be intimidated by complex looking machinery or other seemingly difficult tasks at the workplace. These are doable if one focuses one's mind. While I was familiar with this expression since I was a child, I always took its meaning literally. Its metaphorical implications were lost to me until this was raised in the CI meeting. Again, this is a useful one for encouraging people who may feel that they cannot do certain things.

For me this was like re-visiting the village, for I grew up with these wisdoms, but somehow, living in a mostly exogenous world, these had been pushed into the periphery. Hearing these sayings was like meeting an old relative after many years of separation. To me, it became very important to internalise these expressions which would make sense when communicating with my fellow indigenous employees about work issues, in my role as Human Resources Director, where I may need to encourage, motivate or indeed admonish. It also became important for me to build on this vocabulary and develop the habit of using it so that it comes naturally. Communicating with employees at this level would remove many barriers and enhance objective interaction.

Many irons in the fire

A number of things have been achieved since the CI group commenced its activities. Perhaps the first one was to encourage line management to consult the people on the ground first before changing any parameters in the manufacturing process, and indeed when dealing with other challenges encountered at the workplace. Members of *Denhe re Ruzivo* kept hammering the importance of relationships in an African setting, even a work related one. Second, we had as a CI group revisited the African ways of interacting at the workplace, including the mentoring of younger people instead of just watching them go astray. To this end the company explored the introduction of a peer coaching and mentoring program. Third, the issue of spirituality at the workplace was tabled, and embraced. The Christian prayer is likely to be a permanent feature at work. Fourth, it is important to give people the opportunity to practice a newly acquired skill or knowledge to help with internalisation. Finally, Management was alerted to the gaps in communication, which gaps they then worked towards addressing.

Apart from these issues, the CI group was cognizant of the fact that the target was a much bigger, much more transformative innovation. It also became clear that the issue of relationships was critical in knowledge transfer and creation, and that practice, or doing is what helps people to internalise new knowledge and skills.

Conclusion

There is no doubt that the starting of the *Denhe re Ruzivo* CI group at Turnall raised consciousness at different levels. The CI members became comfortable in their own skin. We all felt free to discuss any issues that came to the table, cognizant of the fact that there are no right or wrong answers. We listened to one another, and felt motivated and excited at the end of each session because we would have discovered new things about one another, about the company and about the African world view. Useful information became available about what was happening in the company (such as workers praying for the fibre situation). We continued to share our hopes and aspirations as individuals and as Turnall employees, and committed ourselves to contribute by coming up with a life changing innovation. We introduced those things that we felt could be introduced, with Management's blessing. As we continued this research journey, there was energetic anticipation of what lay ahead, what it is we will discover and contribute to Turnall. Whatever happens, the bonds have been developed, communication networks established and useful relationships built. This can only benefit the organisation that employees and managers depend on so much for their livelihoods.

At another level, *Pundutso* was instrumental in reinforcing and illuminating some of the concepts and issues that have been raised at *Denhe re Ruzivo*. As we continued in our various researches, *Pundutso* remained a platform where any new concepts and theories that emerged were tried out and verified.

The Management Committee was useful for endorsing the issues that *Denhe re Ruzivo* raised and proposed for implementation, though some members of this committee may have started off feeling sceptical about the group and what they were coming up with. This was in fact an informal extension of *Denhe re Ruzivo,* but the separation was useful in enabling freedom of speech and emancipation in the members of *Denhe re Ruzivo*.

Two critical aspects for successful knowledge creation and transfer emerged. The first one was building relationships first to enable the knowledge transfer process to occur smoothly. The second was to have the opportunity to personally have a practical experience of the knowledge or skill before claiming to have internalised it.

In the next chapter, I will address propositional and practical knowing.

References

Heron, J (1996). *Co-operative Inquiry: Research into the Human Condition.* London: Sage.

Kolb, D. A. (1984). *Experiential Learning.* Englewood Cliffs, NJ: Prentice Hall.

Lessem, R. & Schieffer, A. (2009). *Transformation Management: Towards the Integral Enterprise.* Farnham, England: Gower.

Lessem, R. & Schieffer, A. (2010). *Integral Research and Innovation: Transforming Enterprise and Society.* Farnham, England: Gower.

Mamukwa, E. S., Lessem, R. & Schieffer, A. (2014). *Integral Green Zimbabwe: An African Phoenix Rising.* Farnham, England: Gower.

McIntyre, A. (2008). *Participatory Action Research.* London Sage.

Reason, P. (1988). *Human Inquiry in Action.* London: Sage.

Reason, P. (1994). *Participation in Human Inquiry.* London: Sage.

Reason, P. & Bradbury, H. (2008). *The Sage Handbook of Action Research, Participative Inquiry and Practice.* Los Angeles: Sage.

Reason, P. & Bradbury, H. (2011). *The Sage Handbook of Action Research: Participative Inquiry and Practice.* London: Sage.

Part VI

Contribution

Overview and outcomes of the research

11 The calabash of knowledge creation (Denhe re Ruzivo)

Introduction

In this chapter I will move on to the propositional and practical forms of knowing, having addressed the experiential and presentational forms of knowing in the previous chapter.

It is important that I highlight some of the more critical issues that were raised at *Denhe re Ruzivo* and *Pundutso* pertaining to the way people work and learn. The lessons learnt were many. There were many things that were brought up, accepted as gaps and implemented. Here I will only address the major ones.

I discovered through *Denhe re Ruzivo* that there were many innovations that went unrecognised, particularly on the machines. It became clear that individuals wanted recognition for the improvements they brought to the machines and in other areas. Such recognition would have the effect of improving and increasing innovations at the workplace.

Leadership gaps were identified, where some leadership styles suppressed creativity and innovation. There were perceptions amongst some members of *Denhe re Ruzivo* that some supervisors claimed the innovations of those they led as their own. It was clear that there was need to clarify the measures of different levels of employees at the workplace. For example, if a manager tries to claim the innovation of a welder, then there is something very wrong. Supervisors and managers needed to understand that their success was measured by how successful they were in getting results through people. Therefore, if employees in their departments or sections became innovative, this should be a feather in their cap.

The issue of spirituality, I discovered, is very important where African people are gathered together, be it at work or in the village. It is therefore critical to acknowledge such spirituality at the workplace. These are things that do not cost the companies anything, and yet have an immense impact on productivity and creativity at the workplace. When employees feel that their spirituality is accepted, they become more comfortable in their work environment, and feel that they are more in control of their situation, even in an exogenous work environment. Spirituality is part of the make-up of the African people.

This was further accentuated in my mind when my father died as I was in the middle of writing this chapter. Although our parents raised us in the Methodist Church, they somehow drifted off to a more Pentecostal church later in their lives. Now at my father's funeral there was potential conflict as to which church would preside over the funeral. We negotiated for a position where the Methodist Church would be in charge while we were still in Harare, and the Pentecostal Church would take over when we went to the village. When the Pentecostal Church took the floor, amazing things happened. Although it was basically a Christian ceremony, the way of praise and worship was purely African. People were free to express themselves. The singing was louder and more spontaneous, and the rhythm and movement natural and explosive. It took my mind back to our own employees and the way they insisted on praying. The praying, though fundamentally Christian, is done in an environment and format of the African rhythm, bringing some kind of freedom of expression to the whole situation.

In as much as there are variations in the Zimbabwean Christian worship, so too in the calabash of knowledge, therefore there will by extension be the interaction of different types of knowledge; the exogenous, the hybrid and the indigenous. Even the indigenous will have different variations, depending on whether one's background is Zezuru, Karanga, Manyika or Ndebele; or Kenya, Nigeria, Ethiopia or Mozambique. The creation of knowledge then has to take cognizance of all these dynamics. The calabash will however broadly speak to the African knowledge creator.

On the issue of organisational learning, the issues of relationships and testing (including practice) emerged, and these will be addressed in more details below.

Propositional knowing

The merits of Denhe re Ruzivo

Denhe re Ruzivo became a very interesting platform for information gathering about what really goes on in the company, and what possible solutions could be put on the table. What was unique about this platform was that it was a mixed group in terms of rank, levels of literacy and areas of specialisation. What was highlighted by the group was that, because we were not negotiating for anything, such as the Workers' Committee or Works Council, there was no boxing gloves approach. Individuals were simply sharing their perspectives about what maybe going wrong in the company, and how this may be rectified. Individuals were also free to share the good things that were happening in the company, and discuss ways of making such fractal. The fact that this was working in *Denhe re Ruzivo* means that with these other organs it was possible to completely take the boxing gloves off and pursue the meeting of the minds rather than a win-lose situation. However, this could only happen when the leadership became more people-centric, removing the need in people of fighting for their rights at work.

The fact that there was no rigid agenda and everyone present was encouraged to share something was seen as a recipe for success.

One proposition was that every company needed a *Denhe re Ruzivo* (whatever they chose to call it) to highlight otherwise hidden information and act as a think tank for the organisation.

Denhe re Ruzivo was a significant instrument in that it brought together all levels of the human capital as equals, ready to listen to one another and ready to share. Everyone was willing to share their vulnerability, and who they really are. The agenda was to share who you are, what your strengths and weaknesses are, what you have contributed to the business (and where you have made errors) and your views on what the team needs to do to make the business better. The sharing also covered the good things and as well as the mistakes that have been made by others not necessarily part of the group, and how these can be used as positive learning examples to take the business forward.

For Turnall the proposition was that after the research was complete, *Denhe re Ruzivo* should continue meeting, perhaps on a monthly basis, or at a timing to be agreed upon by the participants. The proposal was that the members should rotate every six months to give more people an opportunity to participate and also share their experiences and their thoughts about knowledge creation in the organisation. The focus of *Denhe re Ruzivo* would be on knowledge creation, sharing and innovation issues only as there were other platforms for other issues. The intention was to continue harvesting and sharing knowledge as well as coming up with innovations that would improve the way we do things at work. *Denhe re Ruzivo* would also propose issues of recognition for successful innovations.

One specific proposal was that going forward there should be a deliberate effort to have a balance of old and young in the grouping to ensure that the younger people also shared their ideas and also became responsible for knowledge creation at the workplace.

How knowledge is transferred at the workplace

The research journey was illuminating with regard to issues pertaining to knowledge creation in the company. With 50% of the company consisting of semi-literate members, it was fascinating to see how they learnt the skills that they possessed. One shared how the machines were operated by some Malawian gentlemen who were very withdrawn from the rest of the workforce. The first step for this individual was to befriend a particular Malawian machine operator then offered to be taught how to operate the machine so that he could relieve the operator at tea break and other such times. When this individual could do the task, the Malawian operator would leave him to tend the machine while he went to look for tobacco at nearby shops. Another shared how a particular operator would fall asleep during the night shift. He would ask his colleagues to watch out for the foreman and wake him quickly when the foreman moved towards him. The others refused, insisting that he should stay awake or meet the wrath of the foreman, but one person agreed. They became friends, and the operator offered to teach his new friend how to drive a forklift, a job he still did at the time of carrying out the research. Yet another shared how he worked with a very ill-tempered white boiler maker who would kick his backside if he failed to follow instructions. While fellow employees in the department refused to work with this "maniac", this particular employee persistently worked with him and put up with the abuse. They developed a love-hate relationship, and this employee was taught how to weld. At the time of carrying out this research he was the best welder in the factory.

There were many other similar stories.

Talking to my friends at *Pundutso* we shared how over the years we had advised Cadets and Graduate Trainees that they needed to develop relationships with the old fellows in the factory if they were to be taught some of the tacit knowledge resident in these older people. Clearly, it was evident that those university graduates who came into the system and could relate to and show respect for the more experienced, semi-literate employees would learn the jobs faster than those who had a more snobbish approach and failed to relate. This became a critical observation.

Nonaka and Takeuchi's knowledge creation spiral

Nonaka and Takeuchi's SECI model highlights the format through which knowledge is transferred from person to person. This model was explained to and shared with the members of *Denhe re Ruzivo* as well as *Pundutso* (at different times of course).

Nonaka and Takeuchi (1995) define four stages in Knowledge creation, namely socialisation, externalisation, combination and internalisation. During socialisation individuals share experiences, and knowledge transfer begins through observation, imitation, brainstorming and asking questions to seek clarification in order to understand and appreciate further. For socialisation to happen effectively there has to be unity of purpose. One person must be willing to share specific knowledge or skills, and another must be willing to learn. Socialisation therefore can only happen when there is acknowledgement on both parties that there is one person who has knowledge worth learning, and another person worth sharing the knowledge or skill with. This then implies that there should be a deeper understanding and appreciation of one another as teacher and learner, and there should be high levels of dialogue.

This debate was carried out very actively in *Denhe re Ruzivo*, with some members arguing that they may be instructed to share a knowledge and skill, but unless the target of such knowledge or skills transfer is willing to learn, such transfer cannot happen. It is very much a case of taking the horse to the river but failing to make it drink unless the proverbial horse is thirsty enough to do so. Others shared the view that these highly schooled young people coming out of universities thought they knew it all and failed to appreciate that they could learn something from the semi-literate people on the line. This is why sometimes we find ourselves in a skills crisis because the "learned" people have failed to learn the simple skills necessary to keep the factories going. However, members highlighted that those with the correct attitudes and disposition towards learning always benefit from such knowledge sharing.

Members also raised the issue of relationships, and contended that it is easier to transfer knowledge to a person with whom one shared a positive relationship. It was agreed after a lot of discussion that yes, knowledge can be shared where there was no relationship, but such transfer was likely to be less effective than where a positive relationship existed. The willingness to share on the part of the transferor might be limited. Therefore, the members suggested, relationship building *(kuvaka hukama)* was a critical pre-requisite for successful and effective knowledge and skills transfer.

Externalisation as a stage of knowledge and skills transfer was then explained to both *Denhe re Ruzivo* and *Pundutso*. It was highlighted that in this stage, it was necessary to commit to writing what has been taught and what has been understood. It was also highlighted by the members of *Denhe re Ruzivo* that, for those who did not have high levels of literacy, metaphors were a good way to remember the stages in learning the skills. It was generally agreed though that, even where the recipient of such knowledge transfer was not very literate, there needed to be a system in the organisation to record the knowledge for posterity. Dialogue levels in this stage needed to remain high to ensure that what was recorded was in fact accurate. In addition, the use of metaphors was very useful to individual learners. Such metaphors would help to relate the new knowledge to things that are ordinary and general so that individual learners can make sense of them in terms of their life worlds.

At the third stage, combination, it was explained that learners are combining various types of explicit knowledge, that is, the knowledge that has just been made explicit through socialisation and externalisation and knowledge that people might already have, as well as knowledge that people may find in the process of dealing with the knowledge at hand to personalise it. Other sources of knowledge, such as the internet and other literature may come in useful here in an attempt to make the newly acquired explicit knowledge relevant to the environment and to self. At this stage it is possible to even modify the original knowledge and skills shared and come up with something more appropriate, using one's knowledge and exposure as well as using the contributions of the sharer. However, at this stage things may still be at an experimental stage, requiring a lot of practice.

According to Nonaka and Takeuchi, the next stage would be internalisation. The learner therefore internalises the knowledge and makes it tacit, waiting hopefully for someone to socialise this knowledge with so that the process begins again. This is what makes it a spiral because the system allows the process to replicate itself over and over again, with the same players in different roles together with new players in the roles of the recipients of knowledge and skills transfer.

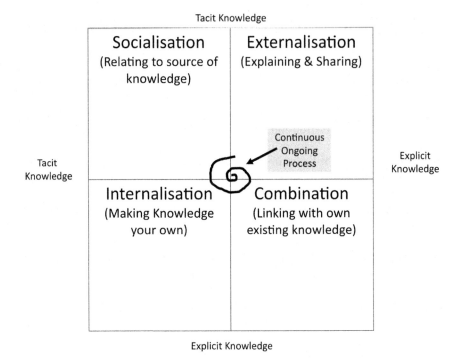

Figure 11.1 Nonaka and Takeuchi's Spiral of Knowledge.
Source: Adaptation and Design: Elizabeth Mamukwa (2019).

Generally, members of the two CI groups were convinced that this model is very relevant to knowledge transfer as well as the creation of new knowledge, where the existing knowledge was used as an anchor for the new knowledge.

What is missing in this model?

Discussions were held as to what we would change in Nonaka and Takeuchi's model to improve it and make it more relevant to us. Two critical issues were identified as missing.

a. Relationship building

Following the vivid discussions that were carried out on the issue of relationship building, *Denhe re Ruzivo* suggested that there could be no way that effective knowledge transfer can effectively happen without relationships. They added that management had a tendency to think in terms of how many people had been exposed to a certain skill without looking deeper to see whether the exposure has been effective or not. They emphasised that the important measure is not the number of employees exposed, but the number of employees who effectively received accurate exposure and information from the transferors of knowledge. This can only happen if the relationships are right.

Von Krogh (Nonaka & Nishiguchi, 2001) touches on this but in a different way, when he identifies a distinction between high care and low care as factors that impact knowledge development. He contends that high care characterises relationships where there is greater propensity to help, high accessibility of individuals, an extensive attentive inquiry, and high lenience. According to Von Krogh, care is a shared value among organisational members. Low care therefore characterises relationships where there is a low propensity for help. Organisational members do not make themselves accessible to one another, attentive inquiry is limited, and members exhibit impatience and lack of leniency towards others. The message that is coming from *Denhe re Ruzivo*, by implication, is that building a positive relationship will automatically result in a high care situation, where bearers of knowledge will develop a greater propensity to help, making themselves available to the recipients of such knowledge. They automatically will develop high levels of attentive inquiry and high lenience.

b. Testing, practice and reflection

The one thing that members of *Denhe re Ruzivo* felt had been completely ignored by Nonaka and Takeuchi was the importance of testing new knowledge and practice in the creation of new knowledge. They felt so strongly about it that they said any amount of knowledge and skills transfer would not be effective unless individual learners were deliberately given the opportunity to try out the skills in practice, and not only once but many times. In addition, to accept new knowledge as a real phenomenon, such knowledge should be tested and confirmed as real through testing, practice and reflection, giving the creators of such knowledge an opportunity to establish its authenticity before sharing it with others. This, they argued, is what promotes internalisation in transferring old knowledge and establishing new knowledge. By trying out the skill several times, they urged, individuals would have the opportunity to correct themselves until they became proficient, leading to a situation where they may even find better ways of carrying out the skills, leading to the creation of new knowledge. Without this practice, they said, people would remain half-baked with regard to skills acquisition and development. This is what contributes to crisis situations such as the one Turnall (and other organisations) had during the hyper-inflationary era. Management was confident that many employees were exposed to certain skills, until one person left and they discovered that the people left behind could not do what this person was doing, even though the other employees were working "closely" with this person. The reason was that these people did not take the trouble to practice what they thought they had learnt and move such knowledge to a level of ownership that made the knowledge their own.

Denhe re Ruzivo therefore came up with the proposition of an expanded knowledge creation spiral.

The calabash of knowledge (for knowledge creation)

First of all, I will dwell on the metaphorical calabash, what it is and why I chose this analogy.

The calabash was among one of the first plants to be cultivated in the world. Although it is edible, it was not cultivated for its culinary qualities but rather for its use as a container, a musical instrument, a bottle or a pipe. In Africa the big calabash is used mostly as a container for water, beer or other non-alcoholic drinks such as *maheu* (an opaque drink made out of fermented maize meal). The smaller size is used as a drinking cup (*mukombe*), and for sharing drink and water. Medium sizes can be used as food containers. The calabash can also be used as a musical instrument (*hosho*) to bring rhythmic harmony to any situation.

Sometimes the calabash is used as a holding container for beer and other fermented drinks so that such drinks can ferment further. It is the African belief that the calabash has natural qualities to enhance this fermentation and continue the brewing process, aided by the natural air which will have certain organisms that will help the process. In the end the taste of the drink or beer is influenced not only by the calabash, but also by the air surrounding the cala bash. This is the analogy that I am using. I see the metaphorical calabash as a "container" where knowledge is allowed to ferment and to develop into new and improved knowledge. The model that is proposed in this chapter centres up on the concept of the calabash.

The calabash of knowledge creation is three-dimensional, as opposed to the SECI model which appears to be two-dimensional. The calabash model therefore has significance in what goes into the calabash and what happens inside there as opposed to what we see on the surface.

What is missing in the SECI model?

It is the proposition of the CI group, *Denhe re Ruzivo* that the knowledge spiral would work better with two added aspects, namely, Relationships (central to the process) and Testing and Practice to test newly developed knowledge.

The way it would work is that relationship building would come first to "soften" the bearer of knowledge and make him want to share his knowledge with a specific person, developing a high care situation. In addition to this, relationships play a central role in the transfer of old knowledge and the development of new knowledge. Only after the development of a reasonable relationship would Socialisation bear maximum fruits. After the building of a relationship, the next three stages (Socialisation, Externalisation and Combination) would follow.

It is clear that we have all along been trying to transfer knowledge in low care situations. Teaching skills to other employees has been a "managerial instruction", and it has never mattered whether one wants to pass on the knowledge or not – that aspect has never before been put into consideration. Therefore, whether one has liked the knowledge recipient or not has never been a factor to consider. What therefore may have happened is that knowledge bearers have gone through the paces of transferring knowledge or skills, and have claimed to have carried out a successful exercise, whether or not the recipient has properly grasped the knowledge or skill. Relationship building will therefore enable the players to create a more conducive environment for knowledge transfer, where the bearer of knowledge will feel bound to genuinely transfer the knowledge to the recipient who will in turn feel free to probe, ask, and say when he needs better explanations. As a result of the high care environment created by the relationship, both parties are likely to do their utmost to share (bearer of knowledge) and receive (recipient).

On Testing and Practice, the learners of knowledge have not been challenged to develop new knowledge from the existing knowledge they are taught. This challenge is what will encourage innovation in this knowledge. The calabash of knowledge is therefore not only about knowledge transfer, but also about taking it further and developing new knowledge (Mamukwa, Lessem & Schieffer, 2014).

The result of this modification of the Nonaka and Takeuchi's SECI Model is as outlined in Figure 11.2.

The calabash of knowledge creation

The first phenomenon, and perhaps the most significant from an African perspective, is that relationships remain the core, the central part, of the knowledge creation process. Without relationships such a process may not be sustainable. Strong relationships therefore are relevant before, during and after the knowledge creation process. The relationships are grounded in ubuntu/unhu, steeped in a healthy environment of mutual love and respect. Combined with relationships is the knowledge spiral – a reminder that knowledge is not static but continues to evolve.

The top half of the calabash places emphasis on dialogue. Relationships are created through dialogue. Socialisation also involves high-level dialogue if it is to bear fruit. The learner needs to ask a lot of questions and seek clarity, while the transferor of knowledge needs to share some subtle aspects of the knowledge or skill which may not be very obvious. During externalisation, as the knowledge is recorded or written down there is also high-level dialogue as the recorders seek clarity and accuracy. More than this, during externalisation there is shared imagination, turning metaphor into analogy. The process of fermentation in the calabash begins to happen more seriously as the interaction between the "calabash" (the environment), the "beer" (existing knowledge) and the "air" (the environments, from the individual's background of existing knowledge to the business environment as well as other environmental factors that may come into play). For externalisation to happen effectively, the receiver of knowledge must have his own context of knowledge which he can relate what he is learning from the transmitter of knowledge. Furthermore, his own imagination must start working to link what he is learning with other things that can enrich the process.

From Externalisation to Combination the learner is now linking the new explicit knowledge with the existing, whether this exists in his own life-world

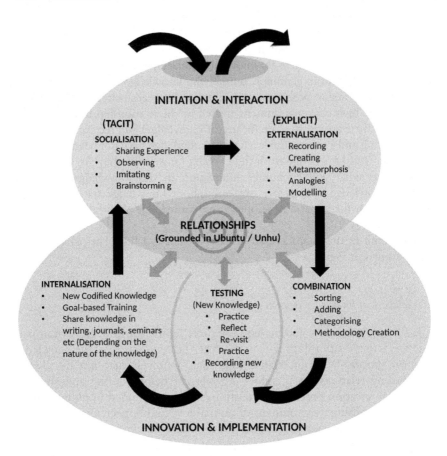

Figure 11.2 The *Calabash of Knowledge Creation: Denhe re Ruzivo.*
Source: Mamukwa, Lessem and Schieffer (2014).

or in other sources. During Combination he also sorts out the methodology for implementing the newly acquired knowledge.

The Testing and Practising stages are critical not only for internalising the newly acquired knowledge, but to challenge it in order to develop new knowledge. The issue is not just to learn from the bearer of knowledge, but to take further what has been learnt and use it as a springboard for new and more enhanced knowledge. The intention therefore, should never be just to learn from the bearers of knowledge, but to develop this knowledge further and come up with new knowledge.

We learn better if we practically apply what we learn, rather than leave it at a theoretical realm. The purpose of practising is also to give the learner practical experience on how to carry out the skill. At this stage she experiments and finds out what works and what does not work. She also has the opportunity to give and receive feedback about her practical experience on the particular knowledge or skill. She must continue to ask questions so that she understands fully why certain things have to be done a certain way (rationalisation). At this stage she can also come up with modifications to the way the particular process is carried out, giving space to the creation of something new, different from what was observed during the process of Socialisation. Where she has come up with new knowledge, she tests it over and over again, reflecting and revisiting to make sure that the new knowledge works. After repeatedly practising this skill or knowledge, she begins to specialise in it – she begins to understand it better than other people, including her original teacher, because the original process is likely to have been modified by this new stage. To a greater or lesser extent, new knowledge has been created, leveraged on the old knowledge learnt during Socialisation.

In Internalisation the learner now becomes the bearer of knowledge. She codifies the new knowledge and may even teach others. She then becomes a target for relationship building by those who may want to learn that new knowledge, skill, or process, and the cycle begins again.

The bottom half of the calabash therefore places emphasis on learning by doing.

The calabash has a very deliberate opening at the top, signifying that the knowledge creation process is not about monopolising knowledge. Knowledge must continue to come into the calabash, and to go out of it. New knowledge will come into the market, which knowledge must be shared in a company or institution. Knowledge must also go out of the calabash, and must be shared with greater society where there are opportunities for such to be improved further, for the greater benefit to all. This will give such knowledge credibility, and will promote the creation of new knowledge in the market. If Nonaka and Takeuchi had kept this knowledge to themselves, I would never have carried out this specific research. Knowledge can never be a closed society issue. Knowledge is constantly changing, therefore the more an enterprise is open to receiving new knowledge and sharing its own the more progressive the enterprise will become. The "opening" also allows the enterprise to throw out archaic knowledge and bring in new, so that it remains current. However, even if the old knowledge is thrown out, it remains a part of those who owned it, and will continue to influence the creation of new knowledge.

Metaphorically the calabash is a vehicle of rhythm and harmony. In knowledge creation and societal learning therefore, this is brought about by a continuous rhythm in the way knowledge is transferred through the five stages, at a continuous and consistent pace. Every day is a day of knowledge transfer and creation, a day of learning new things and passing on old knowledge to others.

Practical knowing

I now get to the final epistemology, Practical knowing. To me this stage is about putting into practice the model that the CI group had developed, asking other people to test it and sharing experiences on it. Should I have found that this model as I have defined it, does not work, then I would have had to go back to the drawing board and explore things further.

Testing the model at Turnall

At the time of developing this model Turnall commissioned a concrete tile machine as mentioned earlier. We came up with a new model of manpower utilisation, with the intention of maximising manpower and reducing manpower levels. The traditional Turnall system was that there were two types of workers in the factory. The first group of people are what was known as "production personnel". Their job was to operate the machines, manufacture the product and ensure that the quality of the product measured up to standard. In addition, they saw to it that the costs of production are contained to ensure productivity. Their task was not only to produce to the required levels, but to ensure that the product measures up to specific quality levels, that the machines were utilised to the targeted capacity level, and that waste levels were kept to a minimum level. These measures were designed to contain production costs and ensure profitability in the production process. On the other hand, there was an Engineering department, consisting of engineers and artisans, whose purpose was to make sure that the machines were available for the production process. Indeed, one of the measures was termed "machine availability".

Now the new Turnall model entailed that we use artisans to run the new concrete tile machine, instead of them simply waiting to fix the machine when it breaks down for any reason. The idea was that if the machine broke down, the same people simply stopped production to repair it, after which they would continue producing.

This seemed to work very well, until we noticed problems with quality. We observed that when quite a significant quantity of the product did not meet the required specifications, this did not deter our engineers turned production personnel from producing. They continued producing regardless of any quality issues. They were excited by their new role of engineers/production personnel, and thought as long as the machine was running, they were doing a good job.

This was a perfect opportunity to bring in the Calabash of Knowledge, particularly the Testing and Practice part. We found that there was need to send home some rationalisation issues. It was important to make our new producers understand the other important issues surrounding productivity, such as quality and lower costs of production. The issue of profitability needed to be emphasised, with reference to how high waste levels negatively impact such. In the Calabash of Knowledge this places emphasis on Testing and Practice, with particular reference to rationalisation, feedback, modification and specialisation. For this particular group of employees, success would be measured by not only how well they could produce in terms of quantity, but also by heightened awareness of quality and profitability issues as well as how they could come up with new improved ways of production. Their specialisation would therefore be broadened beyond simply fixing the machine, but addressing the whole process to cover machine repairs and maintenance and profitable production as well coming up with innovations to improve the process.

Technical Department was introduced to this model and encouraged to use it and give feedback. The members of *Denhe re Ruzivo* were equally encouraged to test this model and give feedback.

Therefore, as part of utilising the last epistemology, this Calabash of Knowledge would be used and critiqued at Turnall.

Testing the model at Astra Paints and at Art Corporation

In order to test the model in different environments, members of *Pundutso* were also given this model and encouraged to use it at both Astra Paints and Art Corporation. Feedback from these entities would also be taken into account with regard to giving credence to this model. My expectations were that depending on the results from these three companies, *Denhe re Ruzivo* would decide to throw the model out altogether, modify it, or accept it as it was.

Conclusion

Nonaka and Takeuchi's Knowledge Creation Spiral bears testimony to how knowledge is passed on from person to person. I may never have met these authors, but in my mind I built a very solid relationship with them (Nonaka in particular). I became very close to them through reading their books. My desire to learn from them was heightened as my respect for them increased every time I came into contact with them through literature.

Through their books I socialised with them. I learnt from them, asked questions and went back to the books for answers. I externalised by drawing their model, understanding it and articulating it in my own words. I also related the knowledge to my own life-world, and tried to make sense of the model in that realm.

During Combination I looked at other models and theories, such as Jaworski's U model (2011), Senge's Fifth Discipline(2006), Charan's "Know-How" (2007), Charan, Drotter and Noel's "Leadership Pipeline" (2001), to name a few. I then reflected on all these theories and models as well as on the Knowledge Creation Spiral specifically, and on other information gathered in the Education phase of my innovation, and information existing in my life-world and experiences. In my life-world, Nonaka's square model did not quite resonate with the African in me. I needed a more wholesome, three-dimensional perspective, and what better analogy than the calabash. I needed a fusion between indigenous and exogenous, and I believe in this model such fusion has been achieved.

This led me to this modified model, which I have come to through my own practical experience, as well as through sharing with *Denhe re Ruzivo, Pundutso* and the Turnall Management Committee. Feedback has been received from these groups, which feedback has resulted in the modification of the new model. In terms of the four epistemologies (Heron 1996), Practical Knowing continued to happen, during which stage there would be an opportunity to refine this model further and for the three CI groups to continue to specialise on it.

References

Charan, R. (2007). *Know-How: The 8 Skills That Separate People Who Perform and Those Who Don't.* New Year: Crown Business.

Charan, R., Drotter, S. & Noel, J (2001). *The Leadership Pipeline: How to build a Leadership Powered Company* (2nd Ed.). San Francisco: Jossey-Bass

Heron, J. (1996). *Co-operative Inquiry: Research into the Human Condition.* London: Sage.

Ichijo, K & Nonaka, I. (2007). *Knowledge Creation and Management: New Challenges for Managers.* New York: Oxford University Press.

Jaworski, J. (2011). *Source: The Inner Path of Knowledge Creation.* Los Angeles: Berret-Koehler Publishers.

Kolb, D. A. (1984). *Experiential Learning.* Englewood Cliffs, NJ: Prentice Hall.

Lessem, R. & Schieffer, A. (2009). *Transformation Management: Towards the Integral Enterprise.* Farnham, England: Gower.

Lessem, R. & Schieffer, A. (2010). *Integral Research and Innovation: Transforming Enterprise and Society.* Farnham, England: Gower.

Mamukwa, E. S., Lessem, R. & Schieffer, A. (2014). *Integral Green Zimbabwe: An African Phoenix Rising.* Farnham, England: Gower.

McIntyre, A. (2008). *Participatory Action Research.* London: Sage.

Nonaka, I. & Nishiguchi, T. (2001). Knowledge *Emergence: Social, Technical, and Evolutionary Dimensions of Knowledge Creation.* New York: Oxford University Press.

Nonaka, I. & Takeuchi, H. (1995). *The Knowledge Creating Company: How Japanese Companies Create the Dynamics of Innovation.* New York: Oxford University Press.

Reason, P. (1988). *Human Inquiry in Action.* London: Sage.

Reason, P. (1994). *Participation in Human Inquiry.* London: Sage.

Reason, P. & Bradbury, H. (2006). *The Sage Handbook of Action Research: Participative Inquiry and Practice* (2nd Ed.). London: Sage.

Senge, P. M. (2006). *Fifth Discipline: The Art and Practice of the Learning Organisation.* London: Random House.

12 The second calabash

Pundutso Centre for Integral Development

Introduction

As highlighted earlier, *Pundutso* (positive transformation) started off as an academic think-tank of three PhD students; Matupire, Chinyuku and Mamukwa (Mamukwa, Lessem & Schieffer, 2014). It was also a CI group for the research to innovation grouping of the three students. This chapter seeks to share the journey of this grouping and its subsequent development into a Trust, and further developments in this realm.

Pundutso's mission, vision and values

Pundutso's Vision is Societal Renewal and Development as well as Restoration of national pride within the Zimbabwean people. This should be achieved through their mission of inclusive and collaborative efforts, through Community Activation, Awakening Consciousness, Research, Transformative education/embodiment of knowledge. Pundutso intends to positively impact Zimbabwe.

Pundutso's values include personal integrity, open communication, authentic collaboration, respect for others, ethical interactions, humane caring and simplicity in all dealings.

What inspires Pundutso

Pundutso sees a gap in what all stakeholders do in Zimbabwe, where there is evident failure to embrace transformational opportunities through our people. There is limited innovativeness in the way problems are addressed. At the time of writing this book most cities in Zimbabwe were getting electricity for seven hours in the middle of the night. There did not appear to be any solution in site to resolve the power issue – in fact there was no evidence of effort. This takes away the notion that it is the rural folk that are marginalised. Zimbabweans are marginalised, wherever they are. As Pundutso then, the focus is on addressing such situations through research to innovation, regardless of location.

People's attitudes need to be influenced so that the expectation of solutions from government is minimised. There is need to encourage self-empowerment in people so that they come up with solutions in their little corners. Who knows, such solutions may then become explicit knowledge shared by many, possibly resulting in its improvement through a process of innovative development, to the benefit of many (Mamukwa, Lessem & Schieffer, 2014).

While at the time of writing this book Pundutso was focused on the improvement of rural life through Integral Kumusha (Lessem, Mawere, Matupire & Zongololo, 2019), there are equally impoverished and suffering urban communities. I see an opportunity for minimising the rural/urban divide by coming up with models that promote the closer association and working together of urban and rural communities.

Another area of capitalisation is the indigenous/exogenous blend where neither indigenous nor exogenous is best, but communities focus on the best of both worlds. While Pundutso seeks to preserve and enhance indigenous and exogenous knowledge systems through research with key stakeholders (Communities, the academia and business fraternity), focus is also placed on the quality of such knowledge as well as the possible benefits of merging the indigenous with the exogenous. It does not help to be sentimental about the African way of doing things if it is not the best way. Pundutso then, seeks to promote a balance in the implementation of transformative initiatives.

What bedevils Zimbabwe in particular and Africa in general (as well as other underdeveloped nations) are issues of poverty, low personal income, starvation, poor water and sanitation, unaffordable health services and unaffordable education. All this leads to poor quality of life. Pundutso sees this as fertile ground for Integral Research to Innovation in an effort to address some of these issues.

Pundutso then seeks to transform rural communities through holistic enterprises development that encapsulates sustainable economic development and learning communities, ultimately transforming these rural communities into vibrant economic zones. It also seeks to enhance profitable and sustainable investments within agriculture production, value addition, clean energy and related industries.

Pundutso sees an opportunity to capacitate commerce and industry through product research and innovation. It also sees an opportunity to positively impact poor urban communities.

What Pundutso does

Pundutso is a catalyst for influencing transformation in Zimbabwe and beyond, which transformation will result in the holistic development of individuals, organisations, communities and societies. As a Catalyst/Pilgrimium, Pundutso will work with other similar catalytic movements locally, nationally, regionally and globally. These are spread over three continents (Africa, Europe, Asia) and eight countries (Zimbabwe, South Africa, Nigeria, Egypt, Jordan, France, the United Kingdom and Pakistan).

Nationally Pundutso enjoys strong links with Econet Wireless Zimbabwe, Schweppes, Providence Human Capital/Kuona and Talent Research Group.

Regionally, Pundutso associates with Paxherbal and Ciser in Nigeria, Aflead in South Africa and Sekem in Egypt. In South Africa, Pundutso also has a very strong link with The Da Vinci Institute through which some of the members read for their PhD degrees. In its role as catalyst Pundutso "superintends" the Da Vinci/Transform PhD students by encouraging and walking with them in their own PhD journeys.

These associations involve the organisation and attendance of seminars, workshops and conferences. These are opportunities to make tacit knowledge explicit, externalise knowledge as well as develop new knowledge. This becomes very exciting because of the cultural diversity which results in different interpretation and further development of knowledge tabled colored by individual backgrounds and interpretations. There are also low hanging fruit situations where specific knowledge, because of its nature and impact, is accepted as it is and immediately adopted. Presentations given from different centres therefore are always met with high levels of anticipation and excitement.

Pundutso as home for PhD students in Zimbabwe

Since 2014 Pundutso has been the academic home for eleven PhD students, including the three pioneers, rendering support and encouragement, and incorporating the new students into the Pundutso vision. At the time of writing this book seven of the eleven had successfully completed their PhD degrees after having delivered on their innovations per the requirements of the Da Vinci program. The other four were on the way to completion. The PhD study has been treated as a process of holistic development for the PhD students themselves as well as for the Pundutso community. Some of the innovations are expected to outlive the PhD period of study and go beyond the confines of the student life.

Pundutso has hosted public lectures (Ubuntu Circles) to showcase the work and innovations done by PhD students. It has also hosted conferences and seminars. Such conferences have served the purpose of stimulating discussion on how challenges faced by Zimbabweans can be addressed. Needless to say, such gatherings have presented opportunities to share the innovations by the members of Pundutso.

Pundutso as catalyst for integral development

More than the issue of PhD qualifications, Pundutso sees itself specifically as a catalyst for integral development. A few examples come to mind:

- Integral Kumusha concept, where the focus is on first of all preserving the rural home concept, restoration of the African heritage as well as enhance the African village (Lessem, Mawere, Matupire & Zongololo, 2019). Almost every Zimbabwean has a rural home. However, most, after experiencing the comforts of urban accommodation, are reluctant to spend meaningful time at the village because of its discomforts. Most such homes have no running water and no power, and there is no meaningful means of economic survival. Rural urban migration has therefore become a norm. The idea of Integral Kumusha is how we can make these rural dwellings comfortable by coming up with a basic model which is within the reach of the average villager. Such a model should be backed up with economic activity in the village to promote sustainability. Taranhike (Lessem, Mawere, Matupire & Zongololo, 2019) has spearheaded this in his place of birth in Buhera, where he has slowly turned the home that he inherited from his parents (his *nhaka)* into an Integral Kumusha. Taranhike has harnessed resources that many did not know existed, including underground water. His wife Christina has turned the place into an economic hub of agricultural activity. This has inspired the neighbours who now want to emulate this, each at his own level of capacity. The Taranhike homestead has therefore been a laboratory for Integral Kumusha. The successful implementation of this to a meaningful extent will most likely contribute to urban–rural migration.

- Taranhike further develops a link with his urban business which produces concrete building materials by providing such to his rural neighbours to avoid the arduous task of making their own bricks in an environment where water and firewood resources are limited. This integration has the impact of reducing the urban rural divide and fostering complementarity.
- Zongololo, through Schweppes (Best Fruits Processers- BFP), (Lessem, Mawere, Matupire & Zongololo, 2019) fostered partnerships with rural communities to build economic capacity for the communities as well as providing raw material for BFP. Potentially, this is a win–win solution for both the rural communities and for BFP. While there could have been challenges in the mindsets of the rural folk, which clashed with the high profit mentality of BFP, such partnerships, if natured, can become a serious success story where economic activity is brought to the village.
- Magodo (Lessem, Mawere, Matupire & Zongololo, 2019) focuses on poverty alleviation in rural communities by ratifying the Africanness in people and building confidence, resulting in successfully improving communities by implementing economic solutions that make people feel comfortable.

In this regard then, Pundutso sees itself focusing, not just on the PhD but also on the Process for Holistic Development (PHD).

Pundutso as sponsor of a research academy

Pundutso operates as sponsor and supporter for Integral Research. It encourages and supports the interaction with current and potential laboratories such as Providence Human Capital (PHC), Schweppes, Kairos Leadership Institute and Tafadzwa ne Chiedza, to name just a few. The impetus of such organisations is not only to review their ways of doing things as organisations, but also to focus on how they interact with the societies in which they operate and make positive contributions for the benefit of such communities. Pundutso catalyses such through the activities of a research academy.

Pundutso supports and encourages work with rural communities such as Buhera, Chikomba, Mamina and others, where there is opportunity to incubate social innovation and societal renewal for the benefit of such communities. Such incubation will create opportunities for walking with the communities and integrally developing new ways of livelihoods for the benefit of such communities as well as the greater society. From the perspective of the Calabash of Knowledge Creation, the incubation process takes such communities through the process of creating new, more effective ways of doing things, collectively tried and tested by the community to a point where the new system is internalised by the said communities but remains open to improvement on an ongoing process. With the Calabash of Knowledge Creation nothing is cast in stone. Change is inevitable and positive change is encouraged. So, Pundutso encourages, inspires and supports the journey to innovation by students or academies.

Working through the academy then, Pundutso focuses on the challenges faced by Zimbabwe with the intention of providing extra-ordinary solutions (following the belief that you cannot solve problems using the same thinking that created such problems). Pundutso is determined to bring new thinking in the solution development carried out by academies, focusing on the 5Cs approach in this regard:

Regenerating Community,
Regenerating Culture,
Regenerating Communication,
Regenerating Capital, and
Regenerating Constitution.

The 5Cs breathe life and energy into difficult situations faced by the Zimbabwean populace.

The academy then will be the centre for social innovation while Pundutso is the Regenerative Pilgrimium that inspires the development of the Academy and encourages the work in the laboratories.

Social innovation

While HIT and Da Vinci focus on prototypes and models, Pundutso focuses on Social Innovation. People's lives can be impacted positively by simply doing things differently, providing that the new way is an effectively researched and developed innovation. Muchineripi and Kada simply identified the correct crop to grow to save the Chinyika people from starvation. They went back to the indigenous (finger-millet) from the exogenous (maize) with exogenous methods (new effective methods of farming). This enabled the Chinyika farmers to address the issue of scale. The result was development from starvation to abundance.

Taranhike in the Integral Kumusha situation did not bring much that was new apart from perhaps a fence for his home, water tanks and solar panels for power. He has achieved the new innovation using the same water and the same soil in Buhera, but mobilised differently. It is then about bringing a social innovation – a new but effective way of doing things. Williams (1993) adds his voice to this by emphasizing the importance of leadership, governance and the way things are done.

Taranhike then, has started the Nhakanomics Research Academy (though it is in its early stages). Pundutso will render any support required, and like everyone else learn from this academy. The Research Academy will work with laboratories such as such as the Taranhike homestead and all the activities that go with it, which include horticulture, environmental conservation, renewable energy as well as water harvesting. The idea is to make a rural home reasonably comfortable while protecting the environment as well as making such self-sufficient and economically viable by selling any excess produce. The outcome is the social innovation, Integral Kumusha.

Pundutso will support other academies yet to come. While the focus from Taranhike's perspective is improving rural, someone will come in the future focusing on improving urban. There are similar challenges in the cities that will warrant the development of urban social innovations to alleviate challenges faced in the urban and peri-urban areas. This is the beginning of a very long journey.

Towards a Communiversity

Social innovation then, is not necessarily about university degrees and PhD programs. It is everything about people and improving their lot. Pundutso has set its eyes on the inception of a communiversity. This is a unique entity, not exclusively an academic enterprise. When it materialises, it will be a vehicle for impacting people's lives, whether such people are highly educated or completely illiterate. The purposes of the communiversity will be:

- To facilitate effective social innovation and transformation within specific cultural, social, economic context.
- To release the GENEius of individuals, communities and society by establishing and addressing imbalances (transcultural, transformational, transdisciplinary and transpersonal). Its purpose is to empower people to change their lot and improve their situation.

The Communiversity will follow the Integral Worlds Model and the GENE. It will start with the local South where Grounding will happen (Community & Nature), moving to the local/global East (Emerging – Culture &

Spirituality), to the global North – Navigating (Systems and Technology), finally moving ultimately to the global local – Effecting (Enterprise and Economics). When the Communiversity becomes fully operational, people from different stations of life will benefit from it, each according to their need. What Taranhike is doing with Integral Kumusha, for example, will end up in the Communiversity where, through a PHD approach, such will be passed on to other people.

Essentially, the Communiversity will be grounded on self-sufficiency, underpinned by *Ubuntu/Unhu* values (I am because you are), focused on people advancement (Budiriro yevanhu) leading to positive and sustainable transformation. For now, the central part consists of Da Vinci and Trans4M, who continue to play a pivotal role by pushing for innovation as part of the PhD requirements. The time will come when it will not be about the PhD program, but about the needs of communities. When this time comes, I have no doubt that Da Vinci and Trans4M will be very happy to walk into the sunset in the knowledge that good things will continue. Figure 12.1 shows the potential structure of the Communiversity. Such a communiversity will be in two parts; the inside out part where the starting point will be academic institutions to the communities, and the outside in one where more focus will be on empowering communities to eradicate poverty and hunger.

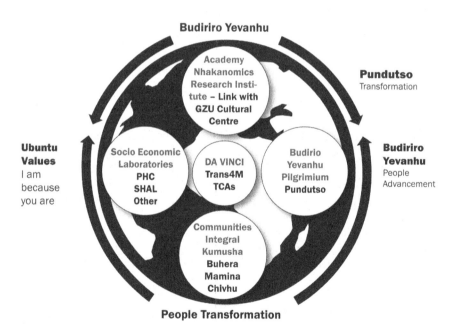

Figure 12.1 Communiversity.

Source: Pundutso Power-point Presentations, 2019, (Adaptation and Design: Elizabeth Mamukwa (2019).

Using the Integral Kumusha Model as an example, the Communiversity is grounded in the practical learning community. It will also be based on the interaction of businesses with the home environment with mutual complementarity. Skills development will be a key component to enable the transformation, such as water harvesting, horticulture and chicken/rabbit rearing for consumption and market. Utilisation of products in the market, such as renewable energy and drip irrigation, and knowledge.

The model will see the closer interaction of urban and rural as skills and commodities cease to be exclusive. The model will preserve and restore the environment and cultural socio-economy – building a heritage and leaving a legacy – nhaka. Community collaboration will be highly encouraged to maximise the learning opportunities and enjoy a meaningful scale of development through community learning. Such community learning will be both indigenous and exogenous in nature. Community collaboration will involve schools and clinics within the community. The model will, most importantly see a triple helix approach where universities, business and government will come together to address the issues bedeviling the economy.

In all this, Pundutso will be the developmental pilgrimium, inspiring, encouraging and resourcing in terms of knowledge. It will be the fountain of knowledge and inspiration. This will all lead to the Nhakanomics Research Academy to develop new research-to-innovation solutions for implementation in the Communiversity. The diagram below summarises the process.

Conclusion

Since its inception Pundutso has acted as a support system for the Da Vinci/ Trans4M PhD program. It has also hosted public lectures (Ubuntu Circles) to share innovations by the PhD students and to heighten consciousness within participants as to what could be possible solutions to the Zimbabwean challenges. Over and above this, it has hosted conferences and seminars to discuss issues challenging the Zimbabwean people and suggesting solutions for such.

Going forward, Pundutso will engage a higher gear by establishing a communiversity as a centre of learning for communities as they participate in processes that enable the improvement of livelihoods and the quality of life. Aligned to this will be the Nhakanomics Research Academy, among other academies, which will come up with research to innovation solutions. Such solutions will feed into the Communiversity for implementation within communities.

References

Lessem, R., Mawere, M., Matupire, P. M. & Zongololo, S. (2019) *Integral Kumusha: Aligning Policonomy with Nature, Culture, Technology and Enterprise.* Masvingo: Africa Talent Publishers.

Mamukwa, E. S., Lessem, R. & Schieffer, A. (2014). *Integral Green Zimbabwe: An African Phoenix Rising.* Farnham, England: Gower

Matupire, P. M. (2017). *Integral Ubuntu Leadership.* New York: Routledge.

Mawere, M. & Nhemachena, A. (2017). *Death of a Discipline: Reflections on the History, State and Future of Social Anthropology in Zimbabwe.* Bamenda: Langaa Research and Publishing CIG.

Mignolo, W. (2011). *The Darker Side of Western Modernity: Global Futures, Decolonial Options.* Durham, NC: Duke University Press.

Williams, C. (1993). *The Re-birth of African Civilization.* Chicago: Third World Press.

13 Conclusion

Introduction

As this book comes to its end, we need to re-examine the real purpose of Knowledge Creation and Innovation. In Chapter 2 I discussed a variety of possible factors that catalyse knowledge creation and innovation. In life, knowledge creation is a combination of passion and curiosity, an example being Aristotle who wanted to study every possible subject and carried out research which resulted in new knowledge then (Ackrill, 1981); real needs, one example being Dr Benjamin Franklin's invention of the flexible catheter because his sick brother needed to use one (Brands, 2010); knowledge is also strategically developed, an example being the Smithsonian Institute where legacy funds were provided for the development of knowledge (Ewing, 2007). This forced America to put a structure in place to promote research and innovation. I could go on. Suffice to say that there are many reasons for knowledge creation. Knowledge creation is not an end in itself. It is a form of emancipation. It is not bound by the past. However, it benefits from the past, interrogates the present and influences the future.

The perceived future of knowledge creation and innovation

The future of knowledge creation and innovation has to be through "research to innovation". Da Vinci Institute/Trans4M and Harare Institute of Technology are some of the academic laboratories. There are also commercial laboratories such as Providence Human Capital and Schweppes, and Integral laboratories such as the Taranhike rural home. Other forms of laboratories might continue to emerge with time. When this happens the various strata of communities need to embrace and work with this for the common good of both knowledge creation and the communities themselves. Knowledge creation is not for the sole purpose of the knowledge itself but must escalate to solving societal/business challenges. It is exciting that our minds are no longer limited to the traditional laboratory concept of test-tubes and chemicals, and that we have opened our hearts and minds to social innovation.

As we continue to navigate the research to innovation journey, systems need to be put in place to enable maximum levels of production, so to speak. Such systems will include the Research Academy, which will feed into a Communiversity. This will build capacity in terms of social innovation as well as societal benefit of such. More importantly, there will be opportunities to re-**GENE-**rate the society.

The role of the Communiversity

The Communiversity is the means through which the results from the Research Academy and its laboratories are propagated to the wider world. The Communiversity will not be limited to academic benefits, but for the propagation of past and new knowledge rhythms to create knowledge pulses. Once in place, the Communiversity will be like a heartbeat which cannot afford to stop, for this will spell death. The heartbeat defines the carrying of fresh blood and fresh oxygen through the body for the survival of the individual. So too must the heartbeat of knowledge through the Calabash of Knowledge Creation. Communities need the continued supply of oxygen in the form of fresh, relevant and appropriate knowledge. Such knowledge must make sense to the community and its needs, whether it is the global community or a single village. Knowledge creation in this so-called global village is no longer specific to a country, city or village, It is universal, and should be a result of indigenous and exogenous rhythms. There are good and not so good things happening in both indigenous and exogenous communities. The creation of new knowledge should be about harnessing the good and useful from both the indigenous and exogenous spaces.

The work of institutions such as Da Vinci and HIT

Such institutions play a critical role. They focus the people to move from the old to the new, by creating options. They empower people to influence the new through their knowledge creation and innovation programs. While HIT focuses on the undergraduate community, Da Vinci focuses on corporate leaders by challenging them to re-think and re-frame the way they solve their work-based (and community-based) challenges. With Da Vinci it is no longer business as usual. It is ideation and creativity through and through in coming up with solutions. It is innovation rather than sticking to the age-old ways of resolving such challenges.

The benefits of knowledge creation and innovation in business

While there are a variety of justifications for deliberate knowledge creation and innovation, it equally has various benefits. From a business perspective, knowledge creation and innovation bring democratisation of learning and teaching to the workplace. This is beneficial as great ideas do not necessarily come from managers, but potentially from all employees regardless of level in the hierarchy. Creativity and innovation become a strong basis not only for learning and teaching, but also for knowledge transfer at the workplace.

As creativity and innovation are embraced at the workplace, collaboration becomes critical. I experienced this at Turnall during our research to innovation journey in 2013. Sharing of ideas and brainstorming become the norm as team members are anxious to come up with innovations that work as they begin to appreciate that successful innovations will secure their jobs.

In innovation-driven organisations, leadership roles are modified as the said leaders appreciate and accept that creativity and innovation can come from anywhere in the organisation. They begin to see their role as that of supporting the team to enable such innovations. The institution will then formally or informally practice an upside-down organogram with the Chief Executive Officer at the bottom, supporting the employees (see diagram below).

Furthermore, some can argue that it is not always possible for the leader to become the source of innovation. As leaders rise higher in organisations, they, of necessity begin to superintend over those they lead, most times in areas they themselves are not familiar with. They therefore depend on those they lead to make things happen in those specialist areas while they play a more supportive role. While they are not subject matter specialists, they play a more supportive role to enable their teams to achieve results and create new knowledge.

Figure 13.1 The upside-down organogram.
Source: Mamukwa unpublished work, (2019).

Tannebaum and Schmidt (1973) came up with the leadership continuum (see diagram below) to describe how there is a change in roles that comes with moving from a subject matter specialist to a leader. However, dependent on the type of leader and his level of motivation and inspiration, this could equally have the impact of promoting innovation. A leader working with a cross-functional team gets to appreciate how everything gels together and can promote wholesome and sustainable innovations that speak to all corners of an organisation.

It makes sense therefore to work with team members and encourage them to be both creative and innovative. Knowledge creation and innovation in business organisations is driven by the need to improve processes and increase productivity which in turn results in improved profitability.

Social innovation on the other hand, is driven by the need to mitigate suffering in communities, improve livelihoods as well as quality of life. Examples are; Muchineripi says "my people are starving" and proceeds to come up with an innovation (collectively with his community) which altogether eliminated starvation in Chinyika; Taranhike sees poverty in his rural home in Buhera and embarks on a journey develop an example of a comfortable and productive rural home, one that his rural neighbours can emulate. The emphasis is not so much on the comfort of such a rural home, but on productivity and sustainability.

Strategies for social innovation

Social Innovation is inspired by communities, be they rural, urban or academic. One of the most common factors leading to social innovation is groups of people facing common problems. The beginning of looking for a solution to a community challenge is usually discourse. People start by sharing common problems and seeking solutions to such. This has been happening since time immemorial. The only difference now is that the likes of Heron (1996), Reason (1988, 1994) and Lessem and Schieffer (2010), to mention a few, have worked on and refined ways of doing this and reduced it to literature so that this can be shared and followed. Of course, having a template helps a great deal because it is no longer trial and error, and success is almost guaranteed when you follow a tried and tested method.

Social innovation has resulted in groups of people deciding on and agreeing to changing the way things are done, hence developing new cultures of addressing societal and community problems. A good example is the Chinyika story which saw hundreds of households adopting a "new" crop and new ways of farming (Lessem, Muchineripi & Kada, 2012). Taranhike's Integral Kumusha is another example (Lessem, Mawere, Matupire & Zongololo, 2019). This is likely to have a positive impact on many rural communities.

Integral research then, is a guaranteed way to achieve social innovation. Communities can embark on a research to innovation journey, communicating in a familiar language, using familiar words and idioms and gradually building consensus on the path they are collectively walking. According to the GENE

Time spent doing technical work reduces and employee rises in an organisation

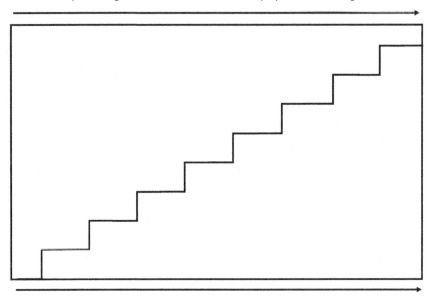

Time spent doing leadership work increases as individual progresses into managerial and leadership roles in the organisation

Figure 13.2 The leadership continuum.
Source: Adapted from Tannebaum & Schmidt, 1973. (Adaptation and Design: Elizabeth Mamukwa, 2019).

rhythm, they start by grounding themselves (re-affirmation of who they are and why they are in this situation), emerging (opening up to possibilities of solutions to the challenge), navigating (researching on the possible solutions) and finally effecting the developed innovations. The final innovation is then based on consensus and experience, and there is little possibility of questioning the integrity of the innovation. The research community then owns such an innovation, believes in it and advocates for it. The implementation of such therefore becomes sustainable.

The importance of propagation and implementation

Without deliberate propagation and implementation, brilliant innovations can die a natural death. It is critical therefore that new innovations are shared and widely used. This way the innovations can be continually interrogated and challenged, leading to new and hopefully better innovations. The subject knowledge is not static. Change is imminent and fast. The Calabash of Knowledge Creation (Mamukwa, Lessem & Schieffer, 2014), is deliberately designed with an opening at the top and a spiral at the centre for this reason. The opening at the top is to allow knowledge to be shared with the outside world and to allow new knowledge into the calabash, which knowledge is equally interrogated and modified if necessary. The spiral is to place importance on iteration in the process of knowledge creation and innovation. There is no end to it – it is a continuous process.

Conclusion

Knowledge creation and innovation is a very active phenomenon in all spheres of life such as science, technology, medicine and other such. Exciting things are happening at the Harare Institute of Technology where the concept of techno-preneurship has been developed and embraced. Da Vinci Institute too has over the years influenced business leaders positively by developing in them the capacity to come up with innovations for addressing work-based challenges in their organisations.

While conventional research continues to happen mostly in the Mode 1 university system, integral research has gained momentum. It is practical in nature and is aligned more with the Mode 2 university spirit. Integral research is particularly useful for social innovation, where communities face challenges that need to be addressed collectively. A number of individuals who have read for their PhDs through Da Vinci/Trans4M have come up with various innovations which have not been effectively marketed and propagated.

Pundutso Centre for Integral Development, through its members and PhD associates is developing a research academy which will feed into a Communiversity, which will also be developed to address issues of knowledge creation and innovation in Zimbabwe. The research academy will step up the development of new innovations as an ongoing activity while the Communiversity will propagate such by training various sectors of society on these innovations as appropriate.

References

Ackrill, J. L. (1981). *Aristotle the Philosopher.* Oxford and New York: Oxford University Press.

Brands, H. W. (2010). *The First American: The Life and Times of Benjamin Franklin.* New York: Random House Digital.

Ewing, H. (2007). *The Lost World of James Smithson: Science, Revolution, and the Birth of the Smithsonians.* New York: Bloomsbury.

Heron, J (1996). *Co-operative Inquiry: Research into the Human Condition.* London: Sage.

Lessem, R., Muchineripi, P. C. & Kada, S. (2012). *Integral Community: Political Economy to Social Commons.* Farnham, England: Gower

Lessem, R., Mawere, M., Matupire, P. M. & Zongololo, S. (2019). *Integral Kumusha: Aligning Policonomy with Nature, Culture, Technology and Enterprise.* Masvingo: Africa Talent Publishers.

Lessem, R. & Schieffer, A. (2010). *Integral Research and Innovation: Transforming Enterprise and Society.* Farnham, England: Gower

Mamukwa, E. S., Lessem, R. & Schieffer, A. (2014). *Integral Green Zimbabwe: An African Phoenix Rising.* Farnham, England: Gower.

Reason, P. (1988). *Human Inquiry in Action.* London: Sage.

Reason, P. (1994). *Participation in Human Inquiry.* London: Sage.

Tannebaum, R. & Schmidt, W. H. (1973). How to Choose a Leadership Pattern. *Harvard Business Review*, 36, 162–180.

Epilogue

Introduction: Where do we go from here?

A lot has been said about knowledge creation and innovation in this book. A lot has been captured of what has been done in this regard. This is the point where we interrogate ourselves in this sphere and chart a definite way forward with regard to what practical actions we take. As they say, talk is cheap. What is required now is action. We now need to chart the way forward regarding how knowledge is created and how innovation is promoted and encouraged as well as how it is effectively shared to impact relevant communities.

There are two action points that are begging to be actualised. The first one is the making of a Research Academy. The Research Academy's purpose will be to promote the envisaged creation of new knowledge. This will promote all kinds innovations, perhaps mostly social innovations, as well as interrogate and integrate the knowledge creation activities. The Research Academy will need to come up with specific strategies so that research quickly becomes the core business of the academy. It will also present opportunities to maximise the use of *Denhe re Ruzivo,* The Calabash of Knowledge Creation (Mamukwa, Lessem & Schieffer, 2014). The Research Academy then, will be an Integral Innovation Ecosystem.

The second is to create a Communiversity, for the primary purpose of propagating research that is seen to be useful to specific communities and to society in general. The Communiversity then, will primarily seek to share the knowledge with others, and also highlight problematic innovations which can be referred back to the Research Academy for further work. The Communiversity's function will primarily be to actualise the Integral Impact of the Research Academy and, more importantly, link up with communities and academia to come up with solutions to community challenges and empower such communities to improve their situations.

Among other things, this book highlights the phenomenon of social innovation. I hope social innovation is not understood to be something that only benefits poor rural or urban people. The truth is, social innovation can be relevant to any grouping of people, be it businesses, academic institutions, or rural/ urban communities, to mention a few.

Social innovation

One may well ask, "What then is social innovation?"

The Stanford Graduate School of Business put it aptly as they define it as follows: "*Social innovation is the process of developing and deploying effective solutions to challenging and often systemic social and environmental issues in support of social progress*". They develop this further by quoting Soule, Malhotra and Clavier, who add that "*Social innovation is not the prerogative or privilege of any organizational form or legal structure. Solutions often require the active collaboration of constituents across government, business, and the non-profit world*" (www.gsb.stanford.edu/faculty-research/centers-initiatives/csi/defining-social-innovation).

Bates (2012, p. xix) defines Social Innovation as *the process of addressing the world's most pressing challenges with "novel solutions ... that [are] better than current solutions, new to the world, and [benefit] society as a whole and not just a single entity"*.

Lessem and Schieffer (2010), bemoan the absence of social innovation in businesses and academic colleges, even though there are many challenges that are screaming for such, such as the pension crisis, human poverty and even climate change, to mention only a few. Corporate leaders are too busy chasing their profit targets instead of looking at possible options in terms of doing things differently and better.

This all sums it up very well in my view. For me social innovation is about resolving social needs by working together with affected parties in order to come up with solutions that are acceptable to them and are sustainable. This then, is where Integral Research (Lessem & Schieffer, 2010) becomes relevant, where research is carried out with the affected communities, and not just by someone who is seen as the specialist researcher. Action Research would ideally be employed through Cooperative Inquiry (CI) or Participatory Action Research (PAR), and this will involve active participation and contribution by representatives of the population affected by the problem or situation (Heron, 1996; Reason, 1988/1994). Solutions should not be imposed but should be the product of collaboration with the affected parties.

The Research Academy

The Research Academy, then, will be a vehicle for working with rural and urban communities, Businesses, Académie and any relevant communities where specific needs are identified or presented. The objective of the Research Academy will be to work together with the relevant communities to develop solutions to common challenges. At the end of the day, the successful innovations must benefit the greater society. This is where the Communiversity comes in.

Consensus within the Pundutso community is that the Research Academy must be put in place as soon as possible. A structure must be immediately put in place to harness past, present and future innovations and re-test the old ones if necessary. This structure will also, with the rest of Pundutso, define what testing can happen in existing laboratories (PHC, Schweppes, Buhera, Mamina and

Chivhu to name only a few). As innovations pass the test, they are then pushed on to the Communiversity for propagation to greater society.

The Communiversity

The word Communiversity is a combination of two words, Community and University. The meaning of Communiversity is therefore "a place where communities can learn". While there will be no limitations on whether the Communiversity will confer degrees or issue certificates, there will equally not be anything to stop even non-literate members of communities from learning something to improve their lives.

Although Pundutso's focus at the time of writing this book was the Research Academy, it is clear that this academy cannot exist without a Communiversity if useful innovations are to be actualised and shared with communities and institutions. In my view, as soon as the Research Academy is launched, work must start on the Communiversity. A structure and Project Team should be equally put in place to develop this and make it operational.

Conclusion

This book will not be just an academic exercise but will be developed into action through the setting up of a Research Academy and following that, a Communiversity. The Research Academy will promote the development of new knowledge and innovations. Such developments will then be escalated to the Communiversity to promote the assimilation of new knowledge and the adoption of the innovations. The result of such will be the empowerment of communities, whether highly educated or not educated at all, whether very affluent or very poor. There is nothing that says that rich people cannot learn, but they may have their own genuine needs. Therefore, the Communiversity will have no limitations as to who goes there apart from the fact of need and relevance. With regard to the size and scope of the Communiversity, this waits to be seen. The sky is the limit as to how far it will grow and what impact it will have on communities and society.

References

Bates, S. M. (2012). *The Social Innovation Imperative: Create Winning Products, Services and Programs that Solve Society's Most Pressing Challenges.* New York: McGraw-Hill.

Heron, J. (1996). *Co-operative Inquiry: Research into the Human Condition.* London: Sage.

Lessem, R. & Schieffer, A. (2010). *Integral Research and Innovation: Transforming Enterprise and Society.* England: Gower.

Mamukwa, E., Lessem, R. & Schieffer, A. (2014). *Integral Green Zimbabwe: An African Phoenix Rising.* Surrey: Gower

Reason, P. (1988). *Human Inquiry in Action.* London: Sage.

Reason, P. (1994). *Participation in Human Inquiry.* London: Sage.

Index

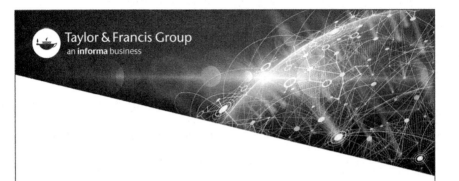

Printed in the United States
by Baker & Taylor Publisher Services